SOCIAL INFORMATICS

Social informatics examines how society is influenced by digital technologies and how digital technologies are shaped by political, economic, and socio-cultural forces. The chapters in this edited volume use social informatics approaches to analyze recent issues in our increasingly data-intensive society.

Taking a social informatics perspective, this edited volume investigates the interaction between society and digital technologies and includes research that examines individuals, groups, organizations, and nations, as well as their complex relationships with pervasive mobile and wearable devices, social media platforms, artificial intelligence, and big data. This volume's contributors range from seasoned and renowned researchers to upcoming researchers in social informatics. The readers of the book will understand theoretical frameworks of social informatics; gain insights into recent empirical studies of social informatics in specific areas such as big data and its effects on privacy, ethical issues related to digital technologies, and the implications of digital technologies for daily practices; and learn how the social informatics perspective informs research and practice.

Social Informatics provides the first book-length overview of Social Informatic research in recent years and will be essential reading for academics and students engaged in the study of information science, internet studies, emerging technologies, digital media, new media studies, computer science, the sociology of communication, and data science.

Noriko Hara is Professor and Department Chair in the Department of Information & Library Science in the Luddy School of Informatics, Computing, and Engineering at Indiana University, Bloomington.

Pnina Fichman is a Professor of Information Science in the Luddy School of Informatics, Computing, and Engineering and the Director of the Rob Kling Center for Social Informatics at Indiana University, Bloomington.

Global Perspectives on Library and Information Science

Global Perspectives on Library and Information Science highlights the wide range of innovative projects and approaches on offer within the LIS field today. Authored and edited by scholars and practitioners, volumes explore the vital work being done by library and information scientists all around the world.

The series contains global and regionally specific volumes and will provide students, researchers, and practitioners in the LIS field with diverse, unique insights into contemporary issues.

To submit a proposal or discuss an idea for a book in the series, please contact the Routledge Editor for Library, Archival and Information Science, Heidi Lowther (heidi.lowther@tandf.co.uk).

The following list includes only the most-recent titles to publish within the series. A list of the full catalogue of titles is available at: https://www.routledge.com/Global-Perspectives-on-Library-and-Information-Science/book-series/GPLIS

Social Informatics
Edited by Noriko Hara and Pnina Fichman

SOCIAL INFORMATICS

Edited by Noriko Hara and Pnina Fichman

Routledge
Taylor & Francis Group

LONDON AND NEW YORK

Designed cover image: Image by DrAfter123

First published 2025
by Routledge
4 Park Square, Milton Park, Abingdon, Oxon OX14 4RN

and by Routledge
605 Third Avenue, New York, NY 10158

Routledge is an imprint of the Taylor & Francis Group, an informa business

British Library Cataloguing-in-Publication Data
A catalogue record for this book is available from the British Library

ISBN: 978-1-032-67850-4 (hbk)
ISBN: 978-1-032-60629-3 (pbk)
ISBN: 978-1-032-67854-2 (ebk)

DOI: 10.4324/9781032678542

Typeset in Times New Roman
by Newgen Publishing UK

In Memory of Rob Kling

CONTENTS

FIGURES

TABLES

CONTRIBUTORS

Kyra Milan Abrams is a PhD candidate in Informatics at the University of Illinois at Urbana-Champaign; she is interested in ways to design technology with marginalized people to provide them with data autonomy. With this approach, she aims to promote digital literacy so that people can advocate for their own data autonomy.

Jošt Bartol is a PhD candidate in Statistics at the University of Ljubljana, Slovenia, and Research Fellow at the Centre for Social Informatics at the Faculty of Social Sciences, University of Ljubljana, Slovenia. His research focuses on methodological and substantive issues related to online privacy, particularly in connection to digital inequalities.

Seung Woo Chae is Assistant Professor in the Department of Journalism and Creative Media Industries at Texas Tech University. Before entering academia, he worked as a TV producer and PR/advertising manager. His last industry role was as a TV producer at the Korean Broadcasting System (KBS), South Korea's largest broadcaster known for its diverse K-culture content. Drawing on this industry experience, his research focuses on digital journalism and communication on social media.

Bevis Hsin-Yu Chen is a PhD candidate in the Media School at Indiana University, Bloomington. His main areas of research focus on media policy, platform governance, disinformation, and online trolling.

Pnina Fichman is Professor of Information Science in the Luddy School of Informatics, Computing, and Engineering and the Director of the Rob Kling Center for Social Informatics at Indiana University, Bloomington. She has published six books and over a hundred peer-reviewed journal articles, conference papers, and book chapters about social informatics, trolling, information intermediation, and communities of practice.

Natalia Grincheva is Program Leader in Arts Management at LASALLE, University of Arts Singapore, and an Honorary Senior Research Fellow in the Digital Studio at the University of Melbourne. She is an internationally recognized expert in digital museum diplomacy and the author of four monographs *Digital Soft Power of Heritage Media* (Cambridge University Press, 2025 forthcoming), *Geopolitics of Digital Heritage* (Cambridge University Press, 2024), *Museum Diplomacy in the Digital Age* (Routledge, 2020), and *Global Trends in Museum Diplomacy* (Routledge, 2019).

Noriko Hara is Professor and Department Chair in the Department of Information & Library Science in the Luddy School of Informatics, Computing, and Engineering at Indiana University, Bloomington. Her current research in social informatics focuses on technology-mediated public engagement with science and technology. Her research has been funded by several organizations, including the National Science Foundation. She has authored various scholarly publications and co-edited a special issue of *Science Communication* titled Public Science in a Wired World.

Bárbara da Rosa Lazarotto is a Marie-Skłodowska Fellow at Horizon 2020 European Union research and innovation funding programme, where she works on business-to-government data sharing. She is a PhD researcher at the Law, Science, Technology and Society Research Group at Vrije Universiteit Brussel in Belgium, where she is an executive team member at the Brussels Privacy Hub and a Lecturer at Sciences Po, Paris.

Azi Lev-On is a faculty member in the School of Communication in Ariel University. His research focuses on the social and political uses and impact of the Internet and social media and particularly on their affordances for and usage by citizens in terms of speech and action, and the corresponding institutional responses. His latest book: "The murder of Tair Rada and the Roman Zdorov affair: Establishment, justice, citizens and social media" was published by Yedioth Books (2023).

Howard Rosenbaum is Professor of Information Science in the Department of Information and Library Science in the Luddy School of Informatics and Computing at Indiana University. He is currently interested in social informatics and critical data studies. He has published in a variety of information science journals and has presented at ASIS&T, iConferences, and elsewhere. He has been involved in social informatics since 1997 and works with collaborators to raise the profile of SI in information science.

Madelyn Rose Sanfilippo is an Assistant Professor in the School of Information Sciences at the University of Illinois at Urbana-Champaign and an expert on data governance, technology policy, and privacy. Dr. Sanfilippo is co-PI of the Workshop on Governing Knowledge Commons and co-Editor of *Governing Misinformation in Everyday Knowledge Commons* (Cambridge University Press, 2024). She received her PhD in Information Science from Indiana University, Bloomington.

Gül Seçkin is Associate Professor of Sociology at the University of North Texas, specializing in medical sociology, digital health, and the intersection of technology, health, and medicine. She holds a PhD in sociology from Case Western Reserve University and an MSG in gerontology from the University of Southern California. Her research focuses on patient-provider dynamics in the digital age, online health information seeking, digital health literacy, e-health information consumerism, patient health empowerment, and the socio-technical transformation of medicine.

Zdeněk Smutný is Associate Professor of Applied Informatics at the Faculty of Informatics and Statistics, Prague University of Economics and Business, Czechia. He is the Editor-in-Chief of the journal *Acta Informatica Pragensia*. His current main academic and research focus includes social informatics, ambient intelligence systems for people with blindness, advances in informatics methodology, and intelligent transportation systems in cooperation with commercial companies.

Patrick Sullivan is a second-year student in the Master of Library Science program at Indiana University's Luddy School of Informatics, Computing, and Engineering. He has worked as a research assistant in the Luddy School's Department of Information & Library Science for the past year. Patrick previously attended the University of Vermont, where he completed a master's thesis in history and served as Executive Editor of the university's student-run history publication.

Vasja Vehovar is Professor of Statistics at the Faculty of Social Sciences, University of Ljubljana, Slovenia. He is also the head of the Centre for Social Informatics (www.cdi.si) at the University of Ljubljana, Slovenia. His main research areas are internet research and various aspects of web survey methodology.

Shengnan Yang is an assistant professor at the Faculty of Information & Media Studies, University of Western Ontario, Canada. She earned her PhD from Indiana University, USA, and a bachelor's degree from Peking University, China. Using a mixed-methods approach, she examines the dynamic relationship between digital technology and human agency in organizations, along with the broader societal impact of technology. Her recent research focuses on information governance, social informatics, and the digital transformation of organizations.

Xiaohua Awa Zhu is an associate professor at the School of Information Sciences at the University of Tennessee, Knoxville. Her work focuses on several themes at the intersection of information policy, social informatics, and libraries: misinformation governance, rights related to digital intellectual properties and digital ownership, open government data and community empowerment, and the impact of digital transformation on libraries. Her work combines qualitative and quantitative methods, often drawing on social theories and historical perspectives.

ACKNOWLEDGEMENTS

We would like to express how grateful we are for the contributions of the many individuals whose support and brilliant work made publishing this book possible. We thank each of the authors of the chapters that were selected for inclusion in this edited volume; their invaluable contributions enhance our understanding of social informatics research. Our sincere gratitude to Patrick Sullivan for providing superb editorial assistance; his help was crucial in making this entire book what it has become. We are also thankful to Heidi Lowther and Manas Roy at Routledge for providing ongoing support during the long process that culminated in the publication of this book; their belief in the merit of the book and their efforts were instrumental.

INTRODUCTION

Noriko Hara and Pnina Fichman

Social informatics (SI) "refers to the study of social aspects of computerization, including the role of information technology in social and organizational change, the use of information technologies in social contexts, and the way that the social organization of information technologies is influenced by social forces and social practices" (Rob Kling Center for Social Informatics, n.d.); it is an interdisciplinary field of study that challenges the "standard model"—assumptions and establishments regarding the understanding of technology uses (Kling et al., 2005). SI was defined by Rob Kling and his colleagues in a 1997 National Science Foundation-funded workshop as follows: "[SI is] the interdisciplinary study of the design, uses and consequences of information technologies that takes into account their interaction with institutional and cultural contexts" (Kling et al., 2005, p. 6).

Kling and his colleagues began investigating the social implications of computing in the late 1970s at a time when computers were new, costly, and primarily adopted and used in large organizations (Kling, 1977; Kraemer & Kling, 1988). At that time, it was a refreshing idea to consider both computers and people as a single unit of analysis, but since then, studies of the social aspects of computing have flourished. Subsequently, various scholars adopted this conceptual framework (see more in Fichman & Rosenbaum, 2014; Meyer et al., 2019).

For a few decades, most of these studies took place in business environments (Sanfilippo & Fichman, 2014). In the 2000s, computer use became commonplace in the broader society (Dutton, 2013; Dutton & Graham, 2014), and it became ubiquitous when the use of smartphones skyrocketed, especially following the popularity of Apple's iPhone, which was first released in 2007 (Merchant, 2017). The combination of the availability of personal devices and the spread of social media have created new opportunities for SI research over the past two decades;

DOI: 10.4324/9781032678542-1

more recently, developments such as generative artificial intelligence chatbots as well as augmented and virtual reality environments have introduced new and unexplored domains for SI research.

SI has undergone stages of forced evolution—not just from external technological and societal forces but also internally from within the field. Sanfilippo and Fichman (2014) identified four stages of evolution in SI. They named these stages "foundational work," "development and expansion," "coherence," and "diversification"; they connected these stages to SI history and development. They noted that before the 1990s, Kling and his colleagues conducted multiple empirical studies to build a strong foundation for SI (e.g., Kling & Iacono, 1989) and began developing theoretical frameworks, such as the Web of Computing (e.g., Kling & Scacchi, 1982). The 1990s became the period of development and expansion of SI theories and perspectives; for example, Kling and his colleagues incorporated sociotechnical perspectives (e.g., Kling & Lamb, 1999) and human-centered systems (e.g., Kling & Star, 1998). During this time, Kling published an edited book entitled *Computers and Controversy* (Kling, 1996), which incorporated these diverse perspectives.

Sanfilippo and Fichman (2014) argued that SI research became most coherent in the early 2000s. Kling's early and unexpected passing in 2003 disheartened many colleagues and scholars (e.g., Lamb & Sawyer, 2005). Since his passing, SI research became less cohesive (Sanfilippo & Fichman, 2014), and some SI scholars identified their works as sociotechnical and used other terminologies, such as the social aspects of information and communication technologies, to describe their work. Different theoretical lenses and methods were incorporated into SI research. For example, the use of social network theory (e.g., Contractor, 2009) and critical perspective (Day, 2007) were integrated during this time.

Since 2014, SI has expanded into new territories, as have its underlying theories, methods, and empirical findings. All of this growth was driven by the development of new digital technologies, new ways in which people design and use these technologies, expanded intended (and unintended) consequences of these technologies, and increased awareness of their sociotechnical implications. Empirical studies that used to be mostly limited within organizations expanded to include individual and online communities' use of technology (e.g., Fichman & Dedema, 2023; Hara et al., 2019), cross-cultural analysis (e.g., Fichman & Hara, 2014; Fichman, 2020), and cross-platform research of online political trolling (e.g., Fichman & Rathi, 2023).

Others located the different SI schools of thought from around the globe (Smutny & Vehovar, 2020). For instance, a special issue of the *Journal of the Association for Information Science & Technology* was devoted to the "Social Informatics of Knowledge" as its focal point (Meyer et al., 2019). The special issue traced the roots of SI and included articles ranging from robotic use in Chinese healthcare systems (Pee et al., 2019) to a large-scale research collaboration between two countries using digital technologies (Ward & Given, 2019) and to the study of ignorance as a framework to inform SI research, especially on denying and obscuring knowledge (Greyson, 2019). The focus on the context of technology use continued to attract SI scholars (Sanfilippo et al., 2017; Fichman & Amidu, 2024). Investigating the unintended consequences of technologies such as misinformation, disinformation, and trolling became an integral part of SI. For instance, Wu and Resnick (2024) redefined how to identify prevalence on social media and demonstrated the framework by examining toxic comments' prevalence on multiple social media platforms.

The interdisciplinary nature of social informatics

Twenty years have transpired since the passing of Rob Kling, one of the founders of SI. Even though most of the field's diversification occurred after Kling's passing, SI research has been interdisciplinary from the beginning as the previously mentioned definition from a 1997 workshop states. Multiple other disciplines influenced SI research. Since SI deals with digital technologies and Kling had a Ph.D. in computer science, earlier works on SI were published in the "computers and society" sub-field of computer science. Kling once reflected that Information Schools would be a better academic home for SI than computer science departments due to the field of Information Science's interdisciplinary nature (Kling, 2002). In fact, the Association of Information Science and Technology is a home for the Special Interest Group in SI, which has hosted the annual research symposium for SI since 2007.

As SI deals with the social aspects and impacts of technology, theories and methods from social science play a major role in SI research; some of the theoretical frameworks in sociology were widely integrated into SI research. For example, structuration theory (Giddens, 1991) was incorporated into the duality of technology by Orlikowski (1992). Scholars in Management of Information Systems, a sub-field of Management, published various SI research concerning topics such as robotics in pharmacy (Barrett et al., 2011), the reconceptualization of users as social actors (Lamb & Kling, 2003), and roles of online knowledge collaborators (Hara & Sanfilippo, 2016, 2017). It makes sense that SI research was embraced by Management of Information Systems scholars as, according to Kling in a personal conversation with one of the authors, business managers appreciated the value of SI research more than computer scientists because managers faced issues entangled with both computers and organizations. Scholars in the communication field have also contributed to SI research since digital technologies are not only computing but also communication devices. Notably, Sproull and Kielser (1991) established studies that focus on the communication aspects of computers within organizations. Their work on computer-mediated communication has influenced studies in SI. Moreover, Contractor, another communication scholar, has used network analysis to examine computing in organizations (e.g., Contractor, 2009; Contractor et al., 2011).

At times, SI research was influenced by theories from science and technology studies (STS). For example, Jarrahi et al.'s (2022) work on digital assemblage was inspired by a theoretical framework, assemblages, which originated from STS scholars such as Latour and Callon. Similarly, Fichman and Dedema's (2023) work on communities of practice, which focuses on boundary objects, was grounded in a theory that originated in STS research—boundary objects (Star & Griesemer, 1989). Another example of STS' influence on SI is co-production of knowledge (Callon, 1999), which was used to analyze public understandings of generative AI on social media (Hara et al., 2024). The ties between STS and SI are also shown in the range of methods that SI scholarship utilizes; as STS is often considered a sub-field of sociology, SI research uses methods that are common in social science research.

SI researchers also focus on privacy and information policy (e.g., Sanfilippo & Shvartzshnaider, 2023; Sanfilippo & Strandburg, 2021; Shilton & Greene, 2019; Yang et al., 2019; Zhu, 2017). For example, privacy issues have been examined in the contexts of public Facebook groups (Sanfilippo & Strandburg, 2021), MagicBands in Disney World (Sanfilippo & Shvartzshnaider, 2023), and privacy policies for mobile apps (Shilton & Greene, 2019). Another focus is governing—which includes, for example—historical analysis of open government data movement in the U.S. (Zhu, 2017) and national policies' influences on crowdfunding platforms for charity organizations in China (Yang et al., 2019).

SI research has also recently expanded to include the analyses of social computing and big data. The availability of massive amounts of data from social media allowed researchers to tap into big data analysis from SI perspectives. For example, Goggins and Petakovic (2014) are two SI pioneers in using large datasets from three online platforms—Facebook, Twitter, and GitHub—to develop a conceptual framework that incorporates context in the analysis of social influence. More recently, Stvilia and Lee (2024) proposed a theoretical framework for assessing data quality in research data repositories.

Outline of this book

In this book, we showcase current SI research from scholars around the world. Chapters cover topics including data and algorithmic governance in Section II, data ethics in Section III, and digital technology domestication in Section IV.

The book is organized as follows:

Section I. Theoretical Framework of Social Informatics (Rosenbaum; Smutny et al.)
Section II. Social Informatics Perspectives on Data (Grincheva; Yang & Zhu; Abrams & Sanfilippo)
Section III. Social Informatics Perspectives on Ethics and Social Justice (Lazarotto; Seckin; Chen & Fichman)

Section IV. Opportunities and Challenges with Digital Technology Domestication
(Fichman & Sullivan; Lev-On; Hara & Chae)

The chapters in Section I discuss how SI perspectives have evolved and expanded. They pay specific attention to recent theoretical developments in SI research (Fichman & Rosenbaum, 2014; Meyer et al., 2019). Particularly, in Chapter 1, Rosenbaum provides an intellectual contemplation on an ontology for SI rooted in sociomateriality and postphenomenology through proposing a path for the future of SI as a thriving field. In Chapter 2, Smutny and his colleagues offer a thorough examination of the methodology used in SI research, which is based on the seven SI approaches ranging from empirical to conceptual, including research beyond English-language SI literature.

We now have unprecedented access to and use of big data in society. Three chapters in Section II shed light on the intersection of big data and society. Specifically, Grincheva, in Chapter 3, critically examines data mapping methodologies to evaluate influences of cultural heritage institutions worldwide. While data can inform people, digital technologies can also be oppressive and introduce negative consequences. Another chapter in this section by Yang and Zhu, Chapter 4, unpacks how algorithmic governance and governance of algorithms affect disinformation policies in the U.S. and China. On the topic of governance, Abrams and Sanfilippo, in Chapter 5, investigate data governance consequences in two U.S. states. Taken together, these chapters' findings have implications for regulations and usages of both data and algorithms.

Section III addresses issues related to social justice in a technology-saturated world, as digital technologies and data are not value-neutral. For example, AI algorithms are intensifying racism (Lee, 2018), and large corporations profit from personal data by way of "surveillance capitalization" (Zuboff, 2023). On one hand, use of digital technologies allows less privileged voices to be heard, such as in the case of Black Lives Matter (Duan et al., 2024). On the other hand, digital technologies may lead not only to unethical behaviors but also challenging privacy issues (Sanfilippo & Shvartzshnaider, 2023). Chapter 6 by Lazarotto interrogates the issues of privacy and inequality when technologies and big data become high-priority in public sectors. Similarly, Seckin, in Chapter 7, investigates AI in the healthcare sector and its consequences for inequality. Furthermore, the increase in misinformation, disinformation, deception, cyberbullying, and trolling are some of the negative consequences of digital technologies (e.g., Fichman & Vaughn, 2021). In Chapter 8, Chen and Fichman provide an innovative approach to examine fake news on TikTok regarding the Russia-Ukraine War. Their expansion of the STIN (sociotechnical interaction network) (Kling et al., 2003) adds a useful new perspective to the existing discourse of the STIN model (e.g., Meyer, 2006, 2014).

The fourth section includes three chapters that examine the domestication of digital technologies. As digital technologies are increasingly prevalent through social media, additional development of technologies' use in everyday contexts has become an interesting topic for SI research. Silverstone (1993) called this process the "domestication" of digital technologies. While similar changes happened with previously adapted technologies at home such as radios and TVs (Silverstone & Haddon, 1996), Agre (2002) suggested in the "amplification model" that digital technologies have the tendency to not change the existing social structures in which they are used, instead amplifying existing phenomena and introducing additional issues. The three chapters analyze, from a SI perspective, the use of digital technologies in everyday contexts such as entertainment, political mobilization, and health/science communication. By examining the domestication of digital technologies, the chapters in this section provide diverse theoretical frameworks for analyses. Fichman and Sullivan, in Chapter 9, focused their attentions on an interesting social media trend—internet challenges—suggesting that they can be understood as organisms of communities of practice that evolve within their socio-ecological contexts. Lev-On, in Chapter 10, used role expansion as a framework to analyze a social media-driven mobilization for justice for an accused murderer who was eventually acquitted 13 years later. The chapter examines how the group, originally formed to advocate for the accused's innocence, broadened its activities to address related social justice issues, illustrating the potential for such movements to evolve beyond their initial scope. In Chapter 11, Hara and Chae proposed two new types of affordances—based on the interview data of COVID-19 scientists who were active on social media—to identify how they interacted with the public during the pandemic.

Altogether, the chapters in this book showcase trailblazing research in the SI field. We hope that this book will provide new insights into how digital technologies are intertwined with people and practices, demonstrating these advances through new empirical findings that push forward SI theories and methods.

References

Agre, P. E. (2002). Real-time politics: The Internet and the political process. *The information society, 18*(5), 311–331.

Barrett, M., Oborn, E., Orlikowski, W. J., & Yates, J. (2011). Reconfiguring boundary relations: Robotic innovations in pharmacy work. *Organization Science, 23*(5), 1213–1522.

Callon, M. (1999). The role of lay people in the production and dissemination of scientific knowledge. *Science, Technology & Society, 4*(1), 81–94.

Contractor, N. (2009). The emergence of multidimensional networks. *Journal of Computer-Mediated Communication, 14*(3), 743–747.

Contractor, N., Monge, P., & Leonardi, P. M. (2011). Network theory | Multidimensional networks and the dynamics of sociomateriality: Bringing technology inside the network. *International Journal of Communication, 5.* https://ijoc.org/index.php/ijoc/article/view/1131

Day, R. E. (2007). Kling and the "critical": Social informatics and critical informatics. *Journal of the American Society for Information Science and Technology, 58*(4), 575–582.

Duan, Y., Hemsley, J., Smith, A. O., Joh, U., Gray, L., & Khoury, C. (2024). Curating virality: Exploring curated logics within# BlackLivesMatter on Twitter/X. *Social Media + Society, 10*(2), https://doi.org/10.1177/2056305124124279

Dutton, W. H. (2013). Internet studies: The foundations of a transformative field. In W. H. Dutton (Ed.), *The Oxford handbook of internet studies* (pp. 1–23). Oxford University Press.

Dutton, W. H., & Graham, M. (2014). Introduction. In M. Graham & W. H. Dutton (Eds.), *Society & the internet* (pp.1–24). Oxford University Press.

Fichman, P. (2020). The role of culture and collective intelligence in online global trolling: The case of trolling Trump's inauguration speech. *Information, Communication & Society, 25*(7), 1029–1044. https://doi.org/10.1080/1369118X.2020.1824006

Fichman, P., & Amidu, G. (2024). The roles of the collapsing contexts and TikTok's features in reciprocal trolling. *Information, Communication, and Society.* https://doi.org/10.1080/1369118X.2024.2391820

Fichman, P., & Dedema, M. (2023). A social informatics approach to online communities of practice of the art recreation challenge on Instagram during COVID-19. In S. Yang, X. Zhu, & P. Fichman (Eds.), *The usage and impact of ICTs during the Covid-19 Pandemic* (1st ed., pp. 67–97). Routledge. https://doi.org/10.4324/9781003231769

Fichman, P., & Hara, N. (2014). *Global Wikipedia: International and cross-cultural issues in online collaboration.* Rowman & Littlefield.

Fichman, P., & Rathi, M. (2023). Trolling CNN and Fox News on Facebook, Instagram, and Twitter. *Journal of the American Society for Information Science and Technology, 74*(5), 493–505.

Fichman, P., & Rosenbaum, H. (Eds.). (2014). *Social informatics: Past, present and future.* Cambridge Scholars Publishing.

Fichman, P., & Vaughn, M. (2021). The relationships between misinformation and outrage trolling tactics on two Yahoo! Answers categories. *Journal of the Association for Information Science and Technology, 72*(12), 1498–1510.

Giddens, A. (1991). Structuration theory: Past, present and future. In C. Bryant & D. Jary (Eds.), *Giddens' theory of structuration* (pp. 201–221). Routledge.

Goggins, S., & Petakovic, E. (2014). Connecting theory to social technology platforms: A framework for measuring influence in context. *American Behavioral Scientist, 58*(10), 1376–1392. https://doi.org/10.1177/0002764214527093

Greyson, D. (2019). The social informatics of ignorance. *Journal of the Association for Information Science & Technology, 70*(4), 412–415.

Hara, N., Abbazio, J. M., & Perkins, K. (2019). An emerging form of public engagement with science: Ask Me Anything (AMA) sessions on Reddit r/science. *PLoS One.* https://journals.plos.org/plosone/article?id=10.1371/journal.pone.0216789

Hara, N., Kim, E., Akter, S., & Miyazaki, K. (2024, July). *Dialogue between scientists and the non-expert public about generative AI.* Joint meeting of the European Association for the Study of Science and Technology (EASST) and the Society for Social Studies of Science (4S), Amsterdam, The Netherlands.

Hara, N., & Sanfilippo, M. R. (2016). Co-constructing controversy: Content analysis of collaborative knowledge negotiation in online communities. *Information, Communication & Society, 19*(11), 1587–1604.

Hara, N., & Sanfilippo, M. R. (2017). Analysis of roles in engaging contentious online discussions in science. *Journal of the Association for Information Science & Technology, 68*(8), 1953–1966.

Jarrahi, M. H., Sawyer, S., & Erickson, I. (2022). Digital assemblages, information infrastructures, and mobile knowledge work. *Journal of Information Technology, 37*(3), 230–249.

Kling, R. (1977). The organizational context of user-centered software designs. *MIS Quarterly, 1*(4), 41–52.

Kling, R. (1978). Value conflicts and social choice in electronic funds transfer system developments. *Communications of the ACM, 21*(8), 642–657.

Kling, R. (1996). *Computerization and controversy: Value conflicts and social choices.* Academic Press.

Kling, R. (2002). Critical professional education about information and communications technologies and social life. *Information Technology & People, 16*(4), 394–418.

Kling, R., & Iacono, S. (1989). The institutional character of computerized information systems. *Information Technology & People, 5*(1), 7–28.

Kling, R., & Lamb, R. (1999). IT and organizational change in digital economies. *Computers & Society, 29*(3), 17–25.

Kling, R., McKim, G., & King, A. (2003). A bit more to it: Scholarly communication forums as socio-technical interaction networks. *Journal of the American Society for Information Science and Technology, 54*(1), 46–67.

Kling, R., Rosenbaum, H., & Sawyer, S. (2005). *Understanding and communicating social informatics: A framework for studying and teaching the human contexts of information and communication technologies.* Information Today.

Kling, R., & Scacchi, W. (1982). The web of computing: Computer technology as social organization. *Advances in Computers, 21*, 1–90.

Kling, R., & Star, S. L. (1998). Human centered systems in the perspective of organizational and social informatics. *ACM SIGCAS Computers and Society, 28*(1), 22–29.

Kraemer, K., & Kling, R. (1988). Political character of computerization in service organizations-citizen interests or bureaucratic control (reprinted from *Computers and the Social-Sciences*, vol 1, pg .77–89, 1985). *Information Age, 10*(4), 229–239.

Lamb, R., & Kling, R. (2003). Reconceptualizing users as social actors in information systems research. *MIS Quarterly, 27*(2), 197–236.

Lamb, R., & Sawyer, S. (2005). On extending social informatics from a rich legacy of networks and conceptual resources. *Information Technology & People, 18*(1), 9–20.

Lee, N. T. (2018). Detecting racial bias in algorithms and machine learning. *Journal of Information, Communication and Ethics in Society, 16*(3), 252–260.

Merchant, B. (2017). *The one device: The secret history of the iPhone.* Little, Brown.

Meyer, E. T. (2006). Socio-technical interaction networks: A discussion of the strengths, weaknesses and future of Kling's STIN model. In J. Berleur, M. I. Numinem, & J. Impagliazzo (Eds.), *Social informatics: An information society for all? In remembrance of Rob Kling* (pp. 37–48). Springer.

Meyer, E. T. (2014). Examining the hyphen: The value of social informatics for research and teaching. In P. Fichman & R. Rosenbaum (Eds.), *Social informatics: Past, present and future* (pp. 56–72). Cambridge Scholars Publishing.

Meyer, E. T., Shankar, K., Willis, M., Sharma, S., & Sawyer, S. (2019). The social informatics of knowledge. *Journal of the Association for Information Science & Technology, 70*(4), 307–312. https://asistdl.onlinelibrary.wiley.com/doi/full/10.1002/asi.24205

Orlikowski, W. J. (1992). The duality of technology: Rethinking the concept of technology in organizations. *Organization Science, 3*(3), 398–427.

Pee, L. G., Pan, S. L., & Cui, L. (2019). Artificial intelligence in healthcare robots: A social informatics study of knowledge embodiment. *Journal of the Association for Information Science & Technology, 70*(4), 351–369.

Rob Kling Center for Social Informatics. (n.d.). https://rkcsi.luddy.indiana.edu/

Sanfilippo, M. R., & Shvartzshnaider, Y. (2023). Technofuturism in play: Privacy, surveillance, and innovation at Walt Disney World. In B. M. Frischmann, M. J. Madison, & M. R. Sanfilippo (Eds.), *Governing smart cities as knowledge commons* (pp. 223–247). Cambridge University Press.

Sanfilippo, M. R., & Strandburg, K. J. (2021). Privacy governing knowledge in public Facebook groups for political activism. *Information, Communication & Society, 24*(7), 960–977.

Sanfilippo, M. R., Yang, S., & Fichman, P. (2017). Trolling here, there, and everywhere: How context impacts trolling behaviors. *Journal of the American Society for Information Science and Technology, 68*(10), 2313–2327.

Shilton, K., & Greene, D. (2019). Linking platforms, practices, and developer ethics: Levers for privacy discourse in mobile application development. *Journal of Business Ethics, 155*, 131–146.

Silverstone, R. (1993, September). Domesticating the revolution: information and communication technologies and everyday life. In *Aslib Proceedings* (Vol. 45, No. 9, pp. 227–233). MCB UP Ltd.

Silverstone, R., & Haddon, L. (1996). Design and the domestication of information and communication technologies: Technical change and everyday life. In R. Mansell & R. Silverstone (Eds.), *Communication by design: The politics of information and communication technologies* (pp. 44–74). Oxford University Press.

Smutny, Z., & Vehovar, V. (2020). Social informatics research: Schools of thought, methodological basis, and thematic conceptualization. *Journal of the Association for Information Science and Technology, 71*, 529–539. https://doi.org/10.1002/asi.24280

Sproull, L., & Kiesler, S. (1991). *Connections*. MIT Press.

Star, S. L., & Griesemer, J. R. (1989). Institutional ecology, 'translations' and boundary objects: Amateurs and professionals in Berkeley's Museum of Vertebrate Zoology, 1907–39. *Social Studies of Science, 19*(3), 387–420. https://doi.org/10.1177/0306312 89019003001

Stvilia, B., & Lee, D. J. (2024). Data quality assurance in research data repositories: A theory-guided exploration and model. *Journal of Documentation, 80*(4), 793–812.

Ward, W. S., & Given, L. M. (2019). Assessing intercultural communication: Testing technology tools for information sharing in multinational research teams. *Journal of the Association for Information Science & Technology, 70*(4), 338–350.

Wu, S., & Resnick, P. (2024). Calibrate-extrapolate: Rethinking prevalence estimation with black box classifiers. *18th International AAAI Conference on Web and Social Media (ICWSM)*, Buffalo, New York.

Yang, S., Zhang, C., & Sang, W. (2019). An analysis on charitable crowdfunding in an authoritarian regime. *Proceedings of the Association of Information Science & Technology, 56*(1), 499–503. https://doi.org/10.1002/pra2.77

Zhu, X. (2017). The failure of an early episode in the open government data movement: A historical case study. *Government Information Quarterly, 34*(2), 256–269.

Zuboff, S. (2023). The age of surveillance capitalism. In W. Longhofer & D. Winchester (Eds.), *Social theory re-wired* (pp. 203–213). Routledge.

SECTION I
Theoretical frameworks of SI

1

SOME REFLECTIONS ON THE GROUNDS OF SOCIAL INFORMATICS

Howard Rosenbaum

Introduction

This chapter is inspired, in part, by Scott and Orlikowski (2013, p. 80), who write that:

> The challenge and opportunity is to turn unsettled and unsettling ideas into inspiration, and differences into analytical edge for deepening understanding so that we might understand the world anew. It flows from this that ruling out novel perspectives and stifling innovation is likely to undermine any field of study. To issue restraining orders on academic views is debilitating, if not deadening.
>
> *(Scott & Orlikowski, 2013, p. 80)*

Social informatics (SI) has been an intellectual and scientific movement since the early 1980s, emerging over the following two decades in several different locations around the world from Norway to Slovenia to Japan to Russia. Fichman et al. (2015) describe the history and development of SI and explain how it has evolved through four main stages since Kling and colleagues began to popularize their version of the approach in the 1980s. In doing so, they review a wide range of research that has been done under the conceptual umbrella of SI. They characterize the current state of SI research in two ways: one is an optimistic sense of transformation in which "researchers started attaching labels to their work other than SI" and began to "address the same problems through different theoretical lens and from different conceptual perspectives" and a more pessimistic sense in which the SI domain is splintering as researchers move in very different directions (Fichman et al., 2015, pp. 23, 24). This latter sentiment is echoed by Smutny and Vehovar (2020), who recently assessed the state of the discipline—noting that while

DOI: 10.4324/9781032678542-3

there had been considerable activity in terms of publications, conference papers, presentations, workshops, etc., it seems to have plateaued by 2015, concluding that SI is "expanding, even as community fragmentation, topical dispersion, and methodological diversity continue to increase" (p. 529).

Are transformation, splintering, fragmentation, topical dispersion, and methodological diversity causes for concern? What is implied for the future of SI if researchers are using different theoretical and conceptual lenses and are less likely to describe their work in print as SI research? Another way to ask these questions is to inquire about the fate of SI as a scientific and intellectual movement (SIM). Applying the framework developed by Frickel and Gross (2005), there could be four different paths that might lay ahead for SI when considered as a SIM. Following the most negative trajectory, SI could simply disappear. The generation of scholars currently involved in SI research could leave the field through lack of interest, retirement, or death without another generation of scholars and researchers coming up to take their place. This approach would then become a footnote in the intellectual history of inquiry into technology and society. In addition to generational change, Vehovar et al. (2022) are concerned that the

> fragmentation and lack of a commonly recognized focus, together with the rise of alternative and competing approaches (e.g., STS [Science and Technology Studies], CSS [Computational Social Science]) addressing similar topics (Petrič and Atanasova 2013; Smutny and Vehovar 2020), can prevent the institutionalization of SI as a discipline and consequently bring about its dissolution as a SIM, in line with the general theory of SIMs (Frickel & Gross, 2005).
>
> *(p. 2)*

A second trajectory is that SI could muddle along under the radar, never quite catching fire. A small number of researchers could continue to publish a small number of papers that would be read and cited by this insular community while the larger community of researchers focused on technology and society would pay them little or no attention. In this case, researchers in cognate domains—such as information science, information systems (IS), new media studies, internet research, digital humanities, digital cultures and heritage, and communications—to name a few, would continue to conduct and publish research that aligns well with SI but would never identify their work as such. A third possibility is that the fragmentation and splintering could abate, and scholarly activity could pick up in a more coherent way, allowing SI to become institutionalized as a legitimate and recognized subdiscipline within the social sciences focusing on the study of people and technology, taking its place alongside cognate forms of inquiry such as STS, CSS, and sociotechnical studies. Sawyer and Tapia (2007) made a case for this path over a decade ago, speculating that it could happen if higher education institutions would foster the emergence and growth of SI research groups or departments with relevant curricula and majors, if there were more conferences devoted to the topic, and if journals would be more receptive to self-identified SI research; however, time has passed and this has not yet happened. A fourth trajectory is that SI becomes a truly revolutionary form of inquiry that significantly changes the way in which we study technology and society.

Assuming that the fourth trajectory is, at this point, highly unlikely, and the first and second should be avoided at all costs, what can be done to help SI move along the third path toward institutionalization? Is it possible to counter the fragmentation and splintering that seems to characterize contemporary SI research? This chapter takes a cautiously optimistic position that it is possible. If this is to happen, progress must be made in several parallel directions, from training the next generation of SI scholars, to developing relevant curricula, to publishing self-identified SI research, to undertaking related initiatives that can be instrumental in the institutionalization of this approach. As a part of this effort, there is also work to be done on SI itself as a form of intellectual inquiry.

It is the assumption of this chapter that as SI enters its fifth decade, there is a need for SI scholars in the brave new world to critically examine its foundations if it is to take its rightful place in the intellectual landscape as an approach focused on the study of the complex interrelationships between society and technology. A brief review of relevant literature will show that there has been little discussion of the grounds on which SI rests. This section will be followed by a discussion of the importance of a social science recognizing and articulating these grounds. A common and widely used definition of SI will be decomposed and four core concepts, technology, people, contexts, and the interplay among the three, will be explored, providing a (hopefully) coherent description of a foundation for SI, or— at the risk of overstating the case—the beginning of a philosophy of technology for SI.

This chapter, if persuasive, will make two main contributions. First, it will address a gap in the literature and answer the call for a common discourse for SI research by initiating a discussion about the philosophical grounds of SI, a topic whose time has come. Second, it will make an explicit case for the importance of social theories in providing these grounds by integrating insights from sociomateriality, structuration theory, and postphenomenology—an integration made possible by the fact that all three share roots in a relational ontology.

What is missing from social informatics and why does it matter?

Consider the North American version of SI, which has been around for more than 25 years. In that time, it has established itself as a viable and useful way to study the mutual shaping that takes place between people and technologies in their many and varied contexts of design and use. As a form of inquiry, SI has been described as problem-centered and has consequently been theoretically and methodologically agnostic (Kling et al., 2005). Researchers have brought a wide range of conceptual frameworks and data gathering strategies to the study of people, technology, and social as well as organizational life and have published and presented their work in a wide variety of venues. What can we learn about the foundation of SI from this literature?

There have not been many extensive reviews of the SI literature that have focused on the approach itself. Vehovar et al. (2022) explain that "while various overviews-and corresponding conceptualizations-of the SI literature have been presented (e.g., Fichman et al., 2015; Smutny, 2016; Smutny & Vehovar, 2020), dedicated empirical studies on SI are rare" (p. 2). Four reviews that have covered the literature are briefly discussed here to demonstrate what is not in the literature.

Early reviews of the literature were conducted by Hoeffner (2012) and Hoeffner and Smiraglia (2012a, 2012b), who used bibliometric and computational methods to assess the extent to which SI exhibited domain coherence at that time. This analysis involved an effort to classify the literature by research focus. Primarily relying on literature from the US version of SI, they analyzed a large corpus of some 7,000 publications to find that the research clustered around computer-mediated communication and information-related topics, including information policy, IS, and the information society. This finding led them to conclude that there was simultaneously increasing diversity and some degree of coherence; interestingly, this finding aligns with the first two stages of the evolution of SI research, expansion, and coherence, in schema proposed by Fichman et al. (2015), discussed below. This review, however, did not surface literature dealing with the grounds or foundations of SI.

Fichman et al. (2015) comprehensively reviewed some 35 years of SI research and organized it in two ways—by chronology and by content. The temporal scheme begins with a foundational period of the 1980s, then expansion seen in the 1990s, followed by a period of coherence from 2000 to 2005, and a transformational period through 2015. They also organized the literature according to the principles, approaches, concepts, topics studied, and main findings published during each period. Examples of principles include:

- Challenges to technological determinism and casting computerization as a sociotechnical phenomenon (foundational);
- Increasing attention to the importance of the social and organizational context, concern for the social impacts of technologies, and the value-laden nature of technology (expansion);
- Mutual shaping of social and technological environments and the importance of a human-centered focus on information and communication technologies (ICT) design and development (cohesion); and
- Differentiation from cognate forms of inquiry into technology and society as well as exploration of approaches such as critical realism and practice theory (transformation) (Fichman et al., 2015).

Examples of concepts include:

- Change, social context, organizational policies, and power relationships (foundational);
- Complexity, computerization movements, dynamics, networks, and unintended consequences (expansion);
- Coordination, governance, and mutual shaping (coherence); and
- Networks and multiculturalism (transformation) (Fichman et al., 2015).

Principles and concepts would seem to be the most likely types of content in which discussions of the grounds of SI could be found, but this does not seem to have been the case. For example, ICT and computerization are frequently mentioned, but their nature is taken for granted. What is the technological artifact at the heart of SI? There is also considerable discussion of the user and—with the possible exception of Lamb and Davidson (2005) and Lamb and Kling (2003), who argued that ICT users are social actors—the nature of the person has not been examined closely. What does it mean to be a social actor? Is this dramaturgical metaphor a conceptually sound way to describe the person who interacts with ICT? There is a significant theme that runs through the SI literature, which characterizes the relationship between people and technology as one of mutual shaping, but what does this mean? And what is the status of the concept of the context that is the backdrop against which and within which people and ICT interact? Reflecting on these questions is one way to open a discourse about the foundations of SI.

Smutny and Vehovar (2020) review a range of more contemporary literature in their analysis of what they describe as the "major schools" of SI. They argue that one of the issues that may have contributed to the current state of the field, which they describe as expanding but fragmented,

> … could also have arisen because, from the very beginning, SI is not a well-defined field (Nakata, 2008), even in the foundational work of Kling, Crawford, Rosenbaum, Sawyer, and Weisband (2000). Consequently, the term SI can be understood in different ways (Kling, 2007).
>
> *(p. 529)*

They explain that there is a fundamental ambiguity in the label because the word "social" could mean a society, a specific group, the act of being social, and a profession (social work) (p. 530); when translated into other languages, even more ambiguities can be introduced. Similarly, the term informatics carries multiple meanings: technology design, computational processes, and information processes. It is therefore not surprising that the different schools of SI (German, Japanese, Norwegian, Russian, Slovenian, UK, and US) have followed somewhat different trajectories as SIMs since the very name of the field exhibits polysemy and has different nuances in different languages and epistemic cultures. Despite this divergence, they do find that research in these different schools that self-identify as SI by and large engages with three main themes:

1 The general interactions between ICT and humans originate in the social sciences. The focus is on the social aspects of ICT implementation, use, and design in general terms.
2 The ICT applications in substantive areas related to the social sciences have origins in informatics (understood in its broadest sense).
3 The ICT applications serving as social sciences research tools have origins in social sciences research methodology … (Smutny & Vehovar 2020, p. 534)

What is clear from their analysis is that there has been little attention paid to the grounds of SI. In fact, one of their recommendations in part addresses this issue:

… Explicit referencing to some SI conceptual basis should become more important in the combined stream of (self-declared) SI research, which often lacks any conceptual grounding. This will help SI to not be just an empty container where scholars talk about SI-related studies without any direct references to SI.

(Smutny & Vehovar, 2020, p. 537)

To use their metaphor, an exploration of its foundations may contribute to the initial stages of filling the container of SI.

Vehovar et al. (2022) return to the SI literature with an exhaustive and rigorous review of trends in the field between 2015 and 2019. They review "scholarly literature, research and educational institutions, conferences, journals, blogs, and presentations at the International Conference on Social Informatics" (p. 1), providing a global view of the state of SI. This review is the latest in a series of empirical studies of the domain conducted by Slovenian scholars since 2006. In their review of prior literature, Vehovar et al. (2022) explain that "the findings of these studies cannot be readily compared, as they each took a slightly different approach to identifying SI-related research" (p. 3). A trend that they noticed in the literature is that more than half of their corpus was theoretical (56%), creating a theoretical core dominated by the US School. Although this work was done earlier and recently (2015–2019), empirical work has been more common (Vehovar et al., 2022, p. 8). Again, there is no indication that among these theoretical publications were those exploring the conceptual foundations of SI.

Echoing their earlier analysis, they describe the current state of fragmentation and some stagnation to the point at which "scholars conducting research in SI-related areas have shown very weak self-identification with SI on a conceptual level" and "the uninformed use of the SI label, which is increasingly used to superficially characterize any form of research dealing with the interaction between ICTs and society" (2022, pp. 1–2, 24). However, this development is mitigated by a more positive assessment that "the field is healthy and that it continuously evolves and adapts to changes related to the interactions between ICTs and society. SI has also become a global research endeavor, with publications coming from an increasingly wide range of regions" (Vehovar et al., 2022, p. 24). Nevertheless, one reason why scholars and researchers show weak identification with SI at a conceptual level is because this level has not received the sustained analytic attention that it needs.

These literature reviews provide cogent analyses of the SI literature but do not provide clear evidence that SI scholars have attempted to provide a rational reconstruction of the conceptual basis of this form of inquiry. To do so would entail describing the philosophical assumptions that underpin the practice of this form of social inquiry. Why is it important for SI (or any social science) to explicitly acknowledge its foundations? According to Langsdorf (2015) "all of our investigations, indeed all of our mundane activities, are based on metaphysical assumptions and convictions, most of which go unnoticed" (p. 45). Woolgar (2012) frames this insight as a question: "what are our fundamental predispositions about the status of entities in the world and how do these organize our thinking and practice" (p. 33)? In the case of SI, this effort aligns with Vehovar et al.'s (2022) recommendation that "different schools of SI work together to find a common denominator of core SI ideas" to articulate the "very broad common discourse" that they see connecting the different schools (p. 24). The task of this chapter, then, is to attempt to foreground what Langsdorf calls assumptions and convictions and Woolgar terms fundamental predispositions.

To do this, it is useful to begin by considering ways in which SI has evolved, which means posing several more questions. What is it about SI that allows it to cast such a wide net and, in a sense, accommodate most participants? Are there common themes that run through the diverse research that makes up contemporary SI? Another way to pose this question is to ask about the research philosophy that animates SI. How is the world constituted when viewed through the lens of SI? This is the question of its ontological grounds. The National Academies of Sciences, Engineering, & Medicine (2022) explains that "Ontologies are essential to science because they identify and clarify the entities and concepts that people want to talk about and study, and they identify the key relationships among those concepts" (p. 14). Given this reality, how can we best come to know this world? This is the question of the epistemological grounds of SI. As Alvesson and Skoldberg (2009) argue, "ontology and epistemology determine good social science" (p. 8). The former is important because it "helps researchers recognize how certain they can be about the nature and existence of objects they are researching" and the latter because it specifies "what constitutes a knowledge claim" as well as how it can be acquired (Moon & Blackman, 2017).

What, then, are the ontological and epistemological foundations of SI? As described above, this question has not received sufficient attention throughout the history of North American SI research, and this chapter provides an initial and exploratory opportunity to highlight a discourse about the foundations of

SI. This chapter will explore this question through a close reading of selected works in sociomateriality, postphenomenology, and structuration theory. For example, from sociomateriality, the materiality of the IT artifact will be considered (Leonardi, 2013), and concepts of entanglement—which focus on "the intimate inter-dependencies within socio-material (and consequently, sociotechnical) arrangements" (Fraunberger, 2019, p. 3)—can be used to explore the relationship between people and technologies. From structuration theory, the articulation of the fundamental relationship between structure and agency can be shown to play a role in the SI discourse about the mutual shaping between people and technology and can provide a useful conceptualization of the context. From postphenomenology, the insights that "technologies [are] actively mediating a person's every-day being ... [and] have the capacity to transform [their] experiences" (Demody & Fritz, 2019, p. 6) can motivate understanding of the ways in which this mediation happens. Taken together, these approaches can begin to provide a basis of a philosophical grounding for SI and spur reflection on a common discourse for SI researchers.

Explorations of ontology and epistemology are the basis of the philosophical grounding of SI, as they are for the social sciences in general (Oppong, 2014, p. 243). The two are distinct but related; as Kant (2014) explains,

> Ontology then is concerned with the nature of reality or existence, which is "apart from the nature of any existent object" (Flew, 1984, p. 255; see Blaikie, 2007, p. 13). It addresses the question of "what is out there to know about" (Grix, 2002, p. 1). In the social sciences ontologies concern the question: "'What is the nature of social reality?'" (Blaikie, 2007, p. 13).

Epistemology studies theories of knowledge, how knowledge is derived (for instance, by reason or experience, which may both take various forms), and the reliability and validity of knowledge claims (Flew, 1984, p. 109; see Grix, 2002, p. 177) (pp. 69–70)

There is ongoing debate about the relation and directionality between the two; there are arguments that: they are distinct, that they should be conflated, that ontology precedes epistemology, and that the reverse is the case (Ferraris, 2020; Kant, 2014; Furlong & Marsh, 2010; Hartel, 2003; Grix, 2002). There is, however, consensus that scientific research presupposes some ontological assumptions about the world and the phenomenon to be studied as well as epistemological assumptions about how the inquiry will be carried out and what will constitute reliable knowledge (Grix, 2002, p. 2). The assumption is made here that these two forms of inquiry are separate. Given this presumption and given the complexity of the debate, this chapter will take up the challenge of exploring the ontological foundations of SI. Should this exploration prove useful and interesting, subsequent analysis will question the epistemology of SI. Ontology, then, provides an account of what general types of entities exist, thereby specifying domains for inquiry. It also takes a position on whether and which of these entities can exist independently of humans and human consciousness and, of particular interest here, of the status of tangible and intangible entities created by humans. What then are the general types of entities found in SI?

What are the grounds of social informatics?

Information and communication technologies from a social informatics perspective

One point of entry into reflections on the grounds of SI is through a widely used definition; it is:

> ... an approach to studying the social aspects of computing that takes into account the complex interplay between information and communication technologies (ICT), the people who design, implement, manage, and use them, and the contexts of their design and use.
>
> *(Fichman et al., 2015, p. 4)*

Embedded in this definition are fundamental entities that can be placed in some relation to each other; these are objects and their materiality, agents, agency, and contexts. It is clear that the primary objects of interest in SI are ICT. SI researchers assume, and in fact now take for granted, that these technologies are always embedded in different social and organizational contexts and then typically go on to investigate how people design, implement, and use them as well as the intended and unintended consequences that follow their adoption and use. This move, while clearly producing valuable insights, seems to sidestep the issue of the impacts of these technologies' materiality. At the beginning of this century, Orlikowski and Iacono (2001) threw down a gauntlet and challenged the IS research community to theorize the information technology (IT) artifact. They begin by asserting that "the field of Information Systems (IS), which is premised on the centrality of information technology in everyday life, has not deeply engaged its core subject matter—the Information Technology (IT) artifact" (p. 121). Consequently, they argue, IS researchers have uncritically adopted a version of the IT artifact that sees it as stable, discrete, independent, and fixed. A little more than a decade later, Akhlaghpour et al. (2013) conducted a replication of this work, examined IS research published in top journals between 2006 and 2009, and found "no drastic advance in terms of deeper engagement with the IT artifact; more than 39% of the articles in our set are virtually mute about the artifact" (p. 150).

It should be noted that since then, there has been debate in the IS literature about the continued viability of the concept of the IT artifact with, for example, Alter (2015) calling for its retirement, and Thomas et al. (2022) arguing instead for the use of the concept of the "information systems artifact." Despite this debate—the engagement with which is beyond the scope of this chapter—the central insight remains that there is a need for some term to represent the object of study so Orlikowski and Iacono's terminology will be used here. Whatever it is called, it has been the case that the IS research community seems to have not been focused on its core object of study, so what then of the theorization of ICT as an IT artifact in SI?

Early SI research was heavily influenced by ideas championed by Kling and colleagues that led to a more nuanced articulation of the IT artifact that moved past its conception as stable, discrete, independent, and fixed. Pushing back against the technological determinism that was prevalent among researchers studying the social impacts of computing in the 1970s and 1980s, alternative conceptualizations were introduced into the literature. One influential example was Kling and Scacchi's (1982) "web of computing" model, which argued that information technologies were never really independent and discrete entities and were in fact always embedded in webs or networks of relationships and arrangements that constituted the social contexts of computing. Researchers subsequently began to explore ICT in organizational and social settings, leading to a set of findings about the IT artifact that have become part of the SI core body of knowledge. For example, information technologies are value-laden, have moral and ethical aspects, are configurable, have multiple and seemingly paradoxical impacts, and tend to favor the status quo. These qualities began to make clear that conceptualizations of the IT artifact in SI research have focused on its social elements; furthermore, the artifact has been described as having social, technical, and institutional natures (Kling et al., 2005; Lamb & Sawyer, 2005; Sawyer, 2005) or, more generally, have been described as sociotechnical network systems (Kling, 2000a, 2000b; Kling & Iacono, 2001; Kling et al., 2003; Lamb & Kling, 2003; Lamb & Sawyer, 2005). From a focus on the IT artifact's social nature, the conceptualization expanded and placed the artifact in a network or ensemble web of computing. While these findings and assumptions begin to describe the IT artifact, particularly its social and network properties, they seem to be hovering around it. What is SI's IT artifact in itself?

Information and communication technologies from a sociomaterial perspective

One way to answer this question is by drawing on sociomateriality, a conceptual lens through which the materiality of technology can be recovered and its role in social and organizational activities clarified. Before discussing the way in which the IT artifact can be conceptualized using this approach, a digression about the nature of sociomateriality is necessary to clarify the version that will figure in the discussion below; a distinction between weak and strong sociomateriality will be discussed and the latter will be relied upon to explore the IT artifact in SI.

Sociomateriality emerged in the early years of the twenty-first century among IS and other researchers engaged in the study of technology and organizations.

According to Jones (2014, p. 896), the approach came to the attention of the field with the publication of Orlikowski (2007). This move was prompted by some researchers' dissatisfaction with approaches that did not seem to be capable of coming to terms with the ways in which modern technologies were impacting organizations, people, and societies. Digital technologies were beginning to blur the previously clear distinctions between "agential humans" and "passive technologies" as these artifacts became ever more deeply embedded in the routines of people's social and work lives. It became clear that these technologies in use could "shape and enact social changes by actively learning and adopting to the social and technological behavior of others" (Niemimaa et al., 2023, p. 182). What were the implications of the increasing ubiquity of digital networked technology? What did this move mean for the ways in which the IT artifact was conceived?

Although not commenting on sociomaterality, Feenberg (2015) offers a perspective that mirrors a key insight that was taken up by early sociomateriality researchers, explaining that technology has always been an essential part of human nature and therefore can be seen as having ontological status:

> We are homo technologicus by our very nature. Technology is not something added on after the fact, like those peculiar little sweaters small dogs are sometimes outfitted with in winter. No. Technology is as natural to human beings as language and culture; its specific content is historically contingent, but it will always be found wherever there are human beings.
>
> *(p. 230)*

Feenberg (2015) argues that technology and humanity have always been bound up in each other. Sociomateriality was introduced into IS research as one way to study the entanglement of humans and technology that makes humans "homo technologicus." There has been considerable debate in the literature since the mid-2000s about the ways in which to account for the relationship between the social and the material, and sociomateriality "stands out as a symbol for the interest in the social and the technical, and in particular, the subtleties of their contingent intertwining" (Cecez-Kecmanovic et al., 2014, p. 809).

Over time, two main versions of sociomateriality have drawn the most interest and critical attention. What distinguishes them is their very different approaches to ontology. Jones (2014) describes these two versions as being "weak" and "strong," differentiated by their ontological assumptions (pp. 918–919). The former assumes that there are independent and discrete entities that constitute the world through engagement with each other, generating sociomateriality, while the latter assumes that the world is fundamentally sociomaterial and made up of entities that only exist in their relation to others. Below, these approaches are compared, and an explanation is offered to support the decision to use strong over weak sociomateriality.

Weak sociomateriality

Weak sociomateriality adopts a substantialist ontology that distinguishes between the social and the material, as well as between humans and technologies, reflecting a dualist perspective in which these elements are seen as independent fundamental substances that interact in shaping the world. Aligned with critical realism (CR), which posits an absolute reality beyond human knowledge shaped by structured interactions of material and non-material agents (Garbutt & Van Den Berg, 2022, p. 3), weak sociomateriality integrates these ideas and defines sociomateriality as the enactment of activities blending materiality with social phenomena like institutions and norms (Leonardi, 2012). Materiality in this context refers to the intrinsic aspects of IT artifacts, separate from their social or organizational context, enduring across time and place but evolving through human or external interventions (Leonardi, 2012, p. 31). Thus, IT artifacts exhibit trajectories of stabilization and change throughout their lifetimes, with interventions introducing new forms of materiality that become stable components. This understanding challenges the notion of materiality as static, emphasizing instead its evolving and dynamic nature.

Weak sociomateriality has undoubtedly enriched our understanding of how the social and material elements interact to shape the social world. However, it has faced criticism, primarily due to its reliance on a substantive ontology reminiscent of Cartesian dualism. This perspective posits that the social and the material are separable and independent entities, akin to enduring realities underlying their observable qualities, which "endure unchanged through the changes of those qualities" (Cecez-Kecmanovic, 2016, pp. 5–6). Such an approach raises challenges in defining these unchanging realities within both realms.

Moreover, weak sociomateriality inherits complexities from its foundation in CR, which advocates for a dualist ontology comprising observable and unobservable levels of reality. Zhang (2023) describes this conceptualization as ontological realism, which is based on the existence of a transcendental reality independent of human awareness or empirical scrutiny (p. 15). This stance, stemming from Bhaskar (1975), delineates an intransitive realm of unobservable structures and mechanisms that influence the transitive realm of observable events (Zhang, 2023). However, this dualist ontology presents a significant challenge: it supports two conflicting versions of reality. One version suggests an empirical process in which observable events emerge from the intransitive realm, facilitating empirical knowledge acquisition. Zhang (2023) sees two problems with this implication:

> First, ontologically, how can the postulate of the real be justified, as no one can possess direct knowledge of the real?
>
> Second, practically, why is the postulate of the real essential for a post-positivist social science paradigm, if ontology also has to come from the observable? Since all human knowledge comes from the observable, the real cannot serve as the source or touchstone of metaphysics …

(pp. 19–20)

The second version is that "the real" generates the observable, which is the source of empirical knowledge, but the real is also the source of ontological knowledge, which is then intransitive. Zhang (2023) states that

> If ontology is understood as a direct representation of the real beyond our knowledge, CR needs to make the troublesome assumption that … some humans possess a cognitive ability that allows them to directly comprehend the transcendental reality without the intermediary of experience or the observable world.
>
> *(p. 20)*

Perhaps recognizing that the substantive ontology of weak sociomateriality actually aligns well with CR and with that which dominates much of IS research (Cecez-Kecmanovic et al., 2014, p. 809), Jones (2014) finds that "in general terms … sociomateriality, particularly in its weak variant, might not appear so different from other, more established research traditions and might, therefore, be considered redundant" (p. 921).

Strong sociomateriality

Strong sociomateriality assumes a relational and practice-based ontology that does not draw distinctions between the social and material or between people and technologies. Strongly influenced by Barad's (1996, 2003, 2007, 2011) agential realism,[1] this version rejects that dualism characterizes the substantialist version of sociomateriality, in which—in IS research—"ontological priority is given to human actors and social structures and, as a result, technological artifacts (and materiality more generally) tend to disappear into the background and become taken for granted" (Orlikowski, 2009, p. 129). Similar to SI, it challenges the technological determinism that posits and reifies technology as an exogenous causal force and the view that technologies are "material artifacts that are socially defined and socially produced, and thus as relevant only in relation to the people engaging with them" (Orlikowski, 2009, p. 131). The former leads to inadequate accounts of human agency, and the latter leads to an equally inadequate account of technology's role in the process of organizing.

Strong sociomateriality has also been criticized but for being too abstract and for not providing clear methodological guidance (Cecez-Kecmanovic et al., 2014; Kautz & Jensen, 2012, 2013). However, the intent of specifying its ontological grounds means that the explanation will be necessarily abstract and requires asserting and defending metaphysical assumptions. The move to develop methodological practices based on such a foundation is a next step. As Niemimaa et al. (2023) explain, their primary objective is to "distil methodological practices tor sociometrical theorizing in IS research founded on the notion of becoming, particularly in agential realism (Barad, 2003, 2007)" (p. 183). A discussion of such a methodological initiative, while intriguing and important, is beyond the scope of this chapter.

A more sustained critique has been offered by Mutch (2013), who described strong sociomateriality as a "wrong turning" because it is incapable of doing justice to the study of material properties' nature and the impact of the material on social and organizational life; also, the strong sociomateriality of Orlikowski and Scott (2008) cannot adequately provide insight into the "combinations of the social and the material" (Mutch, 2013, pp. 32). Scott and Orlikowski (2013) respond, explaining that their version of sociomateriality is not intended to analyze a dualist take on the material and the social because of its reliance on agential realism, which has an "ontology [that] is explicitly opposed to viewing the social and material as separate, and assuming that properties and boundaries are inherent" (p. 78). Furthermore, they (2013) explain that agential realism's

> presumptions of non-separability ("entanglement") and non-essentialism ("indeterminacy") make it unsuitable to studying the "impacts" of technology or how technology "inscribes" aspects of social structure (Mutch, 2013, p. 38).
>
> *(p. 79)*

Scott and Orlikowski also mention two additional issues with Mutch's critique. First, they dismiss Mutch's criticisms of Barad (2003, 2007), from whose work they draw heavily, because he engages in criticism by proxy and "claims fundamental difficulties with Barad's work by examining work done by others" (Scott & Orlikowski, 2013, p. 69). Second, Mutch criticizes their version of sociomateriality because it does not adequately make use of some of CR's basic concepts and ideas, his favored approach. These criticisms do not seem significant enough to derail strong sociomateriality, so it will provide the basis for what follows.

Strong sociomateriality rejects the assumptions of the fundamental ontological status of substance or entities and their independence from each other, and the relegation of relations that could occur among them as secondary. The latter is instead assumed to be the most fundamental element, hence the name relational ontology (Scott & Orlikowski, 2014, p. 878). This is to say that relations, in the form of practices, become the main focus and unit of analysis. Substance or entities become secondary, gaining meaning, significance, and identity through the dynamism of practice. Slife (2004) provides more detail, asserting that each entity, "including each person, is first and always a nexus of relations" (p. 159). The qualities of entities are "temporary distinctions made in the transactional contexts of which they are a part" (Niemimaa et al., 2023, p. 183). The notion of becoming captures the dynamism of practice and implies that the world is an ongoing and open-ended flow of events (Visser & Davies, 2021, p. 1818). The relational nature of the world also means that materiality is as important to the constitution of practices as are humans.

This version of sociomateriality has a very different conception of technology as an IT artifact since it is not seen as substance; according to Orlikowski (2009):

> From such a performative perspective, technologies have no inherent properties, boundaries or meanings, but are bound up with the specific material-discursive practices that constitute certain phenomena.
>
> *(p. 135)*

The IT artifact, then, has materiality and is deeply engaged in the co-constitution of practices and therefore the world. However, as viewed from within agential realism, the IT artifact is not seen as a discrete entity and is entangled with humans and/or other artifacts. It is "matter," as Barad (2003) argues, and is "given its due as an active participant in the world's becoming, in its ongoing 'intraactivity'" (p. 809)—Barad's term for the activity that produces the "resulting entanglements of matter and meaning that produce the world in practice" (Scott & Orlikowski, 2014, p. 876). In this view, the IT artifact is not a "thing"—it is a "relation" and a phenomenon (Barad, 2003, pp. 814, 815). Phenomena are constitutive of reality and are "ontologically primitive relations—relations without preexisting relata" (Barad, 2003, p. 815); furthermore, "Reality is not composed of things-in-themselves or things-behind-phenomena, but things-in-phenomena" (Barad, 1996, p. 177).

Entanglement, then, becomes a core concept of strong sociomateriality. It is ontological and assumes that the boundaries among the entities that are entangled are fluid and changing (Orlikowski & Scott, 2015, p. 699). This is not to say that there are no longer any differences, because "boundaries are iteratively and differentially enacted through situated material-discursive practices" (Niemimaa et al., 2023, p. 183). For example, there are differences between the technology and the person, but they are not fixed or invariant; how these differences are instantiated will be discussed in the "Mutual shaping from sociomaterial and postphenomenological perspectives" Section. What the IT artifact becomes is an emergent phenomenon involving entanglements with the people who use it as well as give it meaning and identity. This development is a form of "interpretive flexibility" (Pinch, 2010, p. 79) because the meaning and identity of the artifact (and the person) can and will change over time. Although agential realism does not privilege either the material or the social (Barad, 1996, p. 180), entanglements can involve assemblages of entities with asymmetric agency and influences, both internal and external. As Kautz and Plumb (2016) explain:

> This 'mutual constitution of entangled agencies' (Barad, 2007) which performs the world in practice is known in Barad's (2003) terminology as intra-action. It is through this intra-action that the practices delineate entities and enact their specific distinctions, boundaries and properties, a local resolution of

determinacy which Barad (2003) refers to as an agential cut; intra-actions within a phenomenon enact local agential separability and agential cuts which affect and allow for local separation within a phenomenon.

(p. 35)

The assumption that there is no distinction between social and material is illustrated by Introna's (2009) comment that

It would not be incorrect to say that our existence has now become so entangled with the things surrounding us (if it even makes sense to use the notion of 'surround') that it is no longer possible to say, in any definitive way, where we end and they begin, and vice versa.

(p. 26)

People and technologies are then seen as ontologically inseparable and, given a relational and practice-based ontology, are constituted—or, in other words, come into being—through sociomaterial practices, which, as relations, precede all other entities (Cecez-Kecmanovic et al., 2014, p. 809). According to Slife (2004),

Strong relationality … is an ontological relationality. Relationships are not just the interactions of what was originally nonrelational; relationships are relational 'all the way down.' Things are not first self-contained entities and then interactive. Each thing, including each person, is first and always a nexus of relations.

(p. 159)

Orlikowski (2009) describes these relations as being enacted performatively[2] through "material-discursive" (p. 135) practices, which are seen as "constitutive, they configure reality, or put another way, they are performative" (Orlikowski & Scott, 2015, p. 700).

The agent from a sociomaterial perspective

When considering the importance of the social aspects of computing to the core of SI, it is clear that research must consider the person as an agent in the complex interplay between ICT and people. The IT artifact as a material object is designed, built, and used by people who bring values, intentions, and goals to the process. Ihde and Malafouris (2019) argue that humans have ontological status as homo faber, the maker, because "… we become constituted through making and using technologies that shape our minds and extend our bodies. We make things which in turn make us" (p. 195). Humans participate in creative material engagement, which involves a long-term commitment to what Malafouris (2014) describes as the discovery of new varieties of material forms, so far as it is possible in a given historical situation, through a saturated, situated engagement of thinking and feeling with things and form-generating materials.

(p. 144)

People as agents are not simply adapting to their social and organizational surroundings; they are engaging in a co-constitutive relationship with them. Through this engagement, in a Heideggerian sense, people change and grow over time because they are "self-conscious fabricators that become ... through their creative engagement with the material world" (Ihde & Malafouris, 2019, p. 200). This view of the person as agent has similarities to an earlier argument by Baker (2002), who finds that persons have ontological status because they

> are real individuals whose appearance in the world makes an ontological difference. They have ontological significance.

In short, the uniqueness of self-conscious beings-of beings who can think of themselves as themselves, who have inner lives-makes it plausible to hold that to be a person is to be a special kind of thing-a thing that has ontological significance in virtue of being of that kind. (pp. 378, 388)

In strong sociomateriality, the person is also given ontological status but as phenomena. Barad (2003) argues that "Bodies are not objects with inherent boundaries and properties; they are material-discursive phenomena. 'Human' bodies are not inherently different from 'nonhuman' ones" (p. 823). This is to say that when constitutive entanglements join together the social and material, the human is similarly entangled and, as Barad (2003) argues, agential realism

> does not fix the boundary between 'human' and 'nonhuman' before the analysis ever gets off the ground but rather enables (indeed demands) a genealogical analysis of the discursive emergence of the 'human.'

(p. 821)

As with the IT artifact, humans are seen as in a state of becoming since they are—in Barad's terms—materialized through the performance of material-discursive practices. In this view, the IT artifact and humans share materiality; they are composed of matter, which "does not refer to a fixed substance; rather, matter is substance in its intra-active becoming—not a thing, but a doing, a congealing of agency" (Barad, 2003, p. 822). Because both are ontological phenomena, they "are constitutive of reality. Reality is not composed of things-in-themselves or things-behind-phenomena, but things-in-phenomena" (Barad, 1996, p. 177).

The context from a structurational perspective

The concept of context in SI is typically seen as being social and/or organizational. Fichman et al. (2015) find that "one of the insights that emerged from early SI work that remains important today is the significance of the context" (p. 2). It has been described as: institutional, cultural (Kling, 1998, 1999), sociotechnical (Sawyer & Eschenfelder, 2002), informational (Lamb, 1996), and as an ICT interaction context (Lamb et al., 2003). There are contexts of design and use, which are sometimes described as sociocultural. Contexts are thought to be dynamic, complex, and changing over time. Fichman and Sanfilippo (2013) argue for the critical significance of context for understanding the ways in which people and technologies act and interact within their contexts because, over time, this activity can lead to changes in all three. Fichman et al. (2015, p. 2) take this reasoning a step further and, using the internet of things as an example, ask: what happens when the technology itself is the context?

There is no doubt that context is another core concept for SI, and its importance is indicated by the variety of ways that it has been used. A wide range of descriptors have been used to describe context, attributing to it a broad variety of qualities. SI studies have found that the organizations in which ICT are designed and built can influence the developmental process. Similarly, the organizational and social settings in which these technologies are adopted and used can shape the ways in which people use them and integrate them into their work and social lives. What is it about these contexts that endows them with this type of limited material agency?

One possible explanation for this aspect of context can be drawn from Giddens' (1984, 1991) structuration theory. Briefly, structuration is an example of what Skinner (1985) calls a "grand theory," meaning that it is an attempt to "construct a systematic theory of the nature of [persons] and society" (p. 3). It provides a complex explanation of the process by which society and individuals are created and recreated through ongoing and routine social practices. Giddens' theory rejects dualism—as does sociomateriality—but this time, it is between structure and agency. At the heart of his approach is the social practice of structuration, which entails that structure and agency are seen as a duality in which both are implicated in "social practices ordered across time and space" that are "key mediating moments between" structure and agency (Giddens, 1979, p. 5). Here, Giddens effectively sidesteps the problem of attempting to account for structure and agency from determinist or structural perspectives by providing a new starting point—social practices. With this move, he (1984) shifts the focus from structure and agency to social practices so that "the basic domain of study ... is neither the experience of the individual actor nor the existence of any form of social totality, but social practices ordered across space and time" (p. 2). Therefore, social practices are "at the root of both the constitution of subject and object" (Giddens, 1984, p. xxii) and "simultaneously constitute society and individual subjects" (Browne, 1993, p. 138).

In structuration theory, the conception of context plays an important role in the constitution of society because people make use of it as they engage in social practices. There are three main components of context that Giddens (1984) describes as modalities of structuration, which "clarify the main dimensions of the duality of structure in interaction, relating the knowledgeable capacities of agents to structural features" (p. 28). These modalities include signification, which refers to meaning and communication structures; domination, which includes structures of power and control; and legitimation, which includes norms and sanctions. According to Giddens, people routinely draw upon all three modalities as they interact, although in different degrees and with different outcomes depending on the context within which and the others with whom they interact.

From the perspective of SI, the question of the ways in which contexts have limited agency can be tentatively answered. Giddens' conception of structure is composed of rules and resources, two concepts that are "recursively implicated in the reproduction of social interaction and social systems." They exist "as time-space presence, only in its instantiations in such practices and memory traces" that orient conduct and action (Giddens, 1984, pp. xxxi, 17). Until it is drawn upon in the enactment of social practices, structure remains a "virtual order of relations, out of time and space" (Giddens, 1984, pp. 304). As people engage in social practices, they make use of rules and resources, and structure is instantiated "in the knowledgeable activities of situated human subjects which reproduce them as structural properties of social systems embedded in spans of time space" (Giddens, 1984, p. 304). This, then, is a structurational conception of context.

Rules are "techniques or generalizable procedures applied in the enactment/ reproduction of social practices" that are trans-situational, allowing a "methodical continuation of an established sequence" (Giddens, 1984, pp. 21, 20). These rules shape and influence social interactions and are components of the social and organizational settings in which the interactions take place. Of interest here are the rules that are drawn upon when people use ICT. For example, there are rules that have developed governing smartphone etiquette and others that govern permissions to access IS. These rules can be constitutive, regulative, or equivalent to habit or routine and structure routine social life through the forming, sustaining, termination, and reforming of social interactions.

Resources, the second important element of context, are means by and through which people can intervene in the world and, with differing degrees of success, pursue their goals and effect change. Resources are not static and are dynamically produced and reproduced through social practices. They are "modes whereby transformative relations are actually incorporated into the production and reproduction of social practices" (Giddens, 1984, p. 17) and are deeply implicated in and necessary components of the exercise of power, which Giddens (1984) sees as "profoundly embedded" in taken-for-granted and "routinized behavior" (p. 176). The two main types of resources are allocative, providing command over objects, and authoritative, providing command over people; both are necessary in the generation of power, as people invoke or make use of them differentially in different contexts. They are deeply intertwined with power relations within society and individuals, and groups have differential access to them based on their positions within social structures. In this sense, rules and resources are both enabling and constraining factors of the social and organizational contexts of social life.

Based on this conception of context, SI research can begin to analyze the contexts within which ICT are designed, developed, implemented, and used— perhaps focusing on the three modalities of structuration, rules, and resources.

Mutual shaping from sociomaterial and postphenomenological perspectives

The complex interplay between ICT, people, and contexts of design and use is perhaps the most critical relation in the definition of SI. It is often described as one of mutual shaping, but the nature and dynamics of this relationship are rarely discussed. The assumption is made that in some way, digital technologies shape people and, in turn, people shape these technologies as they use them. A related assumption is that these technologies are in a similar relationship with the contexts in which they are used. Both have been an accepted part of the SI core of knowledge for four decades, and, most often, ICT are cast into some type of relationship with social and organizational settings in which they are embedded (Kling & Iacono, 1989). Some SI research has made use of sociotechnical theory "to more accurately account for the mutually shaping interactions between social and technical factors" (Fichman et al., 2015, p. 37). This theory has also supported findings that "mutually shaping relationships between ICT and context result from iterated interactions" (Fichman et al., 2015, p. 61).

Mutual shaping is based on the recognition that technological artifacts are not merely passive instruments but instead actively participate in shaping social practices, norms, and institutions. These artifacts must, then, have some limited form of material agency. Conversely, social contexts—such as organizations, institutions, and social groups—in turn influence the development, implementation, and uses of IT artifacts through various factors, including user needs, cultural values, regulatory frameworks, and market dynamics. For example, the design of social media platforms is not solely determined by technical considerations but is also influenced by user behaviors, societal expectations, and economic incentives, leading to complex feedback loops between technology and society.

The relationship of mutual shaping can be approached in two ways. The first draws on strong sociomateriality and requires a reconceptualization of the relationships between people, IT artifacts, and contexts of use. This move will involve a return to sociomateriality's relational ontology. The second draws on postphenomenology to specify the interactions among people, technology, and the world.

Mutual shaping and the agential cut

The concept of mutual shaping does not have a place in strong sociomateriality. This is because the version of the concept that has been a standard assumption of SI research is based on what was called above a "substantivist ontology." Mutual shaping assumes that three separate and independent entities exist—people, the IT artifact, and the context—that can enter into various relationships of influence and change. This interchange is possible because there is some form of agency that is located in them (Introna, 2007, p. 3). Strong sociomateriality rejects these assumptions and instead assumes that the most fundamental ontological entities are phenomena, defined as relations. Humans, IT artifacts, the social, and the material are constitutively entangled, meaning that "there is no social that is not also material, and no material that is not also social" (Orlikowski, 2007, p. 1436). As Barad (2003, p. 816) notes, there are no independently existing entities with inherent characteristics. Entanglement is not a relation of reciprocal or mutual shaping and instead is the "recursive intertwining of the social and material as these emerge in ongoing, situated practice" (Orlikowski, 2007, p. 1436; Scott & Orlikowski, 2014, p. 874). Thus, entanglement replaces mutual shaping in the foundations of SI.

Agential realism, on which strong sociomateriality is based, posits a performative metaphysics (Orlikowski, 2009, p. 135; Orlikowski & Scott, 2015, p. 701) that foregrounds the role of practice, which—as doings and actions— "perform particular phenomena 'ontologically primitive relations—relations without preexisting relata' that are enacted in material-discursive practices" (Barad, 2003, p. 815). Practices are part of a relational ontology and are described as "discursive-material," a phrase that "emphasizes the entangled inseparability of discourse and materiality" (Orlikowski, 2009, p. 699). Both discourse and materiality are instantiated through practice, constituting the world as a contingent and practical accomplishment (Feldman & Orlikowski, 2011, p. 1240; Orlikowski, 2009, p. 700). According to Scott and Orlikowski (2014), strong sociomaterialism assumes that

> ... practices are not bounded in and of themselves but rather are open and ongoing. They do not so much reproduce (in the sense of replicate) the world, but rather, in their historical reconfiguration, they perform the world.
>
> *(p. 875)*

Reality, in this approach, is then seen as the entanglement of materiality, also described as matter, and discourse, also described as meaning, emerging from the intra-action of practice within phenomena. Performative practices produce "distinctions and boundaries (e.g., between humans and technologies) that are stabilized, and destabilized over time" (Scott & Orlikowski, 2014, p. 876). It is important to note that the outcomes of material-discursive practices are characterized by inclusion and exclusion, which are part of the boundary setting process. This is how distinctions, boundaries, and properties of phenomena are made determinate in practice (Scott & Orlikowski, 2014, p. 879).

Barad uses the concept of the "agential cut" to describe the performance of material-discursive practices as enactments that produce and stabilize or destabilize particular distinctions, boundaries, and properties of phenomena; these are not given but are instead "contingently performed in practice" (Scott & Orlikowski, 2014, p. 879). This cut produces local component parts of a phenomenon—say, an information system— "one of which ('cause') expresses itself in effecting and marking the other ('the effect')" (Barad, 2003, p. 824). To be more precise,

> A specific intra-action enacts an 'agential cut' (in contrast to the Cartesian cut— an inherent distinction—between subject and object), effecting a separation between 'subject' and 'object' within the phenomenon. In particular, agential cuts enact a resolution within the phenomenon of some inherent ontological indeterminacies to the exclusion of others.
>
> *(Kleinman & Barad, 2012, p. 77)*

In social and organizational contexts, the agential cut underscores the intricate interplay between human agents and the sociomaterial practices through which reality is enacted as a dynamic web of intra-actions that is being continually shaped and reconfigured. Rather than viewing social phenomena as existing independently of human observation, Barad emphasizes that they are co-constituted through ongoing processes of intra-action.[3] Shotter's (2014) description of agential cuts illustrates their constitutive nature:

> ... in placing the agential cuts, i.e., the distinctions we make between subjective and objective 'things,' in different places at different times, we do not uncover pre-existing facts about independently existing things; instead, we ourselves bring such 'things' into existence.
>
> *(pp. 305, 307)*

Humans and non-humans enact these cuts in different ways, at different points in time, and toward different goals, allowing attention to be paid to different features within the phenomena of interest. Kleinman and Barad (2012, p. 77) state that an outcome of specific agential intra-actions is that the boundaries and properties of "individuals" within a phenomenon become determinate and particular material articulations of the world become meaningful. This result occurs through the enactment of apparatuses, open-ended practices that are "dynamic (re)configurings of the world, specific agential practices/intra-actions/performances through which specific exclusionary boundaries are enacted" (Barad, 2003, p. 826). Apparatuses are a type of material-discursive practice that can, in Barad's terms, materialize components of phenomena in the world.

The agential cut is enacted through specific material-discursive practices. These practices are not neutral but are instead imbued with power relations, cultural norms, and historical contexts that shape what is considered observable and meaningful. Through the agential cut, Barad emphasizes the mutual constitution of the social and the material, challenging dualistic frameworks that privilege human agency over non-human entities or reduce reality to fixed, independent objects. In the social world, the agential cut manifests through various mechanisms of power, discourse, and representation that shape what is considered legitimate knowledge and who has the authority to produce it (Faulkner & Runde, 2011). According to Barad (1996):

> agential realism explicitly shows that boundaries are interested instances of power, specific constructions, with real material consequences. There are not only different stakes in drawing different distinctions, there are different ontological implications.
>
> *(p. 181)*

Social hierarchies, institutional structures, and discursive formations influence the construction of reality by defining which perspectives are privileged or marginalized within dominant narratives. With the concept of the agential cut, Barad highlights the ways in which the constitution of the social world is inherently political, reflecting and perpetuating or challenging existing power dynamics that influence whose voices are heard and whose experiences are valued.

In strong sociomateriality, agential cuts are made on entanglements, which are the intricate relationships between human actors and non-human entities (like IT artifacts or organizational structures) within organizational and social contexts. This is a theoretical move in which the world is conceptualized as intra-actively produced through the cutting together of entangled phenomena at a given point in time. Its use reveals "agential separability – the local condition of exteriority within- phenomena" (Barad, 2003, p. 815), the equivalent of analytic distinctions. That which is ontologically inseparable may appear distinct after the agential cut. For example, the cut may show how technologies and social practices co-constitute each other, influencing behaviors, norms, and organizational dynamics. Entanglements challenge traditional dualisms (such as human vs. non-human or material vs. social) by highlighting their inseparability in shaping everyday life and organizational processes. Understanding these entanglements is crucial for grasping the complex interplay between technology and society in contemporary contexts. Therefore, at a foundational level in SI, entanglements replace mutual shaping by emphasizing the depth and complexity of interactions between human and non-human phenomena within sociomaterial contexts. Unlike mutual shaping, which suggests a more symmetrical influence between these entities, entanglements highlight a more intricate and often asymmetrical relationship in which—in certain instances—IT artifacts or material structures exert significant influence over human behaviors and social practices, and in others, the reverse is the case.

Technological mediation after the agential cut

Assuming that an agential cut has been made and the phenomenon of interest involves the entanglement of people and technology, agential separability means that it is now possible to specify the interactions among people, technology, and the world. As mentioned above, this articulation will be done using postphenomenology, a version of the philosophy of technology that provides insights into the ways in which technology shapes and mediates human experience. It has been defined as "a nonfoundational and nontranscendental phenomenology which makes variational theory its most important methodological strategy" (Ihde, 2009, p. vii). It builds upon phenomenology and recognizes the role of technologies in shaping our perception and understanding of, as well as engagement with, the world (Ihde, 2009). As Ihde and Malafouris (2019) explain, "Humanity has always been inseparable from technical mediation and material engagement" (p. 199).

Technology mediates human experience with the world in four ways (Rosenberger & Verbeek, 2015; Ihde, 1990) and does so "in such a way that the perception of self, world and environment changes" (Giambastiani, 2021, p. 36). Technological mediation involves amplification and reduction; with a given technology, some parts of the experience of the world come into greater detail while others recede. For example, when using binoculars, some part of the visual field can be seen sharply while the rest of the field cannot be seen at all.

An embodiment relation describes an instance in which the IT artifact becomes so integrated into people's daily routines that it "withdraws and serves as a (partially) transparent means through which one perceives one's environment, thus engendering a partial symbiosis of oneself and it" (Brey, 2000, p. 3). The technology unites with the person to experience the world. When using video conferencing, a person is talking to and interacting with another person—not with the conferencing technology, which becomes relatively transparent. A second form of mediation is a hermeneutic relation in which the person "reads" a technology, the output of which is a representation of the world. In this case, the technology has united with the world, and the person experiences the world through the representation. In this sense, astronomers and experimental physicists experience the universe through the imagery and other data generated by their instruments. Physicians read x-rays and MRI imagery to diagnose patient health. A third form of mediation is the alterity relation, in which the person interacts with a technology in anthropomorphic ways. When people interact with a digital voice assistant or a chatbot in ways similar to their interactions with another person, they engage in this type of relation. This is a different type of mediation because the technology is in the foreground and the world recedes. The fourth type of mediation is the background relation, in which the technology recedes and becomes a component of the context.

People experience the world in ways that are shaped by the technology but do not experience the technology directly unless there is a disruption or breakdown. Climate control systems in homes and buildings typically operate below peoples' levels of awareness until they stop.

Concluding thoughts

This chapter has presented a preliminary investigation into the grounds of SI, a global SIM that seems to have reached an inflection point in which it may be fragmenting, splintering, diversifying, or transforming. Possible futures could include disappearance, continued low-level activity in which a small community essentially speaks to itself, the possibility of institutionalization in the intellectual landscape—a positive outcome—and the highly unlikely possibility that it catches fire and revolutionizes the study of people, technology, and society. There have been calls to establish a common discourse and shared conceptual foundation for SI that could provide common ground for SI researchers. This chapter is a tentative entry in the attempt to open and encourage thinking about potential conceptual foundations for the field.

An approach to the grounds of social informatics

A review of several other reviews concerning the current state of SI research indicated that there have been few attempts to investigate the grounds of SI. A popular definition was used as an entry to this exploration based on four key concepts: the IT artifact, the person, the context, and the complex interplay among all three. Three theoretical approaches were employed to analyze these concepts on the path to proposing an ontology for SI. Strong sociomateriality was used to determine the ontological status of the IT artifact and the person. This argument involved clarifying the distinctions between weak and strong sociomateriality as well as arguing for the usefulness of the latter. Structuration theory was used to analyze the concept of context, resulting in a version that focused on context as modalities of structuration, rules, and resources. Finally, strong sociomateriality and postphenomenology were used to analyze the concept of mutual shaping, the most common operationalization of the complex interplay. For reasons explained above, the concept of mutual shaping was set aside and replaced by concepts of constitutive entanglement, intra-action, and discursive-material practices. Taken together, these approaches provide a possible ontological framework for SI by grounding the four concepts that constitute the most commonly used definition of SI.

To summarize, the grounds of SI involve the sociomaterial constitutive entanglement of humans and IT artifacts, a structurationally informed conception of context, and complex interplay among these three—characterized by sociomaterial intra-action through discursive-material practices and a postphenomenological view of human-technology relations. It is hoped that this ontological perspective "offers conceptual and analytical traction for making sense of the world and its possibilities in new ways" (Scott & Orlikowski, 2013, p. 77). Taken seriously, SI researchers who adopt this framework might have to rethink the conduct of certain types of research; an example is provided by Niemimaa et al. (2023).

Relational ontology

One reason for the selection of the three theories used above is that they share several important qualities. All three are practice-oriented approaches, all view relations as fundamental, and all share a relational ontology. A relational ontology is a perspective that posits reality as fundamentally constituted by relationships and interactions among entities, rather than as comprised of independent, self-contained objects. This ontology challenges traditional notions of being and existence by emphasizing the interconnectedness and interdependence of all phenomena. From this perspective, the identities, properties, and meanings of entities emerge through their relational entanglements with other entities within a broader network of interactions. Entities are relational, as their existence is contingent upon their interactions with other entities and the broader contexts in which they are situated. They do not have inherent properties or essences but are instead constituted through their relationships with other entities. This ontological position emphasizes that reality is dynamic and is in a constant state of reconfiguration, co-constitution, or structuration. Furthermore, relationships are not static and continually evolve and transform.

In addition, a relational ontology has implications for understandings of agency and causality. Rather than attributing agency solely to individual entities, in a relational ontology, agency is distributed across networks of relationships. Entities are seen as co-agents whose actions and behaviors emerge through their interactions with other entities within complex systems. Similarly, causality is understood as relational and emergent, with events and phenomena arising through the interplay of multiple factors and contingencies within a relational network.

Limitations and conclusion

This work has several limitations. First and foremost, it is certainly possible that the analysis reflects misinterpretations and misunderstandings of the theories used. For example, strong sociomateriality is a complex theory that is challenging because it is a quite unique approach to the study of people, technology, and society. Second, it is possible that the definition used as the entree into critical reflections on the grounds of SI limited the scope of analysis. Third, the resulting ontological framework may be seen as exclusionary because it diverges sharply from conventional approaches to SI.

This chapter has attempted to address a gap in the literature and answer the call for a common discourse concerning SI research by proposing a foundation for SI based on a relational ontology and three compatible theoretical approaches: strong sociomateriality, structuration, and postphenomenology. In doing so, the case has been made for the key role that social theories play in SI; in a sense, this work is an extended argument for the significance of the social in SI. This analysis of the philosophical grounds of SI is preliminary and is certainly not intended to be the final words on the topic. Instead, it is hoped that this work will open a discussion about the grounds of SI that will ideally lead to the common conceptual grounding for which some have called. Finally, in providing some reflections on the grounds of SI, this chapter is aligned with the sentiment of Orlikowski and Scott (2015), who write:

> We offer these in the spirit of constructive engagement, recognizing that the concepts at stake are necessarily constructs-in-the-making, which for us makes the examination of multiple possibilities all the more generative and valuable.
>
> *(p. 697)*

Notes

1 Agential realism assumes a relational ontology in which the world is understood as intra-related phenomena of entangled agencies. It challenges dualist frameworks by asserting that reality emerges through the entanglement of material-discursive practices. According to Barad (2007), human and non-human agencies do not pre-exist their interactions, but rather come into being through these interactions and co-constitute reality through their interactions and entanglements. It emphasizes the inseparability of the observer and observed, rejecting the idea of an objective reality independent of observation, and it posits that knowledge is always situated within specific practices and perspectives, which actively participate in the constitution of phenomena.

2 "Performing the world" suggests that reality is actively produced through ongoing practices of observation, measurement, and discourse. These practices do not reflect a pre-existing world but rather actively participate in its constitution. Entities and phenomena emerge through performative practices, which shape the boundaries, identities, and possibilities of what is considered real. This perspective challenges fixed notions of reality and emphasizes the role of human and non-human agencies in continuously co-creating and reconfiguring the world through their interactions and interventions.

3 Strong sociomateriality uses "intra-action" to emphasize that human and non-human entities do not exist independently prior to their interactions but rather come into being through these interactions. "Interaction" implies pre-existing entities acting upon each other, while "intra-action" underscores the inseparability and mutual constitution of entities within phenomena. This perspective challenges traditional views of causality and agency, and it is based on a relational ontology.

References

Akhlaghpour, S., Wu, J., Lapointe, L., & Pinsonneault, A. (2013). The ongoing quest for the IT artifact: Looking back, moving forward. *Journal of Information Technology, 28*, 150–166.

Alter, S. (2015). The concept of 'IT artifact' has outlived its usefulness and should be retired now. *Information Systems Journal, 25*(1), 47–60.

Alvesson, M., & Skoldberg, K. (2009). *Reflexive methodology: New vistas for qualitative research.* 2nd ed. Sage.

Baker, L. R. (2002). The ontological status of persons. *Philosophy and Phenomenological Research, 65*(2), 370–388.

Barad, K. (1996). Meeting the universe halfway: Realism and social constructivism without contradiction. In J. Nelson (Ed.), *Feminism, science, and the philosophy of science* (pp. 161–194). Springer Netherlands.

Barad, K. (2003). Posthumanist performativity: Toward an understanding of how matter comes to matter. *Signs: Journal of Women in Culture and Society, 28*(3), 801–831.

Barad, K. (2007). *Meeting the universe halfway: Quantum physics and the entanglement of matter and meaning.* Duke University Press.

Barad, K. (2011). Erasers and erasures: Pinch's unfortunate 'uncertainty principle.' *Social Studies of Science, 41*(3), 1–12.

Bhaskar, R. (1975). Forms of realism. *Philosophica, 15,* 99–127.

Brey, P. A. (2000). Technology and embodiment in Ihde and Merleau-Ponty. In C. Mitcham (Ed.), *Metaphysics, epistemology and technology (research in philosophy and technology* (Vol. 19, pp. 45–58). Elsevier/JAI Press.

Browne, C. (1993). Central dilemmas in Giddens's theory of structuration. *Thesis Eleven, 36,* 138–150.

Cecez-Kecmanovic, D. (2016). From substantialist to process metaphysics–Exploring shifts in IS research. In *Beyond Interpretivism? New Encounters with Technology and Organization: IFIP Wg 8.2 Working Conference on Information Systems and Organizations, IS&O 2016, Dublin, Ireland, December 9–10, 2016, Proceedings,* Springer International Publishing, pp. 35–57.

Cecez-Kecmanovic, D., Galliers, R. D., Henfridsson, O., Newell, S., & Vidgen, R. (2014). The sociomateriality of information systems: Current status, future directions. *MIS Quarterly, 38*(3), 809–830.

Demody, G., & Fritz, S. (2019). A conceptual framework for clinicians working with artificial intelligence and health-assistive smart homes. *Nursing Inquiry, 26*(1), 1–15. www.ncbi.nlm.nih.gov/pmc/articles/PMC6342619/pdf/nihms-988642.pdf.

Faulkner, P., & Runde, J. (2011, July). The social, the material, and the ontology of non-material technological objects. *European Group for Organizational Studies (EGOS) Colloquium, Gothenburg, 985,* 4–8.

Feenberg, A. (2015). Making the gestalt switch. In R. Rosenberger & P. P. Verbeek (Eds.), *Postphenomenological investigations: Essays on human-technology relations* (pp. 229–236). Lexington Books.

Feldman, M. S., & Orlikowski, W. J. (2011). Theorizing practice and practicing theory. *Organization Science, 22*(5), 1240–1253.

Ferraris, M. (2020). To make truth: Ontology, epistemology, technology. In G. Kroupa & J. Simoniti (Eds.), *New realism and contemporary philosophy* (pp. 73–83). Bloomsbury Academic.

Fichman, P., & Sanfilippo, M. R. (2013). Multicultural issues in information and communications technology (ICT). In G. Marchionini (Ed.), *Synthesis lectures on information concepts, retrieval, and services* (pp. 1–87). Morgan & Claypool Publishers.

Fichman, P., Sanfilippo, M. R., & Rosenbaum, H. (2015). Social informatics evolving. In G. Marchionini (Ed.), *Synthesis lectures on information concepts, retrieval, and services.* Morgan & Claypool Publishers.

Fraunberger, C. (2019). Entanglement HCI the next wave? *ACM Transactions on Computer-Human Interaction, 27*(1), Article 2.

Frickel, S., & Gross, N. (2005). A general theory of scientific/intellectual movements. *American Sociological Review, 70*(2), 204–232.

Furlong, P., & Marsh, D. (2010). A skin not a sweater: Ontology and epistemology in political science. In V. Lowndes, D. Marsh, & G. Stoker (Eds.), *Theory and methods in political science* (pp. 184–211). Springer.

Garbutt, M., & Van Den Berg, C. (2022). Theorising sociomateriality in online learning: Cutting through the complexity. *South African Computer Journal, 34*(2), 1–17.

Giambastiani, V. (2021). The asymmetrical relationship between humans and technologies. *Phenomenology and Mind, 20*, 32–40.

Giddens, A. (1979). *Central problems in social theory*. Macmillan.

Giddens, A. (1984). *The constitution of society*. Polity Press.

Giddens, A. (1991). Structuration theory: Past, present and future. In C. Bryant & D. Jary (Eds.), *Giddens' theory of structuration: A critical appreciation* (pp. 201–221). Routledge.

Grix, J. (2002). Introducing students to the generic terminology of social research. *Politics, 22*(3), 175–186.

Hartel, J. (2003). Ontological, epistemological and sociological dimensions of domains. *Knowledge Organization, 30*(3–4), 239–245.

Hoeffner, L. (2012). *The intellectual and social structure of social informatics: Is there evidence of a domain?* [Doctoral dissertation, Palmer School of Library & Information Science, Long Island University].

Hoeffner, L., & Smiraglia, R. P. (2012a). Visualizing domain coherence: Social informatics as a case study. In *Advances in Classification Research Online,* pp. 49–51.

Hoeffner, L., & Smiraglia, R. P. (2012b). Social informatics: Mapping and visualizing an emerging domain. In *Proceedings of the Annual Conference of CAIS/Actes du congrès annuel de l'ACSI*, Wilfrid Laurier University & the University of Waterloo, Waterloo, Ontario, pp. 1–5. https://doi.org/10.29173/cais685

Ihde, D. (1990). *Technology and the lifeworld: From garden to earth*. Indiana University Press.

Ihde, D. (2009). *Postphenomenology and technoscience: The Peking University lectures*. Suny Press.

Ihde, D., & Malafouris, L. (2019). Homo faber revisited: Postphenomenology and material engagement theory. *Philosophy & Technology, 32*, 195–214.

Introna, L. D. (2007, May). Towards a post-human intra-actional account of socio-technical agency (and morality). In *Proceedings of the Moral Agency and Technical Artefacts Scientific Workshop* (NIAS, Hague, 10–12 May 2007), pp. 1–22.

Introna, L. D. (2009). Ethics and the speaking of things. *Theory, Culture & Society, 26*(4), 25–46.

Jones, M. (2014). A matter of life and death: Exploring conceptualizations of sociomateriality in the context of critical care. *MIS Quarterly, 38*(3), 895–925.

Kant, S. L. (2014). The distinction and relationship between ontology and epistemology: Does it matter? *Politikon: The IAPSS Journal of Political Science, 24*, 68–85.

Kautz, K., & Jensen, T. B. (2012). Debating sociomateriality: Entanglements, imbrications, disentangling, and agential cuts. *Scandinavian Journal of Information Systems, 24*(2), 5.

Kautz, K., & Jensen, T. B. (2013). Sociomateriality at the royal court of IS: A jester's monologue. *Information and Organization, 23*(1), 15–27.

Kautz, K., & Plumb, M. (2016). Strong versus weak sociomateriality: Neither subordinate nor privileged-A rejoinder to "New technology and the post-human self: Rethinking appropriation and resistance." *ACM SIGMIS Database: The DATABASE for Advances in Information Systems, 47*(4), 34–40.

Kleinman, A., & Barad, K. (2012). Intra-actions. *Mousse Magazine, 34*(13), 76–81.

Kling, R. (1998). A brief introduction to social informatics. *Canadian Journal of Information and Library Science – Revue Canadienne des Sciences de l'Information et de Bibliotheconomie, 23*(1–2), 50–85.

Kling, R. (1999). What is social informatics and why does it matter? *D-Lib Magazine, 5*(1), 1082–9873.

Kling, R. (2000a). Learning about information technologies and social change: The contribution of social informatics. *Information Society, 16*(3), 217–232.

Kling, R. (2000b). Social informatics: A new perspective on social research about information and communication technologies. *Prometheus, 18*(3), 245–264.

Kling, R., & Iacono, S. (1989). The institutional character of computerized information systems. *Information Technology and People, 5*(1), 7–28.

Kling, R., & Iacono, S. (2001). Computerization movements: The rise of the Internet and distant forms of work. In J. Yates & J. V. Maanan (Eds.), *Information technology and organizational transformation: History, rhetoric, and practice* (pp. 93–136). Sage Publications.

Kling, R., McKim, G., & King, A. (2003). A bit more to it: Scholarly communication forums as socio-technical interaction networks. *Journal of the American Society for Information Science and Technology, 54*(1), 47–67.

Kling, R., Rosenbaum, H., & Sawyer, S. (2005). *Understanding and communicating social informatics: A framework for studying and teaching the human contexts of information and communication technologies.* Information Today, Inc.

Kling, R., & Scacchi, W. (1982). The web of computing: Computer technology as social organization. In M. C. Yovits (Ed.), *Advances in computers* (Vol. 21, pp. 1–90). Elsevier.

Lamb, R. (1996). Informational imperatives and socially mediated relationships. *Information Society, 12*(1), 17.

Lamb, R., & Davidson, E. (2005). Information and communication technology challenges to scientific professional identity. *Information Society, 21*(1), 1–24.

Lamb, R., & Kling, R. (2003). Reconceptualizing users as social actors in information systems research. *MIS Quarterly, 27*(2), 197–235.

Lamb, R., King, J., & Kling, R. (2003). Informational environments: Organizational contexts of online information use. *Journal of the American Society for Information Science and Technology, 54*(2), 97–114.

Lamb, R., & Sawyer, S. (2005). On extending social informatics from a rich legacy of networks and conceptual resources. *Information Technology & People, 18*(1), 9–20.

Langsdorf, L. (2015). Why postphenomenology needs a metaphysics. In R. Rosenberger & P. P. Verbeek (Eds.), *Postphenomenological investigations: Essays on human-technology relations* (pp. 45–54). Lexington Books.

Leonardi, P. M. (2012). Materiality, sociomateriality, and socio-technical systems: What do these terms mean? How are they related? Do we need them? In P. M. Leonardi, B. A. Nardi, & J. Kallinikos (Eds.), *Materiality and organizing social interaction in a technological world* (pp. 25–48). Oxford University Press.

Leonardi, P. M. (2013). Theoretical foundations for the study of sociomateriality. *Information and Organization, 23*(2), 59–76.

Malafouris, L. (2014). Creative thinging: The feeling of and for clay. *Pragmatics and Cognition, 22*(1), 140–158.

Moon, K., & Blackman, D. (2017). *A guide to ontology, epistemology, and philosophical perspectives for interdisciplinary researchers.* https://i2insights.org/2017/05/02/philoso phy-for-interdisciplinarity/

Mutch, A. (2013). Sociomateriality – Taking the wrong turning? *Information and Organization, 23*(1), 28–40.

National Academies of Sciences, Engineering, & Medicine. (2022). *Ontologies in the behavioral sciences: Accelerating research and the spread of knowledge: Digest version.* The National Academies Press.

Niemimaa, M., Schultze, U., & van den Heuvel, G. (2023). Methodological practices for enacting "strong" sociomateriality in qualitative IS research. In R. M. Davison (Ed.), *Handbook of qualitative research methods for information systems: New perspectives* (pp. 182–196). Edward Elgar Publishing.

Oppong, S. (2014). A critique of the philosophical underpinnings of mainstream social science research. *Academicus International Scientific Journal, 10*, 242–254.

Orlikowski, W. J. (2007). Sociomaterial practices: Exploring technology at work. *Organization Studies, 28*(9), 1435–1448.

Orlikowski, W. J. (2009). The sociomateriality of organisational life: Considering technology in management research. *Cambridge Journal of Economics, 34*, 125–141.

Orlikowski, W. J., & Iacono, C. S. (2001). Desperately seeking the "IT" in IT research–A call to theorizing the IT artifact. *Information Systems Research, 12*(2), 121–134.

Orlikowski, W. J., & Scott, S.V. (2008). Sociomateriality: Challenging the separation of technology, work and organization. *The Academy of Management Annals, 2*, 433–474.

Orlikowski, W. J., & Scott, S. V. (2015). Exploring material-discursive practices. *Journal of Management Studies, 52*(5), 697–705.

Pinch, T. (2010). On making infrastructure visible: Putting the non-humans to rights. *Cambridge Journal of Economics, 34*(1), 77–89.

Rosenberger, R., & Verbeek, P. P. (2015). *Postphenomenological investigations: Essays on human-technology relations.* Lexington Books.

Sawyer, S. (2005). Social informatics: Overview, principles and opportunities. *Bulletin of the American Society for Information Science and Technology, 31*(5), 9–12.

Sawyer, S., & Eschenfelder, K. (2002). Social informatics: Perspectives, examples, and trends. *Annual Review of Information Science and Technology, 36*, 427–465.

Sawyer, S., & Tapia, A. (2007). From findings to theories: Institutionalizing social informatics. *The Information Society, 23*(4), 263–275.

Scott, S. V., & Orlikowski, W. J. (2013). Sociomateriality — Taking the wrong turning? A response to Mutch. *Information and Organization, 23*, 77–80.

Scott, S. V., & Orlikowski, W. J. (2014). Entanglements in practice. *MIS Quarterly, 38*(3), 873–894.

Shotter, J. (2014). Agential realism, social constructionism, and our living relations to our surroundings: Sensing similarities rather than seeing patterns. *Theory & Psychology, 24*(3), 305–325.

Skinner, Q. (Ed.). (1985). *The return of grand theory in the human sciences.* University of Cambridge Press.

Slife, B. D. (2004). Taking practice seriously: Toward a relational ontology. *Journal of Theoretical and Philosophical Psychology, 24*(2), 157–178.

Smutny, Z. (2016). Social informatics as a concept: Widening the discourse. *Journal of Information Science, 42*(5), 681–710.

Smutny, Z., & Vehovar, V. (2020). Social informatics research: Schools of thought, methodological basis, and thematic conceptualization. *Journal of the Association for Information Science and Technology, 71*(5), 529–539.

Thomas, M. A., Li, Y., & Lee, A. S. (2022). Generalizing the information systems artifact. *Information Systems Research, 33*(4), 1452–1466.

Vehovar, V., Smutny, Z., & Bartol, J. (2022). Evolution of social informatics: Publications, research, and educational activities. *The Information Society, 38*(5), 307–333.

Visser, L. M., & Davies, O. E. (2021). The becoming of online healthcare through entangled power and performativity: A posthumanist agential realist perspective. *Organization Studies, 42*(12), 1817–1837.

Woolgar, S. (2012). Ontological child consumption. In B. Sandin, A. Sperman, & J. Sjoberg (Eds.), *Situating child consumption: Rethinking values and notions of children, childhood and consumption* (pp. 33–52). Nordic Academic Press.

Zhang, T. (2023). Critical realism: A critical evaluation. *Social Epistemology, 37*(1), 15–29.

2

SOCIAL INFORMATICS THEMATIC-METHODOLOGICAL FRAMEWORK

Zdeněk Smutný, Vasja Vehovar, and Jošt Bartol

Introduction

This chapter deals with social informatics (SI) from an international perspective (Smutny & Vehovar, 2020). The core of this view includes seven SI schools of thought identified in the literature, which are typically labeled according to their country of origin: German, Japanese, Norwegian, Russian, Slovenian, UK, and US (e.g., Smutny & Vehovar, 2020; Rosenbaum, 2014). In addition to the conceptually defined SI core, there is also self-declared SI research that is conceptually outside of SI schools, i.e., a self-labeled SI approach. Within the latter, scholars use their own definition of SI without placing it in a wider regional or international perspective, such as works by Pantell et al. (2020) or Karthik et al. (2023).

The notion of SI has evolved over the last 50 years in a similar way to the development of the social (people) and technical (computing and information technologies) components of sociotechnical systems (Fichman et al., 2015; Smutny & Vehovar, 2020; Smutny, 2016; Vehovar, 2006). The above-mentioned seven SI schools exist in parallel and create a rather fragmented community of social informaticians. Their views on SI differ mainly due to each region's different historical, cultural, social, economic, ideological, and scientific circumstances (Rosenbaum, 2014), which also affects their conceptual and methodological apparatuses (Smutny & Vehovar, 2020).

One such difference is in how dissimilar SI schools understand the concept of *informatics*. In continental Europe, the notion of informatics is generally associated with all computer-oriented disciplines (Informatics Europe, 2023) and is divided into many subfields (e.g., engineering, applied, or theoretical informatics). In other words, informatics includes: computer science, information science, computer engineering, information systems, and other computer-oriented fields. Informatics

DOI: 10.4324/9781032678542-4

in the US has roots in information science; exceptions are medical and health informatics, which have specific historical circumstances in the US (Mašić, 2020; Hersh, 2009; Smutny & Vehovar, 2022). From the US point of view represented by the National Center for Education Statistics, informatics "focuses on computer systems from a user-centered perspective and studies the structure, behavior and interactions of natural and artificial systems" (National Center for Education Statistics, 2023). Even more differences and controversies appear with the English term *social*, particularly because it can take on different meanings when translated into other languages and vice versa (e.g., direct translation can refer to *societal* or *social work*), which further complicates the orientation of researchers (Smutny & Vehovar, 2020).

An international perspective of SI that includes all known SI schools brings with it not only a broader outlook, but also some issues and challenges (see Smutny & Vehovar, 2020, 2022). The most recent overview of research, publication, and teaching activities related to SI offers interesting insights into the endeavors associated with the notion of SI in the world over the last 35 years (Vehovar et al., 2022). The overview found that the field of SI is active and evolving, although this varies by type of activity and country. The number of publications referring directly to SI has increased every decade, and the number of conferences has been rising. However, the number of research centers remained constant, although rising in some regions and decreasing in others. For educational activities, the number of study programs is decreasing, but at the same time, the number of educational courses is increasing. The latter may indicate that SI is considered less as a research and educational field, and more as a complementary subject to help students become acquainted with the social aspects of information and communication technology (ICT) implementation and use. It can thus be summarized (Vehovar et al., 2022) that the numbers of articles, educational courses, conferences, and bibliographic hits in bibliographic databases are rising. At the same time, conceptually grounded SI literature—SI research centers, study programs, and blogs—are largely stagnating or decreasing. These trends vary from one country (and SI school) to another; they are generally declining in the US and UK, which is specifically true for the share of bibliographic output related to the US school (Vehovar et al., 2022, p. 329). On the other side, SI activities are increasing in some European and Asian countries.

To assist scholars in navigating the varied landscape of SI research and promote global convergence of different SI schools, this chapter proposes a thematic-methodological SI framework. Frameworks are high-level-oriented artifacts that outline relationships and connections, and they can therefore support or guide researchers in their endeavors (Smutny, 2020, p. 92). The current framework is developed based on published overview and conceptual articles dealing with an international view of SI and combines the scientific as well as research approaches and methods used in SI with the thematic focuses of the seven SI schools. This endeavor is crucial in the current moment, when SI scholarship is proliferating but lacks a common approach to classifying its research activities under a unified and international perspective of SI. The thematic-methodological framework proposed here can also be used by researchers worldwide when planning their own research, or for justification and anchoring their research in SI from an international perspective.

Since SI ideas from the US dominate worldwide, at the end of this chapter, we discuss the methodological perspective of the US school and compare it with the international SI perspective presented here. For this purpose, we use a book by Fichman et al. (2015), which presents an overview of approaches and methods used in the US school with roots in the 1980s.

The next section discusses the inclusion of informatics and SI in basic science classification. Subsequently, two primary research approaches and their connection with three SI thematic areas are identified. The "Social informatics scientific methods of reasoning" and "Social informatics research methods" sections offer an overview of scientific approaches to reasoning (basic scientific methods) and instruments used to conduct research (research methods) related to SI. The synthesis of the above views resulted in the SI thematic-methodological framework presented in the "Presentation of social informatics thematic-methodological framework" section. The "Discussion and conclusion" section concludes the chapter.

Thematic and scientific classification of social informatics

From the European perspective, informatics is understood as a broad and computer-oriented discipline that focuses more or less on three directions (Mounier-Kuhn & Pégny, 2016): (i) computational processes (emphasis on numerical use of computers), (ii) information processes (emphasis on non-numerical use of computers), and (iii) computer design and construction. In all seven SI schools of thought, SI is strongly connected to (ii) information processes (Smutny & Vehovar, 2020). This linkage also corresponds to the current concept of informatics in the US, which stems from information science. However, in recent years, we can also see the expansion of the notion of SI into the area of computational social science, i.e., (i) computational processes (Vehovar et al., 2022). This development relates to a broad, implicit, and general understanding of the notion of SI as a floating label for any research addressing combinations of ICTs and social research (Smutny & Vehovar, 2020) alongside the conceptually established regional SI notion. Therefore, the use of the SI notion is limited to the seven SI schools of thought and is occasionally used by scholars from computational social sciences. With reference to the SI schools of thought, SI research can appear in three thematic areas or streams according to research origin (Smutny & Vehovar, 2020; Vehovar, 2006):

1 **Social sciences.** The general interactions between ICT and humans focused on (a) personal, (b) organizational, or (c) societal levels (referred to as ICT and society).

2 **Informatics.** ICT design and applications in areas related to the social sciences. It includes (a) computer modeling of social sciences data, (b) ICT services and solution design, and (c) structuring, conceptualization, and processing of information (referred to as ICT for society).
3 **Social science methodology.** ICT design and applications as tools for social science research. It includes ICT in various stages of the social science research process: (a) ICT-supported analysis, (b) ICT-assisted data collection, and (c) ICT infrastructure for social sciences research (referred to as ICT as a research tool).

Based on this thematic classification, SI

> can be broadly defined as a research field that focuses on the research of sociotechnical interactions at different levels in connection with the development of the information society, including the social aspects of computerization and informatization, which can be structured into three main areas: interactions between ICT and humans, ICT applications in the social sciences, and ICT applications as a social sciences research tool.
>
> *(Smutny & Vehovar, 2020, p. 537)*

The connection of these three thematic areas with typical research focuses of the seven SI schools can be found in Smutny and Vehovar (2020).

From a methodological point of view, SI predominantly draws from the social sciences, where its historical roots lie (Kling et al., 2003). However, SI is formally classified under informatics, which extends—according to the traditional view of science—across three main scientific areas (Dresch et al., 2015; Aken, 2004; Beth, 1959):

- **Natural and social sciences** explore the world and contribute to the empirical knowledge base; they use quantitative and qualitative research methods to understand phenomena, e.g., biomedical and health informatics.
- **Formal sciences** investigate formal systems and, using mathematical proof, provide information about the structures used to describe our world and what conclusions can be drawn about them, e.g., theoretical informatics.
- **Applied or design sciences** propose solutions using design methods, thereby creating artifacts (objects made by humans) and changing the sociotechnical setting of the world in which humans find themselves, e.g., engineering or applied informatics.

Informatics also has interdisciplinary overlaps with the humanities, which are not classified as sciences in Anglophone countries (Wilson, 1999), from where it gathers inspiration for its research. In the following text, we will focus only on the SI perspective.

In any regional understanding, SI does not seem to include research in the formal sciences, as an overview of SI did not identify any studies using mathematical proofs or models as a research method (Vehovar et al., 2022). By its very nature, SI is primarily associated with empirical approaches to investigating the technosphere in which people live. SI is closest to the social sciences, which are primarily a posteriori, using inductive reasoning as they primarily derive knowledge from empirical findings. In contrast, formal sciences are a priori, using deductive reasoning, and their conclusions can be independent of empirical data.

Empirical and systems approaches relevant to understanding the interaction between societal systems and ICTs are used in social and applied sciences. It should be noted that the Japanese SI school understands humans as part of the environment and looks at them from a systems perspective, which is why even research classified under SI is thematically close to natural sciences, such as the proposal to "expand the coverage of social informatics into socio-ecological informatics" (Tanaka, 2023, p. 22). It can be concluded that from an informatics perspective, SI is connected in particular with the two research approaches related to the issue of the design and use of artifacts (e.g., constructs, models, methods, instantiations, design propositions):

I **Design-oriented research** is related to the design of an artifact, i.e., the design of a useful solution to a defined problem. For this purpose, design science methods are used (Wieringa, 2014; Dresch et al., 2015), which also employ quantitative and qualitative research methods to understand the problem's context and evaluate solutions. Design-oriented research has practical (I.a) and scientific (I.b) focuses:

a **Design of artifact** (or solution) solves a defined problem, e.g., how to provide remote home care support. The result of the artifact design is a useful solution to the given problem, e.g., a mobile application for remote home care support. This resolution can include not only practical but also research-oriented artifacts that help researchers, e.g., Web Survey Methodology or WebSM (Callegaro et al., 2015) and sociotechnical interaction networks or the STIN strategy (Kling et al., 2003).

b **Artifact research** as part of artifact design can be approached in two ways:

i Research into how an artifact was designed with the goal of contributing to the knowledge base about artifact design in a particular area. The results will be used as best practices by future designers of similar solutions.

ii Research into the usefulness of the pre-final version of the artifact in the target deployment context. The aim is to verify the usefulness of the proposed solution practically and empirically, such as whether future users are willing and ready to use the proposed solution in their practice. The results of this research can still directly influence the final design of the solution (as designers participate in it).

II **Analytically oriented research on sociotechnical interaction** examines existing or potentially existing sociotechnical systems in which a particular solution is used. It deals with the investigation of artifact use (i.e., acceptability, acceptance, and adoption). In contrast to the research on the usefulness of the pre-final version of the artifact in the target context (I.b), in this case, the designers of the investigated solutions are not directly involved in the research. Thus, the conclusions of the research can only affect future solutions. In sociotechnical interaction research, multiple artifacts or solutions providing similar functions/services can also be investigated simultaneously. An example can be research on user attitudes toward employing various digital contact tracing app specifications during the COVID-19 pandemic (Trang et al., 2020). This research approach uses quantitative and qualitative methods, and methods of processing extensive data about interactions and their modeling.

In design-oriented research, SI is oriented toward quantitative and qualitative research, either before (explorative research of problem contexts) or after (evaluation of solutions) artifact design. SI is not primarily concerned with the design of artifacts. Examples of exceptions are designs of methodologically oriented artifacts, including: STIN, SI research in Japanese and German schools (e.g., design of aids for the social work sector), and self-declared SI research that is conceptually outside of SI schools.

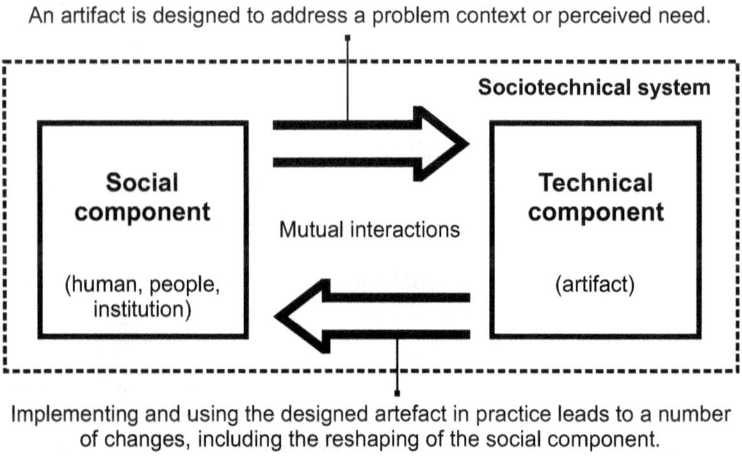

FIGURE 2.1 The principle of mutual constitution of the social and technical components of the sociotechnical system.

Note: These mutual interactions are important for all SI schools, as they focus on interactions between ICT and humans.

Source: Prepared by the authors.

This section classified SI, considered as a part of informatics, into essential branches of science. On this basis, two primary SI research approaches (I and II) were identified. The first is focused on the issue of artifact design (synthesis), and the second on the issue of using the artifact in practice (analysis). Furthermore, the previously published and used classification of SI research was presented, representing thematic areas where SI research relevant from an international perspective can appear. The three thematic areas—(1), (2), and (3)—are combined in scholarly practice and can be connected with (I) and (II) research approaches focused on design and analysis.

The above corresponds to a sociotechnical approach (Guest, 2022) or coevolutionary approach (Kolin, 2021), in which based on an understanding of the problem's context (behavioral and social research), a solution can be proposed that is useful for its users (design science research) while the proposed solution affects the user's behavior in retrospect. There is mutual shaping of the social and technical components of the sociotechnical system, as presented in Figure 2.1.

Social informatics scientific methods of reasoning

It is largely accepted that there are three distinct but closely related methods of scientific reasoning (Baur, 2019; Campos, 2011; Minnameier, 2010; Flach, 1996):

- **Deduction** refers to deriving claims based on theoretical propositions.
- **Induction** relates to generalizing empirical findings into general statements.
- **Abduction** relates to making speculative explanatory claims based on some predefined or observed conditions.

Each of these reasoning methods can be used independently, but they can also be combined in a single study (Baur, 2019). For example, theory is used to derive a set of hypotheses (deduction), which are then empirically tested (induction) while surprising findings are explained through innovative propositions (abduction) (Minnameier, 2010). Such combined approaches are preferable, as they enable scholars to comprehensively develop and test their theories (Campos, 2011).

While SI scholars use all three methods of reasoning in their research, Smutny and Vehovar (2020) have noted that the dominant methods are induction and abduction. Most SI schools are a posteriori in their approach to knowing the world—i.e., empirically based—and therefore use induction as the primary scientific method of reasoning. Analytically oriented SI research is mainly inductive and builds on individual cases of a particular phenomenon to formulate the concepts and theories about it. Design-oriented SI research is also mostly inductive, designing or investigating artifacts with the intent to provide useful solutions and, based on these experiences, build the design knowledge base (best practices) in a particular field.

Some SI schools, most notably the Russian and Japanese schools (Kolin, 2021; Hagiya, 2015), also use the systems approach, which is based on abduction. The systems approach, in short, is a purposeful way of thinking in which the investigated phenomena or elements and their interrelationships are examined as a whole in different internal and external contexts with respect to a defined system (Habr & Veprek, 1986). The researcher defines the elements, interrelationships, context, and boundaries of a system—based on existing knowledge, practice, and observations—and introduces different perspectives on a problem (Smutny & Vehovar, 2020). The aim is to find the best possible explanation of the problem in question (Habr & Veprek, 1986).

While the Japanese school applies empirical and systems approaches (mostly together) due to its teleological nature, the Russian school prefers a systems approach without empirical background for historical-ideological reasons (Skovajsa & Balon, 2017). In addition to the systems approach in the Russian SI school, Kolin (2021) also mentions information and coevolutionary approaches, which are additionally closely connected with systems thinking.

The independent use of a systems approach without direct support in conclusions from empirical research cannot be considered a research method, but rather a methodological principle (Burianek, 2017; Clegg, 2000). Unfortunately, in the countries of the former Eastern Bloc, the systems approach was or still is understood as a research method. This is the consequence of the legacy of previously very limited possibilities for empirical research due to ideological reasons (e.g., research results must not contradict the official position of the Communist Party). If the systems approach is used independently without direct connection to empirical data, it allows reality to be bent according to the needs of the researcher—as it depends on the knowledge and practice of the researcher—into which a (totalitarian) ideology can be projected. This possibility contrasts with empirical research, in which it would be necessary to modify or falsify obtained data.

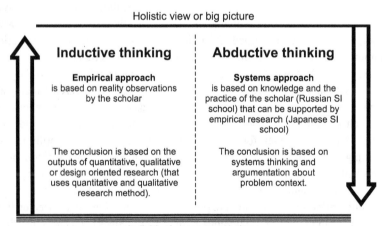

FIGURE 2.2   Inductive and abductive thinking as used in SI.

Source: Prepared by the authors based on Smutny and Vehovar (2020) and modified.

The systems view can also be found in other SI schools, mainly in an implicit form, including in the STIN strategy presented by US scholars (Kling et al., 2003) and in the sociotechnical approach used in the UK school (Davenport, 2008)

To summarize, SI seems to be based mainly on two scientific methods of reasoning: induction and abduction. Different ways of reasoning can complement each other, but when conducting research, emphasis should be placed on the use of research methods and approaches that are empirically based. Both ways of thinking and related methodological practices in SI are summarized in Figure 2.2. Finally, it should be noted that SI scholars engage in all forms of reasoning when conducting research, but induction and abduction—and their specific use in different SI schools as described here—are dominant trends in SI research.

Social informatics research methods

Research methods build on scientific methods of reasoning and allow scholars to conduct the research itself. An overview article (Vehovar et al., 2022) dealt with methodological aspects of SI concerning articles from 1985 to 2019 that refer to the term *SI* in the title, abstract, or keywords. This overview offers an international view of SI discourse, as the first authors of the reviewed articles come from 42 countries (mostly from the US, followed by the UK, Australia, and China at a long distance). Most articles were non-empirical (56%) and mainly reviewed past literature or put forward ideas and speculations; data from observations played only a supporting role. Only 44% of documents were empirical. Interestingly, empirical research has dominated the last period of 2015–2019. Among empirical articles, 48% adopted a qualitative approach, 33% a quantitative approach, and 19% a mixed methodological approach. The dominance of the qualitative approach may be related to the fact that most articles (64%) in the review are associated with the US school of SI, which focuses on in-depth insights, usually at the organizational level.

Since this section focuses on SI research methods in relation to SI thematic areas, the data from Vehovar et al. (2021) were re-analyzed. The re-analysis deals with how research methods are connected to themes addressed in the articles. It is done only for articles that include the term *SI* in the title, abstract, or keywords. The number of articles in the overview article was N = 275. In the re-analysis, only papers that addressed one of the three thematic areas were selected and analyzed (N = 255): (1) ICT and society, (2) ICT for society, or (3) ICT as a research tool. In addition, each article could be coded with up to three (sub) themes; here, we took only the first (and most important/prevalent) thematic area for each.

Table 2.1 includes all articles addressing one of the three thematic areas with any research method (N = 255). Table 2.2 excludes articles that conducted conceptual studies and literature reviews (N = 142), and the analysis is made on N = 113 articles that used empirical methods as well as addressed one of the three thematic areas. It should be added that of the three research approaches, only (I) Design-oriented

TABLE 2.1 Number of articles according to thematic area and research methods (N = 255)

Research methods	Thematic areas					
	(1) ICT and society		(2) ICT for society		(3) ICT as a research tool	
	N	%	N	%	N	%
Action research	1	1	2	6	0	0
Case study	**39**	**20**	**6**	**17**	2	6
Concept implementation	0	0	**5**	**14**	**5**	**14**
Content analysis	6	3	0	0	0	0
Data analysis	3	2	0	0	**4**	**11**
Field study	8	4	0	0	0	0
Interview	6	3	1	3	0	0
Laboratory experiment (computer)	0	0	2	6	1	3
Laboratory experiment (human)	0	0	1	3	0	0
Literature analysis/conceptual/ meta analysis	**119**	**60**	**16**	**46**	**7**	**20**
Multi-method	3	2	1	3	1	3
Survey	15	8	1	3	0	0
Total	200		35		20	

Note: In bold are research methods used in more than 10% of documents related to each theme.

and (II) Analytically oriented approaches are relevant for the found documents associated with empirical research; 91% are analytically oriented research related to natural and social sciences, and 9% are design-oriented research related to applied or design sciences. Design-oriented research uses analytical methods in some research phases, but the primary output is solution design. Therefore, we count only concept implementation because it is the sole research method that refers purely to design. No mathematically oriented research related to formal sciences was found.

The re-analysis shows that literature and conceptual analyses are prevalent across all thematic areas (Table 2.1). Among empirical studies, the most often used methods are case studies and concept implementation (Table 2.2). This finding is not surprising, as case studies are suitable for a deeper understanding of ICT use in an organization to define the problem's context or as a method for evaluating solutions. On the other hand, concept implementation deals with the design and evaluation of sociotechnical artifacts and, given the importance of such activities for SI research, it is appropriate that scholars use this method. SI also uses a plethora of other methods, whose utilization differs across thematic areas. For studying (1) interactions between ICT and society, researchers use case studies, field studies, and surveys—less often, interviews, content analysis, or a combination of methods (i.e., multi-method studies). In the case of (2) focus on ICT for society, methods used include mainly case studies and concept implementation—less often, action

TABLE 2.2 Number of empirical articles according to thematic area and research methods (N = 113)

Research methods	Thematic areas					
	(1) ICT and society		(2) ICT for society		(3) ICT as a research tool	
	N	%	N	%	N	%
Action research	1	1	**2**	**11**	0	0
Case study	**39**	**48**	**6**	**32**	**2**	**15**
Concept implementation	0	0	**5**	**26**	**5**	**38**
Content analysis	6	7	0	0	0	0
Data analysis	3	4	0	0	**4**	**31**
Field study	**8**	**10**	0	0	0	0
Interview	6	7	1	5	0	0
Laboratory experiment (computer)	0	0	**2**	**11**	1	8
Laboratory experiment (human)	0	0	1	5	0	0
Multi-method	3	4	1	5	1	8
Survey	**15**	**19**	1	5	0	0
Total	*81*	*100*	*19*	*100*	*13*	*100*

Note: In bold are research methods used in more than 10% of documents related to each theme.

research and laboratory experiments as well as other methods. Methods used by studies aimed at (3) developing ICT as a research tool for social science research include concept implementation, data analysis, and case studies; other methods are used less often.

We now compare the above view based on well-known SI schools with another view that is not conceptually anchored in SI schools but refers directly or indirectly to the notion of SI. We can look at the research methods used in so-called self-declared SI research, which often lacks any conceptual grounding (e.g., it lacks a reference to any literature on SI, yet the authors classify this research under SI) or self-labeled approach, in which the authors present their definition of SI without placing it in a wider regional or international perspective (see, for example, Smutny and Vehovar (2022)). Both approaches are increasingly common in international discourse, and they are also the principal drivers for rapidly expanded usage of the term *SI* in bibliographic databases (Smutny & Vehovar, 2020, p. 535). In this context, Vehovar et al. (2022) established that the self-declared SI approach is most typically represented by the International Conference on Social Informatics (SocInfo), in which out of the 476 conference papers examined (in 2009–2019), only three explicitly refer to the term *SI*. This conference thus supports the general usage of the term *SI*, which is understood as a label for any connection of social sciences with informatics, while no conceptual elaboration is offered for SI.

Articles published at SocInfo deal predominantly with (2) ICT for society and (3) ICT as a research tool. Therefore, it is not surprising that the identified research methods differ. Among the most used methods in empirical articles (N = 451) published on SocInfo is concept implementation, i.e., solution design and evaluation (44%) as well as data analysis (23%). The remaining methods have a share of less than 10%. With its focus and thematic composition of articles, SocInfo overlaps with the fields of computational social science and social computing.

Presentation of social informatics thematic-methodological framework

Combining SI's scientific, thematic, and methodological approaches, a broad thematic-methodological SI research framework can be developed (Figure 2.3). The framework considers the conceptual foundations of all seven SI schools and draws on a recent comprehensive literature review (Vehovar et al., 2022) to identify the most often used methods and their connection to thematic areas of SI research (i.e., based on Tables 2.1 and 2.2). The framework characterizes the English and conceptually grounded international SI discourse and does not refer to thematic areas or research methods outside of the seven SI schools. In addition, unifying rather than divergent aspects are emphasized, which also lends itself to potential future convergence of SI.

The framework is organized in a sequential order following from the most general and abstract level to the most specific and concrete. The arrows between levels indicate the most applicable sublevel and can both describe the SI research field as well as help researchers in guiding their studies.

Specifically, at the very general level, SI covers two areas of scientific inquiry: applied or design sciences on one side as well as natural and social sciences on the other. The research approach best suited for applied or design sciences is naturally (I) design-oriented research, which is aimed at addressing themes related to (2) ICT design and application in areas related to the social sciences as well as (3) ICT design and application as tools for social science research. Concretely, such research would focus on designing specific solutions for real-world problems, either related to society or (social) sciences. Examples include a privacy management tool for Facebook (Lee et al., 2011) and tools for key-word co-occurrence analysis (Cech, 2017).

On the other hand, activities related to natural and social sciences are usually approached through (II) analytically oriented research. This research predominantly focuses on themes related to (1) interactions between ICT and humans, although it can also investigate ICT design and application for (2) society and (3) as a research tool. Here, the research problems are addressed through the analytic orientation, meaning that they examine existing sociotechnical systems to identify potential issues and propose solutions for future development. For example, Paul et al. (2015) explored the facilitators and barriers of ICT use among Indian women,

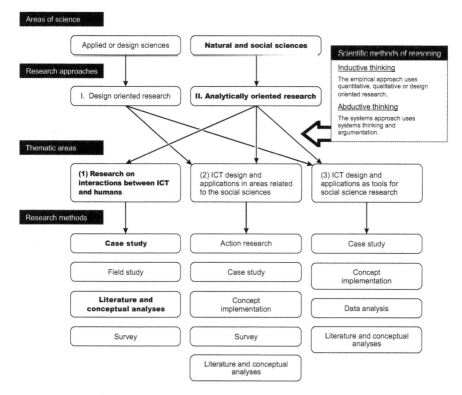

FIGURE 2.3   Social informatics thematic-methodological framework based on the conceptual basis of seven SI schools and bibliographic analysis of SI literature explicitly referring to the notion of SI.

Source: Prepared by the authors.

Note: The most common practices in SI are marked in bold.

while Pee et al. (2019) examined information value cocreation in Xiaomi's online user community.

Research approaches are not limited to their scientific methods of reasoning, although they should be chosen with care since they restrict the choice of methods and potential outcomes. It is also possible to combine different reasoning approaches, which is often preferable because it enables holistic evaluation, extension, or development of a theory (Minnameier, 2010). Nevertheless, inductive and abductive reasoning seem to be predominant in SI research (see also Figure 2.2).

Finally, although most themes can be explored by a variety of research methods, the framework indicates the most often used methods in relation to each theme. Perhaps unsurprisingly, literature analysis or conceptual studies are an important method across all themes. In case of theme (1), the most often used methods are case studies, field studies, and surveys, which is understandable since these methods can study the interactions between ICT and humans in a variety of contexts at different levels of depth. Theme (2) is typically approached through action research, case studies, and laboratory experiments, which presumably address efforts to deploy an ICT or evaluate its deployment, while concept implementation refers to the design and evaluation of a particular sociotechnical artifact. Research methods for theme (3) are similar, although these studies also use data analysis to test and evaluate the proposed tool. A concise description of each research method can be found in the Appendix to Vehovar et al.'s (2022) study.

Discussion and conclusion

This chapter discussed the scientific classification of SI, its thematic focus, methodological approaches, and its research methods. These aspects were integrated into an innovative thematic-methodological SI framework that not only describes this vibrant field of scientific investigation, but also provides scholars with a helpful guide for positioning their research and selecting the most appropriate approach. In respect to the latter, scholars can consider whether they are interested in developing a new sociotechnical artifact (research approach I) or analyzing existing ones (research approach II). Subsequently, keeping in mind the thematic focus and adopted scientific methods of reasoning, the most appropriate research methods can be selected. To see examples of SI studies that adopted different approaches, the dataset prepared by Vehovar et al. (2021) can be useful.

Alongside its practical significance, the framework can also act as a means for unifying the SI field of study. Given that it integrates the thematic and methodological characteristics of all seven SI schools, it provides fruitful grounds for mutual convergence. Specifically, the framework offers a classification of SI knowledge and research methods, which is one of the criteria for a field of study to become a scientific discipline (Krishnan, 2009). This key component is especially important given the current time and space of SI development, which is facing a certain turning point. Namely, self-declared SI research is rapidly expanding and becoming a dominant stream of SI research, while conceptually grounded SI research seems to be at a certain stagnation, failing to evolve itself into a formal discipline (instead staying a specific scientific and intellectual movement). This development is due to the diversity and isolation of SI schools, lack of established global SI identity (e.g., an international professional association), and limited expansion in studying the interactions between ICT and society. As the framework incorporates different schools and approaches, it allows scholars to refer to it in order to classify their research as part of a larger whole of SI and identify important SI themes. Over time, this outcome would strengthen the position of the SI field at the global level and help to establish its global identity.

Furthermore, the framework expands regional approaches to SI. In a book characterizing the US school, Fichman et al. (2015) describe four periods of SI's development and present methodological approaches and research methods used in SI research during the last nearly 45 years. In their view, SI has an interdisciplinary nature and adopts a multitude of theoretical lenses and approaches, including the concepts of: sociology, political science, economics, and communication studies. The use of theoretical concepts and paradigms determines the methods used in SI research (Fichman et al., 2015). Analytical-oriented research is mainly based on qualitative research, which is supplemented by quantitative research focused on network analysis, especially in the later years. The stated conclusions are in line with the focus of the research on (1) interactions between ICT and humans (personal and organizational level), for which a deeper understanding of the problem's context is needed. Fichman et al. (2015) identify case studies and interviews as the main research methods, while SI research also uses content analysis (document analysis, discursive analysis, and policy analysis), field studies (ethnography), and network analysis. In practice, multiple research methods are often combined to achieve a comprehensive understanding of the analyzed problem.

Comparing the proposed framework to Fichman et al.'s (2015) understanding of SI, it can be observed that the framework does not challenge or change past understandings of SI, but instead extends it to design-oriented approaches and associated research methods. It also introduces a specific application of abduction that is popular in some SI schools. Thus, the framework offers a truly international view of SI and can help to bridge the gaps between different SI schools.

Some limitations must be kept in mind when considering the proposed framework. First, the framework was developed based on conceptual foundations of the seven SI schools of thought. While these schools represent the core of SI, there exists other SI literature that is not linked to any of the schools of thought, and the framework does not account for such approaches. Secondly, the re-analyzed dataset included only articles in English that explicitly referred to SI (i.e., mentioned SI in either the title, abstract, or keywords; see Vehovar et al. (2022)). Thus, the framework might not provide a complete picture of the state of SI, and considering additional SI references might somewhat change the indication of methods' popularities. Third, the framework is based on practices from past literature and does not consider future developments. This aspect is especially relevant in the case of research methods, as new developments in ICT might necessitate novel methodological approaches. Indeed, Vehovar et al. (2022) note that

> from 2010–2019, methods that were not used previously, such as action research, concept implementation, data analysis, interviews, and multi-method studies, are also gaining ground [in SI research]. The most likely reason for this is that

the interactions between ICT and society are becoming more extensive, and new methods are needed to analyze these emerging social dynamics.

(p. 329)

Therefore, the list of methods should not be seen as exhaustive, and scholars are welcome to adopt new methods that they consider appropriate for addressing the research problem at hand.

In conclusion, this chapter provides an innovative thematic-methodological SI research framework that can both be a useful guide for future research and help in activities aimed at SI global convergence. Although the framework is substantially grounded in past conceptual analyses and literature reviews, the SI field is likely to keep evolving as it explores new forms of ICT-human interactions and designs new sociotechnical artifacts. The framework can be easily refined or extended to accommodate such developments.

References

Aken, J.E. (2004). Management research based on the paradigm of the design sciences: The quest for field-tested and grounded technological rules. *Journal of Management Studies, 41*(2), 219–246. https://doi.org/10.1111/j.1467-6486.2004.00430.x

Baur, N. (2019). Linearity vs. circularity? On some common misconceptions on the differences in the research process in qualitative and quantitative research. *Frontiers in Education, 4*, Article 53. https://doi.org/10.3389/feduc.2019.00053

Beth, E.W. (1959). Science and classification. *Synthese, 11*, 231–244. https://doi.org/10.1007/BF00486414

Burianek, J. (2017). Přístup systémový. In Z.R. Nespor (Ed.), *Sociologická encyklopedie* [Encyclopedia of Sociology]. Academia. https://encyklopedie.soc.cas.cz/w/P%C5%99%C3%ADstup_syst%C3%A9mov%C3%BD

Callegaro, M., Manfreda, K.L., & Vehovar, V. (2015). *Web survey methodology*. Sage. https://doi.org/10.4135/9781529799651

Campos, D.G. (2011). On the distinction between Peirce's abduction and Lipton's inference to the best explanation. *Synthese, 180*(3), 419–442. https://doi.org/10.1007/s11229-009-9709-3

Cech, F. (2017). Exploring emerging topics in social informatics: An online real-time tool for keyword co-occurrence analysis. In G.L. Ciampaglia, A. Mashhadi, & T. Yasseri (Eds.), *Proceedings of the 9th international conference on social informatics* (pp. 527–536). Springer Nature. https://doi.org/10.1007/978-3-319-67256-4_42

Clegg, C.W. (2000). Sociotechnical principles for system design. *Applied Ergonomics, 31*(5), 463–477. https://doi.org/10.1016/s0003-6870(00)00009-0

Davenport, E. (2008). Social informatics and sociotechnical research — A view from the UK. *Journal of Information Science, 34*(4), 519–530. https://doi.org/10.1177/0165551508091011

Dresch, A., Lacerda, D.P., & Antunes, J.A.V. (2015). *Design science research: A method for science and technology advancement*. Springer Cham. https://doi.org/10.1007/978-3-319-07374-3

Fichman, P., Sanfilippo, M.R., & Rosenbaum, H. (2015). *Social informatics evolving*. Morgan & Claypool.

Flach, P.A. (1996). Abduction and induction: Syllogistic and inferential perspectives. In P.A. Flach & A. Kakas (Eds.), *Proceedings of the ECAI 96 workshop on abductive and inductive reasoning* (pp. 31–35). ECCAI.

Guest, D.E. (2022). The sociotechnical approach to work organization. *Oxford Research Encyclopedia of Psychology*. https://doi.org/10.1093/acrefore/9780190236557.013.905

Habr, J., & Veprek, J. (1986). *Systémová analýza a syntéza* [System Analysis and Synthesis]. SNTL.

Hagiya, M. (2015). Defining informatics across Bun-kei and Ri-kei. *Journal of Information Processing, 23*(4), 525–530. https://doi.org/10.2197/ipsjjip.23.525

Hersh, W.R. (2009). A stimulus to define informatics and health information technology. *BMC Medical Informatics and Decision Making, 9*(1), Article 24. https://doi.org/10.1186/1472-6947-9-24

Informatics Europe. (2023). *Informatics Europe – mission and history*. Informatics Europe. www.informatics-europe.org/about/mission-and-origins.html

Karthik, N., Pawar, S.R., Pramodhini, R., & Shukla, A.K. (2023). Swarm intelligence embedded data mining for precision agriculture advancements. *ICTACT Journal on Soft Computing, 14*(2), 3218–3223.

Kling, R., McKim, G., & King, A. (2003). A bit more to it: Scholarly communication forums as socio-technical interaction networks. *Journal of the Association for Information Science and Technology, 54*(1), 47–67. https://doi.org/10.1002/asi.10154

Kolin, K.K. (2021). Social informatics: 30 years of development of Russian scientific school. *Acta Informatica Pragensia, 10*(3), 289–300. https://doi.org/10.18267/j.aip.150

Krishnan, A. (2009). *What are academic disciplines? Some observations on the disciplinarity vs. interdisciplinarity debate*. NCRM Working Paper. National Centre for Research Methods. https://eprints.ncrm.ac.uk/id/eprint/783

Lee, R., Nia, R., Hsu, J., Levitt, K.N., Rowe, J., Wu, S.F., & Ye, S. (2011). Design and implementation of FAITH, an experimental system to intercept and manipulate online social informatics. In *2011 International conference on advances in social networks analysis and mining* (pp. 195–202). IEEE. https://doi.org/10.1109/ASONAM.2011.86

Mašić, I. (2020). The history of medical informatics development – An overview. *International Journal on Biomedicine and Healthcare, 8*(1), 37–52. https://doi.org/10.5455/ijbh.2020.8.37-52

Minnameier, G. (2010). The logicality of abduction, deduction, and induction. In M. Bergman, S. Paavola, A.-V. Pietarinen, & H. Rydenfelt (Eds.), *Ideas in action: Proceedings of the applying Peirce conference* (pp. 239–251). Nordic Pragmatism Network.

Mounier-Kuhn, P.-É., & Pégny, M. (2016). AFCAL and the emergence of computer science in France: 1957–1967. In A. Beckmann, L. Bienvenu, & N. Jonoska (Eds.), *Pursuit of the universal* (pp. 170–181). Springer. https://doi.org/10.1007/978-3-319-40189-8_18

National Center for Education Statistics. (2023). *Detail for CIP Code 11.0104:2020, informatics*. National Center for Education Statistics. https://nces.ed.gov/ipeds/cipcode/cipdetail.aspx?y=56&cip=11.0104

Pantell, M.S., Adler-Milstein, J., Wang, M.D., Prather, A.A., Adler, N.E., & Gottlieb, L.M. (2020). A call for social informatics. *Journal of the American Medical Informatics Association, 27*(11), 1798–1801. https://doi.org/10.1093/jamia/ocaa175

Paul, A., Thompson, K.M., & Heinström, J. (2015). After access: An inquiry into ICT use factors for Indian women. *Proceedings of the Association for Information Science and Technology, 52*(1), 1–10. https://doi.org/10.1002/pra2.2015.145052010035

Pee, L.G., Pan, S.L., Li, M., & Jia, S. (2019). Social informatics of information value cocreation: A case study of Xiaomi's online user community. *Journal of the Association for Information Science and Technology, 71*(4), 409–422. https://doi.org/10.1002/asi.24252

Rosenbaum, H. (2014). Social informatics as a scientific and intellectual movement. In H. Rosenbaum & P. Fichman (Eds.), *Social informatics: Past, present and future* (pp. 2–28). Cambridge Scholars Publishing.

Skovajsa, M., & Balon, J. (2017). *Sociology in the Czech Republic: Between East and West.* Palgrave Pivot London. https://doi.org/10.1057/978-1-137-45027-2

Smutny, Z. (2016). Social informatics as a concept: Widening the discourse. *Journal of Information Science, 42*(5), 681–710. https://doi.org/10.1177/0165551515608731

Smutny, Z. (2020). *Diskurz sociální informatiky: Metodologická východiska, myšlenkové školy a tematická konceptualizace* [Discourse of Social Informatics: Methodological Backgrounds, Schools of Thought and Thematic Conceptualization]. Professional Publishing.

Smutny, Z., & Vehovar, V. (2020). Social informatics research: Schools of thought, methodological basis, and thematic conceptualization. *Journal of the Association for Information Science and Technology, 71*(5), 529–539. https://doi.org/10.1002/asi.24280.

Smutny, Z., & Vehovar, V. (2022). On the current connection and relation between health informatics and social informatics. *Journal of Medical Internet Research, 24*(9), e40547. https://doi.org/10.2196/40547

Tanaka, K. (2023). *Spatio-temporal variation of dugongs' habitat use and vessel traffic revealed by underwater acoustics information: Toward harmonized coastal management* [Unpublished doctoral dissertation]. Kyoto University. https://doi.org/10.14989/doctor.k24936

Trang, S., Trenz, M., Weiger, W.H., Tarafdar, M., & Cheung, C.M.K. (2020). One app to trace them all? Examining app specifications for mass acceptance of contact-tracing apps. *European Journal of Information Systems, 29*(4), 415–428. https://doi.org/10.1080/0960085x.2020.1784046

Vehovar, V. (2006). Social informatics: An emerging discipline? In J. Berleur, M. Nurminen, & J. Impagliazzo (Eds.), *Social informatics: An information society for all? In remembrance of Rob Kling* (pp. 73–85). Springer. https://doi.org/10.1007/978-0-387-37876-3_6

Vehovar, V., Smutny, Z., & Bartol, J. (2021). *Overview of social informatics scientific activities (1985–2019): Three datasets* (Version 1) [Data set]. Zenodo. https://doi.org/10.5281/zenodo.5788186

Vehovar, V., Smutny, Z., & Bartol, J. (2022). Evolution of social informatics: Publications, research, and educational activities. *The Information Society, 38*(5), 307–333. https://doi.org/10.1080/01972243.2022.2092570

Wieringa, R.J. (2014). *Design science methodology for information systems and software engineering.* Springer.

Wilson, E.O. (1999). *Consilience: The unity of knowledge.* Vintage.

SECTION II

Social informatics perspectives on data

3

FROM INNOVATIVE METHODOLOGIES TO CREATIVE MYTHOLOGIES

Measuring GLAM soft power through data-driven research

Natalia Grincheva

Introduction

Vast repositories of digital footprints that we leave behind, from online transactions and search queries to social media interactions, shape a contemporary landscape of global media communications. In the past decade, data-intensive research, along with data visualization and mapping, as key methods of data analysis have greatly contributed to the development of academic scholarship across different domains. This chapter explores data mapping methodologies applied to public and cultural diplomacy evaluation studies to identify their strengths and expose their limitations and weaknesses. As one of the instruments in a state's arsenal to manage its international relations, global image, and even a reputational status quo via cultural activity, cultural diplomacy has always been centered on cultivating international audiences and managing human perceptions.

While being a central concern of national governments, which have always sought to convincingly justify their international cultural outreach investments, impact evaluations of cultural diplomacy activities have remained a challenging task (Banks, 2011). The long-term nature of cultural diplomacy's possible impacts, the elusiveness of its direct effects on people, and the vagueness of its specific outcomes in relation to foreign policy goals explain why evaluating cultural diplomacy has presented a significant methodological difficulty. However, with the rise of the internet and mobile communications, datafication processes have considerably enriched diplomatic evaluation activities—offering new methods to measure global public engagement, track opinion formation, and assess attention span (Bjola et al., 2020). In the domain of arts and culture, big data collected from audiences by cultural organizations and government agencies increasingly inform the evaluation of local and global activities to support decision-making processes,

DOI: 10.4324/9781032678542-6

becoming "a source of national, indeed international, obsession" (Gilmore et al., 2018).

Recently, geo-visualization approaches to mapping cultural activities have also been employed in cultural and creative industries research to categorize the size, economic significance, and growth patterns of creative industries, looking at the geographic distribution of both global cultural imports and exports with accompanying analysis of "cluster effects" (Duxbury et al., 2018). Going beyond global economics, political implications of cultural activities taking place on the global stage have been addressed through both academic scholarship and professional experimentation in cultural mapping (Manovich, 2020; Grincheva, 2018). The case study that informs this chapter contributes to this scholarship. This chapter describes an experience of designing a geo-visualization system to understand, map, and measure the complex phenomenon of soft power.

Coined by Joseph Nye, *soft power* refers to intangible forms of power, such as culture, ideology, and institutions, which allow countries to achieve their foreign policy objectives (Nye, 2004). In the context of the knowledge-based global economy, soft power is a more sophisticated tool to influence international politics, in contrast to military or economic coercion. Nye (2004) argues that a country possesses soft power if it is capable of exploiting information and culture to shape and inhabit the "mind space" of another country through the persuasive powers of attraction by both appealing to and promoting common cultural values and principles. Furthermore, the extent of a nation's soft power is increasingly subject to data-driven measurements, with many ranking systems produced by national governments and private actors providing convincing evidence of this trend (Monocle, 2024; SP 30, 2019). However, these ranking systems have provoked severe criticism in academic literature for their considerable knowledge gaps and inconsistencies in assessing soft power, driving competition among actors for better scores while inciting the processes of data colonization—inequalities in data access, ownership and power to interpret results, shape narratives, and manipulate opinions (Grincheva, 2022).

Indeed, while computational methods significantly increase the scope of data that could be effectively analyzed in a much shorter time, this analysis comes with limitations and biases that should be properly acknowledged. Quantitative data usually gives an impression of extreme objectivity that is misleading, as the algorithms used to generate them reflect the cognitive biases and epistemological prejudices of their designers (Kitchin, 2014). Second, data-intensive metrics offer only limited insights that can be used to evaluate impacts of cultural diplomacy. Therefore, qualitative methods, storytelling, and analysis of "thick data" must be equally employed to complement data analytics (Grincheva, 2022). Absent the latter methods, data-driven methodologies tend to create narratives that are a subject to mythologization.

Data mythologies are deeply woven narratives embedded in the fabric of our digital lives, shaping how we interact with and make sense of the vast information ocean. These myths can be seductive, promising predictive power or personalized truths and data objectivity based on algorithmic calculations and affected by the biases of their collection and analysis. However, we should be aware of the mythological implications that arise from working with big data while also understanding the key technological factors and social conditions at play that give these mythologies a ground to emerge and develop. This chapter aims to deconstruct these mythologies and explore key factors behind the existing biases and limitations that usually emerge in data visualization from the perspective of social informatics. In the context of big data, social informatics is a crucial tool for deconstructing the underlying narratives that inform human understanding of this phenomenon.

According to the original definition, social informatics is "the interdisciplinary study of the design, uses and consequences of information technologies that takes into account their interaction with institutional and cultural contexts" (Kling, 1999). Social informatics questions how people relate to, explore, and employ information. It is mainly a problem-driven research domain based on assumptions that technological solutions and tools are always a result of human choices, imaginaries, and biases while they simultaneously are the platforms that shape social perceptions and relationships. Social informatics seeks to understand how the production, dissemination, and consumption of information shape cultural norms, power dynamics, and individual identities. This chapter specifically draws on the *critical orientation* of social informatics that, in this case, refers to examining data mythologies from multiple perspectives, including both their production as a social process and their social implications.

In particular, it focuses on examining possible "failure modes and service losses, as well as idealized expectations of routine use" (Sawyer & Rosenbaum, 2000, p. 90). As a problem-driven research domain, social informatics work in most cases is empirically focused and characterized by the problems being examined rather than the theories or methods used in the research. In this regard, it allows us to explore various technological issues and direct social implications when certain tools are being used for specific purposes. Such a design of social informatics research is at the basis of this chapter. It helps to identify, describe, and interrogate data narratives for the purposes of highlighting important insights that can generate new vision and understanding of soft power while exposing technological limitations and revealing data mythologies as intricate constructs—imbued with power dynamics and laden with inherent biases.

Specifically, this chapter shares results of the critical digital practice research project "GLAM and Digital Soft Power in the Post-pandemic World," completed in 2022 in collaboration with the Digital Diplomacy Research Centre at the University of Oxford to explore computation methods for the purposes of mapping and assessing the soft power of cultural heritage institutions on a global scale. It identifies and explores boundaries between innovative data-driven methodologies and creative data "mythologies," which emerge as a result of contextual limitations that current big data aggregation and analysis tools possess. This chapter shares advancements in soft power measurement—aiming to identify avenues for further developments, signaling current boundaries, and flagging limitations in data-driven computational methodologies.

Case study: Designing the data to power prototype

This chapter draws on the case analysis of the Data to Power mapping prototype, designed as a new computational tool to measure, map, and predict the soft power of galleries, libraries, archives, and museums—or GLAM institutions (see Figure 3.1). Drawing on collaborations and consultations with 25 museum professionals from Europe and Asia-Pacific—including the Victoria & Albert Museum in London, the Museum of Asian Civilizations in Singapore, and the Australian Museum—the project explored illuminating and provocative examples of GLAM digital soft power effects. It also generated knowledge through critical reflexive praxis, exposing cultural mechanics, political technologies, media strategies, and global target responses of digital soft power exercised by contemporary cultural heritage institutions.

The project employed reflexive praxis methodology, which is based on an agile, incremental, iterative approach to facilitate the knowledge generation process through creative practice, informed by theory but enhanced through focused collaborative reflections on the processes. On the one hand, the project emerged through a serious of online international research sessions, focus groups, and community discussions that brought together more than one hundred GLAM sector professionals, academics, policy makers, and diplomatic actors. These individuals

FIGURE 3.1   Data to power 3D mapping visualization sample. © Victoria Software.

collaborated to facilitate a productive knowledge exchange that explored, scoped, and critically assessed current practices and perceived challenges and opportunities existing in the global communication space. On the other hand, the project employed the method of critical digital practice, which is a practice-led epistemic approach in media research supporting tools development through critical engagement with digital media as both objects and instruments of investigation. The project drew on experimentation with various sets of data collected from participating museums in different countries to prototype a new software solution: the Data to Power interactive mapping application for assessing and predicting soft power of GLAM institutions.

The Data to Power application employed multilayered mapping empowered by GIS that allowed for a focused integration of different types of data through their cartographic display on multiple layers. Multilayered mapping is used in research to visualize and evaluate interrelationships, coexistence, and processes of complex phenomena predominantly by exposing and comparing different data across layers. In the project, GIS provided an effective tool for a more accurate aggregation of different sets of research data across institutional resources, outputs, and impacts to expose correlations of data and processes happening on different levels of the soft power conversion process and analysis.

The mapping system interface is designed for users to easily navigate various tasks including data aggregation, collection, categorization, and analysis to geo-visualize and explore the soft power of GLAM actors on the global map. It allows users to make important decisions on all levels of data visualization, including: selecting which raw data can be aggregated and how; creating formulas for data indices by determining the weight of different variables; compiling mapping layers on the basis of aggregated data; shaping visualizations for different audiences depending on different purposes; and considering different access levels to sensitive data. The system taps into the processes enabled by an Application Programming Interface (API), which is an automatic aggregation of data and metadata from existing Open Access data repositories. Employing the API, the app accommodates a dynamic and automatic aggregation of large data sets—for example: social demographics for each country on the globe from Open Access repositories, such as World Bank Open Data.

In conversation with GLAM professionals from 25 different organizations in Europe and Asia-Pacific, the project tested, critically assessed, and trialed the Data to Power Prototype as a tool for more intelligent, data-informed soft power evaluations and mapping. The project explored the prototype's capabilities to create maps, timelines, and data cuts for a comparative soft power analysis across geographies, time periods, and programs. Drawing on the results of this project, this chapter discusses current practices and advancements in computational technologies that could provide new avenues for understanding soft power, while flagging barriers and limitations in data-driven research. Employing a social informatics approach, the following three sections expose how data-driven methodologies and tools help GLAM actors to explore the phenomenon of their attraction power on the global map. While the first two sections focus on the insights that data analytics could bring to better understand soft power reach, appeal, and engagement across countries, the last section identifies data mythologies that arise from limitations associated with data access and data contexts.

Mapping GLAM soft power through cultural reach and appeal

GLAM artifacts and collections have always been a strong source of cultural and political power to shape cultural and political discourses, build citizenry and sense of national identity and belonging, and construct public perceptions and understandings of reality at home and abroad (Bennett, 1995; Luke, 2002). The geographic diversity of cultural collections is a very important variable that makes GLAM institutions influential actors on the world stage. Objects from the collections offer important anchors that connect these institutions to cultural communities of their origin. They become important assets in cultivating international cultural relations through loans, repatriation activities, exchange projects, educational and archival programs, co-curated exhibitions, and even cultural and political missions organized on higher diplomatic levels (Sylvester, 2009; Grincheva, 2020). Mapping collections' geo-diversity brings to light important details about museum audiences and stakeholders—exposing important moments about GLAM histories and their connections to partner institutions, communities, and stakeholders in different parts of the world.

Understanding and visualizing a potential soft power reach of GLAM actors and their resources requires a systematic and accurate geo-visualization of their collections' origins and histories, which can help to highlight areas on the world map where this soft power could be generated. In other words, this geo-visualization can assist with identifying where museum collections and their legacies could serve as meaningful bridges to connect institutions, audiences, and communities across borders. The first layer of the Data to Power Prototype calculates a Collection Reach Power Index for each of the 250 countries on the global map, indicating where the collection could make a greater reach and potential appeal or an increase in awareness of the country's population concerning a remote institution. This index is a weighted sum of several key normalized indicators based on several critical types of data, including institutional data of a GLAM actor and Open Access data. The scale from 0 to 100 for each of these indices should be interpreted in a linear fashion, focusing on absolute scores progressing equally on the scale. For the Collection Reach Power layer, the total Layer Score allows users to compare different countries in terms of the scope of the collections' reach and appeal to people living in this geographic area (see Figure 3.2).

In the Data to Power mapping system, institutional data on collection diversity is automatically aggregated via the Museum Collections' API. Accessing the collections' API via a provided link, the mapping solution searches the collection for the geo-location information of each object, extracts these data, and automatically

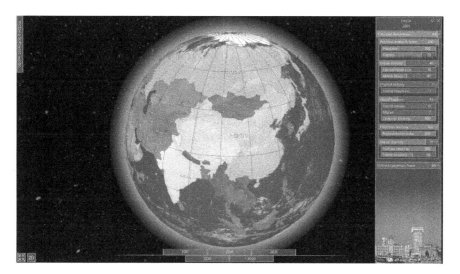

FIGURE 3.2   Data to power prototype: collection reach power in India in 2021 of the Science Museum Group. © Victoria Software.

distributes the geo-data across all countries on the globe. In this way, each country receives its unique index of collection diversity, which indicates how many holdings in the heritage institution collection originate from this country. In the layer, these data correlate with the Digital Diversity Index that demonstrates how the country is represented by the institution in its feeds on different social media channels, focusing on the number of references made to each country on the globe.

This index is an important indicator that reveals how cultural heritage assets of soft power are activated in the global media space targeting specific audiences to generate attraction power and provoke a target response. For example, a museum might possess rich and rare collections originating from another country. However, without exposing the collections to wider audiences and creating meaningful and engaging onsite or online activities around these artifacts, it is not possible for the institution to attract relevant communities and involve them in interactive learning and sharing. In the global media space, social media conversations targeting people from specific countries are a great way to not only expose a museum collection's diversity, but also to generate "soft power" through cross-cultural exchange and collaborations. In the Data to Power system, the data for the Digital Diversity Index is automatically aggregated by the social media channel's API—specifically in the experimental mapping exercise, which focused on Twitter and YouTube channels.

Reflecting on mapping the Victoria & Albert (V&A) Museum's Collection Diversity and Digital Diversity, Kati Price (2022), the Head of Digital Media, stressed the usefulness of this geo-visualization exercise—highlighting important insights from a vast volume of data generated by 17 national collections featuring over 2 million objects in the possession of the museum: "I think it tells us some interesting top level views on the history of our collections, our collecting policy and how those collections are received by our audiences." For example, their visualization of the Collection Reach Power layer highlighted Japan as a country with a high index for both Collection Diversity and Digital Diversity. Not only did such a visualization of data demonstrate the V&A' rich holdings representing Japanese culture and heritage, but it also exposed the most recent digital conversations happening on social media in regard to an exhibition called Kimono: Kyoto to Catwalk. This exhibition covered the whole history of the kimono and its influence on contemporary culture. As Price (2022) confirmed, the museum featured many objects from the V&A collection as part of their digital outreach campaign, which fueled social media engagement, especially on YouTube. Reading this visualization as a brief but convincing snapshot of activating digital soft power is helpful for making strategic decisions in terms of leveraging rich and diverse collections' cultural assets to better understand how they could affect the museum's communication with audiences from different countries (Price, 2022).

Similarly, Craig Middleton (2022), Senior Curator, Digital Innovation & Strategy at the National Museum of Australia, emphasized that such a mapping exercise could be a valuable strategic tool for finding the gaps within its collection as well as within its current international cultural relations policies and practices. For example, he shared that the top three countries that provide the most permanent migrants to Australia are India, China, and the United Kingdom. He additionally explained that while China and the United Kingdom shine brightly on their Data to Power museum's visualization, exposing rich connections to the heritages of both countries through the museum collection holdings, India is not very strong in its visual representation. "There's an opportunity, I can see, that we could use to think about the collection as not necessarily representative" of particular cultures that are important for our local audiences (Middleton, 2022).

On the other hand, the cultural diversity visualization of the National Museum of Australia's collections piqued Middleton's curiosity about rich institutional holdings representing indigenous cultures of Papua New Guinea, which at some point appeared as an "unexpected" visualization result for him. Digging through the institutional archives, he discovered two collections: the Lady Helen Blackburn Collection and Miss Beth Dean Carol Collection. The former features about 500 seashells collected from Australian beaches, reefs, and islands, many of which come from the shores of Papua New Guinea, a colony of Australia from 1902 to 1975. The latter collection features cultural items collected by the dancer Beth Dean Carroll throughout her travels to the Pacific and Papua New Guinea. "These were really interesting insights," Middleton (2022) pointed out, "as they revealed a potential reach power of our institutional cultural resources," which at that point were not really activated for the benefit of a more engaging communication with source communities from New Guinea.

Complementing the Diversity Indices, the Collection Reach Power layer also draws on the Open Access data of various social demographic variables—such as Potential Audience Scope, Global Exposure, and Physical and Digital Mobility of populations—that point to the extent to which audiences in each geo-location are actually able to interact with the digital content of GLAM actors, considering digital divide threats that still exist in many rural communities. Indeed, through mapping collection reach power across museums from the UK, Singapore, and Australia, it was revealed that vast geographic areas in Africa or Southeast Asia still remain difficult to engage online for many institutions—even though their collection diversity index is quite high—inviting potential outreach and meaningful communication. Jolan Wuyts (2022), Collections Editor from the Europeana Collections Engagement Team, pointed out that data visualization on the Collection Reach Power layer can be "used as a way to decolonize or create a post-colonial collection" by drawing attention to "structural inequalities, the historical dominances or oppression" exercised by Western institutions.

A detailed global mapping of collection diversity, especially in correlation with Digital Diversity and Open Access Data exposing digital and cultural divides, could be used as a strategic tool to develop diplomatic routes and channels to engage with "underrepresented communities, or oppressed communities" to help them share their stories and narratives—exposing their rich cultures and traditions (Wuyts, 2022). As this section has illuminated, the research sessions with professionals who experimented with Data to Power is evidence that data-intense approaches—as well as mapping and correlation of large data sets ranging from collection geo-data to social demographics of audiences—is a helpful methodological approach to reveal important insights in soft power assessments of GLAM actors.

From the social informatics angle, the new technological capabilities implemented through the Data to Power app work with big data to help create meaningful and insightful narratives concerning museums, their collections, historical legacies, and potential audiences with which they could engage. These new narratives and interpretations of museum collections can make a significant step forward toward a more equitable digital landscape. By facilitating a detailed mapping of collection diversity alongside digital access and open data availability, the app exposes existing digital and cultural divides. This knowledge can empower GLAM actors to develop targeted diplomatic strategies that address existing historical colonial legacies. Social informatics here helps to reveal the power dynamics inherent in online spaces to foster a more inclusive digital environment where diverse stories and cultural narratives can be shared. Such an approach to audience analysis can allow GLAM institutions to move beyond assumptions created by social media analytics and develop strategies to engage with audiences in a more meaningful way.

Mapping GLAM soft power through audience engagement metrics

The online audience is an important dimension of digital soft power that depends on virtual participants' trust, understanding, and respect of GLAM media, which is usually assessed through their levels of online engagement. The Online Engagement Power Layer of the Data to Power Prototype was designed to provide a convenient tool for aggregating organizational web and social media analytics, and for correlating these data with Open Access census data collected from each country on the global map. The layer aims to expose areas across countries where a GLAM actor could enjoy greater digital attention and engagement, and where it requires further efforts to involve online audiences. This index, measured on a scale from 0 to 100, is a weighted sum of several key normalized indicators based on two critical types of data: institutional data and Open Access data of different social demographic variables. From the institutional perspective, the layer relies on the data collected by museums through Google and Social Media Analytics, specifically focusing on geographic distribution of "Average Session Duration." This data refers not to the number of visits, but to the total time spent by online visitors on the institutional web resources, while automatically "cleaning" it from the bias created by "ghost spam" and "bot traffic" (Mokalis & Davis, 2018). To put the platform analytics data into context, the layer correlates it with audience profile social demographic data in each country in terms of the Potential Audience Scope as well as its Digital Mobility, the latter of which refers to the population's digital access and literacy skills concerning traversing the global web. This data points to the extent to which audiences in each geo-location are able to interact with digital GLAM institutions and their collections (see Figure 3.3).

FIGURE 3.3 Data to power prototype: online engagement power in India in 2021 of the Science Museum Group. © Victoria Software.

Reflecting on the Online Engagement Power visualization of the Science Museum Group, Rosie Cardiff (2022), Website Editor, shared that such a mapping significantly advances the understanding of potential and real online audiences as compared to the data that they usually collect from their institutional analytics. As she mentioned:

> a lot of the colors on the map kind of correlated with what we would expect to see from our Google analytics in terms of where most of our traffic comes from – the UK, USA, India, but what was quite interesting when you see that Google data correlated with the open-source data. These sort of pink areas – China was one, Brazil was another – where there is a large potential audience scope for us.
>
> *(Cardiff, 2022)*

She elaborated that such a snapshot of potential audiences vividly exposed countries with "quite large populations, quite high digital literacy," and prompted her to think that their institution could do a much better job on its digital outreach activities to better communicate to their global audiences, especially those that are currently not engaged. One of the key questions that comes out of this research and data visualization, Cardiff (2022) stressed, is how GLAM actors could diversify their audiences. In other words, how could they reach communities that are currently not on their radar and what steps could be taken? While the Data to Power tool certainly does not have the exact answer, "it does show the potential for audiences in other countries" and expose missed opportunities (Cardiff, 2022).

Raymond Tham (2022), Senior Manager of Digital Marketing and Corporate Communications at the Asian Civilizations Museum in Singapore, seconded these observations, sharing that the visualization was very helpful in revealing an urgent need for the museum to improve its efforts in certain countries:

> I was very surprised when I looked at the data visualization that our closest neighbor Malaysia, which we are just a bridge away from, had very low traffic or a very low score. This is our closest neighbor, we share a lot of cultural similarities, a lot of people similarities, with which we actually cross the border almost every day. We have a lot of family members from across both nations, so it's shocking that it has a low score on online engagement. The learning for us is to continue to ramp up our efforts there, which we have not really done, compared to a country like Indonesia, which is also our second closest neighbor.
>
> *(Tham, 2022)*

Katie Moffat (2022), the Head of Sector Engagement Europe at Substrat, stressed that Data to Power is "a very interesting tool to help museums and cultural institutions to remind them that online audiences are not just one homogenous group of people." People's motivations, their interests, and unique online behaviors vary from country to country, and "what a tool like this does, it helps people to start thinking much more about how audiences differentiate among countries"—even among different time periods (Moffat, 2022). Understanding the digital engagement of audiences in different countries as a dynamic variable, the Online Engagement Layer offers a timeline setting that allows users to explore audience engagement not only across different countries, but also through time. For instance, in geo-visualizing the Science Museum Group's digital audiences from 2017 to 2021, the layer exposed and interrogated quite modest changes in audience geographical reach and cultural diversity taking place during those five years. Switching across years on the visualization timeline, one would spot no significant differences in the museum's online audience scope or geographic reach.

Cardiff (2022) shared that this mapping appeared to be quite accurate and corresponded to their own online audience research results. While the Museum Science Group experienced a large increase in traffic to its website, especially during the COVID-19 pandemic crisis, "it was always the same core audiences that we had already always been reaching," targeting the same countries (Cardiff, 2022). This finding shows that digital engagement patterns are hard to change over time if no efforts are undertaken on the institutional side to understand their target audiences beyond their usual scope and reach, and to direct their digital activities toward them—activating digital soft power. For example, in contrast to the Museum Science Group's digital audience stagnation over the past five years, the visualization of the Asian Civilizations Museum's Online Engagement Power on the timeline exposed a high spike of online Chinese visitors to the museum website and collections in 2020, right as the pressure of border closures during the pandemic hit. As Tham (2022) revealed, during that time, the Asian Civilizations Museum collaborated with the National Museum of China on an online campaign, which in fact sparked "some hundred million views in China alone for some of our content" and eventually dramatically increased traffic to the museum's online resources.

Also, that same year, the museum sent 168 treasure artifacts from the Tang Shipwreck exhibition to the Shanghai Museum in China to commemorate the 30th anniversary of diplomatic relations between the two countries. As the Shanghai Museum's first international collaborative exhibition to take place post-lockdown, it was also the first on such a large scale in China to exhibit the Tang Shipwreck collection. Tham (2022) explained that the Tang Shipwreck exhibition has traditionally been the most popular among the museum's Chinese visitors onsite and online, considering its ancient age—dating back to the ninth century—and size as the single biggest collection of Tang Dynasty artifacts found outside of China. It is not surprising that this exhibition caused such an increase of online traffic from China in 2020. It also excellently demonstrated a strong connection between physical and online audiences, which complicates the phenomenon of digital soft power. This example shows that a targeted digital response can be caused by physical activities and online campaigns that can attract onsite visitors.

From a social informatics perspective, the Data to Power app facilitates the creation of narratives that can reveal and challenge assumptions about online audiences, going beyond monolithic representations of diverse online communities existing across countries in the digital domain. These data-driven narratives paint a picture of audiences with distinct online behaviors that vary geographically and temporally. This finding challenges the notion of a homogeneous global online viewership or engagement, encouraging GLAM institutions to tailor their digital strategies in order to resonate with specific target cultural and linguistic groups. From the social informatics angle, Data to Power's capabilities of visualizing and exposing potential and actual GLAM audiences create a tool for understanding the online public beyond basic demographics and delve into the "why" behind online engagement. This capability can enable cultural institutions to craft more meaningful interactions, fostering a richer and more inclusive digital environment. Ultimately, Data to Power's role in constructing these audience narratives aligns with social informatics' core principles of promoting social awareness of technological capabilities, especially in relation to aggregation and analysis of the big data that stand behind online users and their digital traces.

The Online Engagement Power Layer proved to be helpful for understanding the audience scope, reach, and level of target response. However, mere engagement metrics focusing on quantitative data do not necessarily lead to understanding feelings and perceptions of digital GLAM audiences. For instance, Price (2022) from the V&A Museum pointed out:

> The challenge of social media is that it doesn't necessarily say anything about the quality of that engagement, and I think the idea of sentiment and how one might use it for data analysis is very important. Instead of measuring just reach and volume, the quality of engagement, this is what matters.

Indeed, the soft power conversion model of Joseph Nye (2004) identifies audience perceptions as the most important component that can help with understanding impacts. Social media provides a perfect tool for recording qualitative data that can be aggregated to understand audiences, motivations, opinions, preferences, and ideas (Grincheva, 2018). This data can offer important insights that are especially valuable for measuring GLAM soft power in order to better understand changes in public opinions.

However, as the following section will illuminate, the project revealed significant challenges in creating reliable computational systems to map public sentiment and opinion. It identified several levels of barriers that currently exist, which significantly challenge a dynamic and automatic big data analysis that could be reliable for GLAM institutions to better understand their audiences.

GLAM soft power mythologies: Capturing public perceptions

As many museum professionals stressed—beyond just quantitative analysis of online audience engagement in terms of likes, shares, and views—it is very important to understand virtual visitors' intrinsic motivations, interests, and passions or concerns, which requires in-depth qualitative analysis. While, indeed, social media data offers a rich source of evidence for studying the structure of networks, the dynamics of online behavior, and the speed and reach of informational spread over time (Lerman, 2013), understanding why people do what they do online using in-depth qualitative analysis remains a complex task. To meet this challenge, marketing researchers have long been advocating for complementing big data analytics with so-called "thick data" analysis (Latzko-Toth et al., 2017). "Thick data" is required to get insights on human perceptions, as what is measurable in terms of clicks is not necessarily valuable (Wang, 2016). Not surprisingly, in the past few years, there has been a rise of netnographic or digital ethnographic and data anthropological research that has allowed for an in-depth analysis of "people with complicated lives, existing in rich cultural ecosystems" who stand behind big data's quantitative summaries (Rassi, 2017). However, this research is very limited in terms of the scope of the data that could be collected and meaningfully analyzed, and there have been constant interrogations as to whether real data-intensive, large-scale, qualitative research is possible.

Myth #1: Universal big data access

Through interactive datathon research sessions, we revealed significant challenges in creating reliable computational systems that map public sentiment and opinion on a massive scale. One of the most widespread myths concerning social media platforms is that they have given researchers universal access to massive quantities of data for analysis that can help to understand human behavior. However, in terms of automatic data aggregation on a massive scale, scraping textual qualitative data such as audiences' comments from social media sites comes with significant limitations. While scraping this data from social media through the platform's API is technically possible, due to the data's commercial value, most of the major sources' data platforms such as Facebook or X—previously known as Twitter—do not provide affordable and comprehensive data access. Both Twitter and Facebook, for instance, offer very limited archiving capacities, which creates a bias toward working with the most recent data or data of the immediate past.

In early 2022, for example, Data to Power could—using free public API access—aggregate and scan for search words in a corpus of up to 3200 of the latest tweets posted by any organization on Twitter (Twitter, 2020). This limit was the maximum number of tweets one could gather using a free account to analyze the chronology of an organization's posts and online conversations. Currently, X offers different tiers with differentiated level of access to public posts corresponding to higher monthly subscription costs (up to several hundred thousand dollars) in order to access larger amounts of data. Nevertheless, the social media platform limits the number of API requests that one can make within a specific timeframe and restricts access to private data points like user comments. One might not be able to access data from private accounts or posts with certain privacy settings that restrict visibility. Moreover, the available data points that one might access are filtered, meaning that access to the full content of all messages and tweets is not possible. Even for public comments, web scraping using bots or scripts violates X's terms of service and can lead to account suspension or termination.

Similarly, even within one's own Facebook group, scraping user comments data comes with significant limitations and potential risks. While the Facebook Graph API allows access to some group data, it specifically excludes comments due to privacy concerns. Techniques like browser automation or custom scripts might be technically possible, but they violate Facebook's terms of service and can lead to account termination. In terms of geographic distribution of users—which is particularly important for mapping exercises that use tools such as Data to Power—Facebook Insights, for instance, currently offer location data only for the past 28 days. While this ability helps with gauging recent audience demographics, it does not cover a long timeframe. In terms of data retention, Facebook typically anonymizes or deletes older data after a certain period. While the exact timeframe is not publicly disclosed, it is unlikely that detailed individual location data persists for at least a decade. Due to the emphasis on users' privacy, even group owners cannot access individual members' precise location information. Any data provided would likely be aggregated and anonymized, potentially limiting granularity and insights (Facebook, 2022).

Social media API limitations imposed by different platforms are quite necessary tools for managing and protecting user privacy, which also directly relates to ethics. Indeed, addressing ethical considerations when collecting data from social media is crucial for not only academic, but also professional GLAM research. It is a common misconception that it is acceptable to treat online spaces as if the usual ethical rules do not apply (Franzke et al., 2021). Public communication in institutional online spaces might apply restrictions on how it could be accessed and used by others.

In academic scholarship, it was argued that the existing ethical guidelines usually applied to small-scale qualitative digital ethnographic research and have little to do with big data research. Automated data scraping on social networking sites makes the concept of informed consent, for instance, practically infeasible (van Schie et al., 2017), leading to academic debates regarding ethical practices that preserve users' privacy and develop research integrity (Al-Zaman et al., 2024). While there are no standard approaches that can be used to determine ethical social media research, the main guiding principle is to understand context and apply a "situative" approach that should arise directly from the specific practices and contingencies of the environment (Vonderau, 2021). However, this approach, which is tailored specifically for anthropological and ethnographic purposes, is very difficult if not impossible to establish if GLAM institutions employ automatic aggregation tools to collect qualitative data on their audiences. Hence, the user privacy question becomes a hot platform issue, leading to restrictive policy regarding data access.

These technical data access affordances—or rather, limitations—create significant barriers for an all-encompassing compilation of research samples that could be comprehensively analyzed and mapped. It is important to acknowledge data mythologies that are prescribed by platforms' data access limitations to accurately interpret big data narratives. For example, limitations on the number of API data access requests per second unintentionally leads to more data collected during peak hours of users representing a specific demographic profile, marginalizing opinions and views of people who belong to other demographic groups. Furthermore, it is important to account for much higher engagement generated around content created by public figures, influencers, or even AI bots. As a result, limited API access leads to the collection of a data sample that might be over-representative of a specific niche view that seems to only look more popular than it actually is. This outcome skews the narrative of big data, leading to false representations of social and cultural trends that are niche rather than mainstream.

From a social informatics perspective, these limitations become the basis for data mythologies, emerging not necessarily from intentional malice, but rather from the inherent biases within the data aggregation processes—shaped by platforms' policies as well as functionalities and amplified, on the one hand, by data monetization measures, and by user retention strategies concerning personal data access, integrity, and ethics on the other hand. Social informatics, through its focus on the interplay between technology and social structures, helps to reveal here how data limitations become a lens that shapes big audience research, which requires more nuance in the context of GLAM soft power analysis. These mythologies could lead to quite dangerous consequences if based on biased data, as they influence GLAM international cultural relations strategies and policy decisions. However, beyond automated aggregation of a reliable data sample, there are data analysis limitations that must be considered.

Myth #2: Meaningful big data analysis

The research sessions with museum professionals stressed that the possibility of dynamically and responsively analyzing high volumes of qualitative data generated by online audiences in order to extract meaningful insights remains an unresolved dilemma. There are two ways that audience perception or sentiment analysis could be conducted, but both come with significant limitations. First, if audience perception or sentiment analysis is conducted by museum professionals, the approach comes with substantial limitations in terms of the research sample's size, the time required for such an in-depth analysis, and human resources that could be allocated for this task. Second, if research is conducted with the help of

Natural Language Processing (NLP) and AI tools, the quality of such an analysis could be quite low.

AI tools could mainly be employed to identify key themes, patterns, and major trends, but they are poorly equipped to grasp the context, nuance, and sentiment behind user comments. While AI can automate some tasks, human oversight and interpretation are still crucial for accurate qualitative analysis of audience perceptions, attitudes, and opinions. Although some museums experimented with NLP using off-the-shelf commercial tools, they have been a subject of academic criticism that has outlined multiple limitations and biases of these systems, which are usually developed for businesses to target clients with a higher purchase potential (Murphy & Villaespesa, 2020). There are currently no solutions specifically tailored for GLAM needs, or more so, for soft power analysis purposes.

Moreover, it is important to understand that human communication, especially on the cross-cultural level, is incredibly complex and requires appropriate contextualization. Even with a successful extraction of qualitative data from social media, which has proven to come with its data access biases, the text data of audience communications might lack context or formatting, making accurate interpretation difficult or even impossible. When one deals with digital audiences, one needs to consider not only social, political, economic, and historical contexts, but also linguistic, cultural, and religious contexts. All of these factors play important roles in defining online practices adopted by different audiences concerning their interactions with heritage institutions.

A good illustration of this reality is a Virtual Museum of the Pacific platform developed by the Australian Museum to engage indigenous and aboriginal communities from across the Pacific. Despite the museum's aspiration to democratize digital communications, decolonize their collections, and involve their source communities in digital storytelling to expose their cultures and traditions, the portal generated zero engagement from the targeted audience. It resulted in a silent protest in the online environment and the deterioration of the relationship with aboriginal communities in the physical realm of Sydney (Grincheva, 2020). A silent online protest, though, would not necessarily be visible to an AI tool, and only a careful exploration of this silence's context can reveal hard moments of truth about audiences' attitudes, perceptions, and concerns.

From the social informatics perspective, data mythologies emerging about AI-biased reading or interpretation of qualitative data become self-fulfilling prophecies. To demystify them, a certain data interpretation and contextualization flexibility is required in order to acknowledge the cultural contexts and diverse communication styles of online communities. Developing AI that can interpret silence, nuance, and non-participation alongside active engagement is crucial for bridging the gap between technology and the richness of human experience as well as its actual meaning. Ultimately, a socially informed approach to AI development could help to ensure that these tools serve as bridges for communication rather than tools for exclusion. Due to the current rapid advancement of AI technologies, it would be valuable to focus on efforts to develop more sensitive NLP tools that could deploy a so-called "interpretative flexibility of platform grammars" to better understand, analyze, and accurately interpret different meanings associated with various online textual, audio, and visual practices of digital audiences (Gerlitz, 2016, p. 28).

Conclusion

This chapter shares some advancements in soft power measurements as applied to contemporary heritage institutions actively operating in the digital domain and engaging online audiences across continents. It employs a social informatics framework to explain how new data-driven computational tools change the narratives created about GLAM institutions and their global impacts.

In this way, the Data to Power app's technical capabilities enabled by data-intense research redefine soft power as a continuing and multi-staged process that is differently shaped across various geographic contexts depending on local barriers and possibilities. As two sections in this chapter devoted to mapping cultural reach and appeal as well as measuring audience engagement documented, the Data to Power mapping system enables a valuable research exercise through which one can pose critical research questions and draw spatial patterns, correlations, or discrepancies to expose complexities of soft power's geographical reach and spread. However, this system is currently limited to a more comprehensive big data analysis, leaving aside qualitative approaches in exploration of the "thick data," which require a more focused strategic research design and approach on a much smaller scale.

While the project identified significant limitations of understanding soft power target responses, conversations with participants during online focus groups were instrumental, as they shared some valuable solutions to these challenges. For example, building on the capability of the Data to Power tool to create different mapping layers based on various data sources—both automatically aggregated via API and collected manually by researchers—Moffat (2022) suggested that the mapping system should incorporate "other types of data that could be useful to layer on top." She emphasized that GLAM institutions should conduct their own primary qualitative research, especially one that helps to reveal audiences' motivations and interests, to be effectively integrated with more automatic data aggregation tools that could measure online audience engagement and reach but not necessarily their sentiment.

While this chapter exposed important data platform affordances and limitations for qualitative audience analysis, future social informatics research should further scrutinize this topic in order to find new avenues for a more robust large-scale audience research, which remains one of the most sophisticated tasks—especially in soft power assessments.

References

Al-Zaman, M.S., Khemka, A., Zhang, A., et al. (2024). The defining characteristics of ethics papers on social media research. A systematic review of the literature. *Journal of Academic Ethics 22*, 163–189. https://doi.org/10.1007/s10805-023-09491-7

Banks, R. (2011). *A resource guide to public diplomacy evaluation*. Figueroa Press.

Bennett, T. (1995). *The birth of the museum: History, theory, politics*. Routledge.

Bjola, C., Cassidy, J., & Manor, I. (2020). Digital public diplomacy. In N. Snow & N. J. Cull (Eds.), *Routledge handbook of public diplomacy* (pp. 405–412). Routledge.

Cardiff, R. (2022). Datathon: Understanding and mapping digital museum audiences. Retrieved May 4, 2023, from www.datatopower.net/datathon2

Duxbury, N., Garrett-Petts, W.F., & Longley, A. (2018). *Artistic approaches to cultural mapping: Activating imaginaries and means of knowing*. Routledge.

Facebook. (2022). Terms of service. *Facebook*. https://m.facebook.com/legal/terms

Franzke, A.S., Muis, I., & Schäfer, M.T. (2021). Data Ethics Decision Aid (DEDA): A dialogical framework for ethical inquiry of AI and data projects in the Netherlands. *Ethics and Information Technology*. https://doi.org/10.1007/s10676-020-09577-5

Gerlitz, C. (2016). What counts? Reflections on the multivalence of social media data. *Digital Culture & Society, 2*(2), 19–38. https://doi.org/10.25969/mediarep/941

Gilmore, A., Arvanitis, K., & Albert, A. (2018). Never mind the quality, feel the width. In G. Schiuma & D. Carlucci (Eds.), *Big data in the arts and humanities* (pp. 27–40). Auerbach Publications.

Grincheva, N. (2018). Mapping museum "Soft Power": Adding geo-visualization to the methodological framework. *Digital Scholarship in the Humanities, 34*(4), 730–751.

Grincheva, N. (2020). *Museum diplomacy in the digital age*. Routledge.

Grincheva, N. (2022). Beyond the scorecard diplomacy: From soft power rankings to critical inductive geography. *Convergence: The International Journal of Research into New Media Technologies, 28*(1), 70–91.

Kitchin, R. (2014). *The data revolution: Big data, open data, data infrastructures and their consequences*. Sage.

Kling, R. (1999). What is social informatics and why does it matter? *D-Lib Magazine, 5*(1) at www.dlib.org:80/dlib/january99/kling/01kling.html

Latzko-Toth, G., Bonneau, C., & Millette, M. (2017). Small data, thick data: Thickening strategies for trace-based social media research. In L. Sloan & A. Quan-Haase (Eds.), *The SAGE handbook of social media research methods* (pp. 199–214). Sage.

Lerman, K. (2013). Social informatics: Using big data to understand social behavior. In P. Michelucci (Ed.), *Handbook of human computation* (pp. 751–760). Springer.

Luke, T. (2002). *Museum politics: Power plays at the exhibition*. University of Minnesota Press.

Manovich, L. (2020). *Cultural analytics*. The MIT Press.

Middleton, C. (2022). Datathon: Mapping potential appeal of heritage collections: From API to geo-visualization. Retrieved May 4, 2023, from www.datatopower.net/datathon1

Moffat, K. (2022). Datathon: Understanding and mapping digital museum audiences. Retrieved May 4, 2023, from www.datatopower.net/datathon2

Mokalis, A.L., & Davis, J.J. (2018). *Google analytics demystified*. CreateSpace Independent Publishing Platform.

Monocle. (2024). Soft power survey. *Monocle*. https://monocle.com/search/Soft%20Power/

Murphy, O., & Villaespesa, E. (2020). AI: A museum planning toolkit. Retrieved May 4, 2023, from https://themuseumsai.network/toolkit/

Nye, J. (2004). *Soft power: The means to success in world politics*. Public Affairs.

Price, K. (2022). Datathon: Mapping potential appeal of heritage collections: From API to geo-visualization. Retrieved May 4, 2023, from www.datatopower.net/datathon1

Rassi, M. (2017). 'Thick data' helps marketers humanize big data. *Marketing News Weekly*, www.ama.org/publications/eNewsletters/Marketing-News-Weekly/Pages/thick-data-humanized-big-data.aspx

Sawyer, S., & Rosenbaum, H. (2000). Social informatics in the information sciences: Current activities and emerging directions. *Informing Science: The International Journal of an Emerging Transdiscipline, 3*, 089–096.

Soft Power 30 (SP 30). (2019). Soft power. *Soft Power 30 (SP 30)*. https://softpower30.com/

Sylvester, C. (2009). *Art/museums: International relations where we least expect it*. Paradigm Publishers.

Tham, R. (2022). Datathon: Understanding and mapping digital museum audiences. Retrieved May 4, 2023, from www.datatopower.net/datathon2

Twitter. (2020). Twitter terms of service. *Twitter*. https://twitter.com/en/tos

van Schie, G., Westra, I., & Schäfer, M.T. (2017). Get your hands dirty: Emerging data practices as challenge for research integrity. In K. van Es & M.T. Schäfer (Eds.), *The datafied society: Studying culture through data* (pp. 183–200). Amsterdam University Press.

Vonderau, P. (2021). Ethics in media industries research. In P. Mcdonald (Ed.), *The Routledge companion to media industries* (pp. 518–526). Routledge.

Wang, T. (2016). Why big data needs thick data. *Ethnography Matters*. https://medium.com/ethnography-matters/why-big-data-needs-thick-data-b4b3e75e3d7

Wuyts, J. (2022). Datathon: Mapping potential appeal of heritage collections: From API to geo-visualization. Retrieved May 4, 2023, from www.datatopower.net/datathon1

4

UNDERSTANDING ALGORITHMIC GOVERNANCE AND GOVERNANCE OF ALGORITHMS THROUGH A DISINFORMATION POLICY ANALYSIS

Shengnan Yang and Xiaohua Awa Zhu

Introduction

The widespread adoption of algorithms across various fields has sparked significant discourse about the "power" of algorithms (Saurwein et al., 2015), which is presented as both computational capacity and regulatory power (Introna, 2016). As suggested, algorithms constitute, rather than merely mediate, our lives (Beer, 2009). Through applications like news feeds, search rankings, and recommendation systems, this power influences human behaviors including consuming information, engaging in electronic commerce, and participating in politics, often in a technologically unconscious manner (Beer, 2009; Danaher et al., 2017; Pasquale, 2015). Concerns over such power and influence have been discussed in academia for several decades across different disciplines (Gillespie, 2014; Lash, 2007; Lessig, 1999; Musiani, 2013). However, the evolvement of algorithmic culture has ignited much "awe and terror that overrides rational thought" among the public (Ames, 2018, p. 1), and the recent hype concerning generative artificial intelligence (AI) has further triggered substantial political, academic, and public debates that transcend legal regulations and highlight the importance of governance of algorithms.

One reason for the complexity of such debates is algorithms' paradoxical characteristics—they are both the origin or amplifier of many social challenges and often taken-for-granted solutions in technological discussions as well as public imaginations (Just & Latzer, 2017). Scholars and policymakers have engaged in discussions about how to understand and manage algorithms' influences, stressing the need for leveraging and regulating algorithmic power. These discussions have generated insights and recommendations for public policy interventions to address

DOI: 10.4324/9781032678542-7

challenges to social justice and individual rights such as privacy (Cath, 2018; De Gregorio & Stremlau, 2021; Jobin et al., 2019; Ziewitz, 2016). The disinformation problem, one of the most cited risks attributed to algorithms (particularly AI), has inspired many technological "solutions" such as: AI-based disinformation detection, offering a unique opportunity to study the complexity of algorithms' governing capacities (governance by algorithms or algorithmic governance), and the need to regulate algorithmic power (governance of algorithms).

Disinformation is not a new social problem but has become increasingly challenging and prominent during critical moments such as the COVID-19 pandemic and contentious political periods. Governments around the globe have been pouring resources into mitigating the spread of disinformation, yet achieving tangible progress remains elusive. The governance of disinformation remains challenging for many reasons, including: censorship concerns, lack of consensus and collaboration, the commercial nature of social media platforms, the international nature of information dissemination, and the fast development of AI technology itself (Graves, 2018; Marsden & Meyer, 2019; Villasenor, 2020). In this chapter, we add to current discussions about algorithms and governance, in addition to disinformation studies, by providing a comparative case study of disinformation policies in distinctive countries: China and the US. We examine the ostensible dilemma of using algorithms to battle against disinformation generated by algorithms.

The disinformation problem is broadly defined in this study to encompass the spread of false information, misleading misinformation, rumor, fake news, malign information, and conspiracy theories. Researchers have defined these concepts in various ways, using multiple dimensions such as: intent, facticity, authenticity, falsifiability, and accuracy (e.g., Gibbons & Carson, 2022; Tandoc et al., 2018; Wardle & Derakhshan, 2017). Different governments also tend to use different terms to label related issues; for example, "rumor" and "false information" are commonly used in China, "disinformation" is the most prevalent term in Europe, and "misinformation" as well as "fake news" appear more frequently in the US. We use "disinformation" because it is often characterized by the intention to deceive, its falseness, and the potential harm that it may cause (Wardle & Derakhshan, 2017), which underscore the rationale for governance to intervene.

This chapter poses a critical research question: what is the role of algorithms in the governance of disinformation? Inspired by Trosow's (2010) comprehensive model for studying information policy through a critical lens, we conduct a critical policy analysis, tracing discourses within policy documents. Building upon Wijermars and Makhortykh's (2022) problem-solution-outcome framework, we expand the critical perspective by integrating Bacchi's (2012) problem representation and assumptions. This critical perspective responds to assumptions within social informatics, further enriching our analysis by acknowledging the interplay between technology, society, and human behavior.

Literature review

The examination of the nexus between algorithms and governance engages scholars across various disciplines, such as: law (Yeung, 2018; Yeung & Bygrave, 2022), media studies (Gillespie, 2014; Gorwa et al., 2020), political science (Campbell-Verduyn et al., 2017), and science and technology studies (Wijermars & Makhortykh, 2022). Discussions in this domain primarily focus on two key themes: the recognition of algorithms' considerable impact and their roles in governance (governance by/through algorithms) as well as debates surrounding effectively regulating these powers (governance of algorithms). As Danaher et al. (2017) point out, these two discussion themes pivot around distinct governance objectives—efficiency and fairness, respectively. In this section, we first briefly summarize some key literature on the concepts of algorithms and governance to establish a context for our analyses, and then we review relevant literature on the two themes.

Defining algorithms and their power

Acknowledging algorithms' power and their socio-material nature is a prerequisite of appropriate governance (Introna, 2016). An algorithm "is a finite, abstract, effective, compound control structure, imperatively given, accomplishing a given purpose under given provisions" (Hill, 2016, p. 47). Algorithms are well-structured, named entities that direct the execution flow within a program or computational process to operate and achieve a desired outcome or to address practical problems. They serve as the foundational instructions that drive information systems, dictating how data is processed to create computational capabilities. They shape the functionality of these systems and are decisive despite relying on computing power, hardware, and software for execution (Sastry et al., 2024).

One of the most critical high-level shifts concerning the design of algorithms in recent years is the move from "top-down" algorithms (in which a programmer or team of programmers exhaustively defines the ruleset for the algorithm) to "bottom-up" machine learning algorithms (in which the algorithm is given a learning rule and trained on large datasets to develop its own rules). In other words, machine learning algorithms—particularly those dealing with big data—operate on a training-testing-generating model, utilizing vast and often unstructured data sets for computational operations (Dourish, 2016).

Algorithms have both capacity and governing power. They perform various functions including recommendation systems, news feeds, and content filtering (Latzer et al., 2016). Advances in algorithmic design, such as the Transformer architecture, have improved the efficiency of model development, allowing significant enhancements in information systems without proportional investment increases (Sastry et al., 2024). Manovich (2013) emphasizes that "software takes command" by supplanting diverse technologies to manage cultural artifacts.

Algorithms exhibit flexibility and adaptability when executed by humans, as they can incorporate steps that involve selecting or using arbitrary values. By doing so, algorithms enable the functionality of complex decision-making systems that affect many aspects of modern societies, from individual daily routines (Latzer & Festic, 2019) to broad institutional practices (Latzer et al., 2016).

Algorithms also have a regulatory dimension, constituting and shaping our lives by influencing behavior, preferences, and content production (Beer, 2009; Napoli, 2013). They are not just code, but also regulatory forces within digital architecture, enabling or restricting actions. This concept is known as "Code as Regulation," as described by Lessig (1999). These rules can either empower or constrain, depending on their design. Demonstrating their socio-material nature, algorithms actively participate in crafting reality through performativity. They generate and sustain knowledge and practices, impacting what is perceived as empirically valid and normatively acceptable. Embedded within a socio-material context that intertwines digital infrastructure with social dynamics, algorithms are part of the fabric of society (Introna, 2016).

Governance concerning algorithms

Governance, as described by Rhodes (2007), encompasses a novel process of governing, a transformed state of ordered rule, or a fresh methodology of societal regulation. This concept is crucial for navigating the challenges posed by new technologies, with some approaches viewing governance through the lens of management and others emphasizing rule-making, diverse structures, practices, and multi-stakeholder engagement (Hofmann et al., 2017). In the contemporary landscape, governance transcends the conventional confines of government and is characterized by agile and interactive decision-making responsive to the swift and intricate dynamics of society. It signifies a transition toward cooperative strategies essential for realizing objectives in a time surpassing the capabilities of centralized mechanisms alone.

In this chapter, we adopt the work of Hofmann et al. (2017) and Katzenbach and Ulbricht (2019), who define governance as a system of social ordering rooted in rule-based coordination among actors, which aligns with Stoker's (1998) perspective that governance is about "creating the conditions for ordered rule and collective action" (p. 17). Moving beyond the traditional view that governance is primarily within the government's rule-making capacity, this broader definition acknowledges governance as both a capacity and a complex network of dynamic relationships among varied actors and actions. Governance is fundamentally about navigating and managing networks, which involves a continuous process of interaction and negotiation among members to exchange resources and establish shared objectives. The boundaries between public, private, and voluntary sectors are no longer rigid, but are instead fluid and overlapping, reflecting the dynamic and interconnected nature of governance in the modern world (Hofmann et al.,

2017; Rhodes, 2007). It represents a social order born from interactions among various autonomous yet interdependent entities (Gorwa, 2019). This perspective underscores the complexity and collaborative nature of governance, emphasizing the importance of cooperation and coordination over mere hierarchical control.

Regarding behavior, governance encompasses deliberate, regulatory-like coordination (Black, 2001) as well as unintentional coordination (Hofmann et al., 2017). Distinct from ephemeral social structures without rule-based foundations, governance demands stability that is vital for actors to form expectations, which is crucial for achieving coordination (Katzenbach & Ulbricht, 2019). Thus, governance is not just about capability; it is a vibrant and detailed mosaic of interactions across diverse actors and behaviors, facilitating ordered rule as well as collective action (Stoker, 1998).

Algorithmic governance

Building upon the broader definition of governance, algorithmic governance is characterized as a specific type of governance that is rule-based and integrates complex, computer-based epistemic procedures for social organization, necessitating coordination among actors (Katzenbach & Ulbricht, 2019). In essence, algorithms function as instruments of governance. Latzer and Festic (2019) describe algorithmic governance as encompassing both the intentional and unintentional steering effects exerted by algorithmic selection systems. Algorithms are instrumental in navigating governance processes, with the capacity to significantly alter power dynamics and the allocation of resources (Gritsenko & Wood, 2022; Latzer & Festic, 2019). They also play a critical role in decision-making, with algorithmically processed knowledge systems being deployed to execute or guide decisions, particularly those pertinent to regulatory governance (Yeung, 2018). In the view of legal and political scholars, algorithmic governance represents a unique mode of governance that operates differently from traditional forms, with an increasing reliance on design-based and self-executing regulation and governance (Gritsenko & Wood, 2022; Yeung & Bygrave, 2022).

Governance of algorithms

The scholarship on the governance of algorithms began its discourse by identifying critical issues associated with algorithms—such as inaccuracy, unfairness, opacity, and unintended consequences (Danaher et al., 2017)—alongside the dominance of large platforms that secure unfair market advantages (Introna, 2016). Viewing algorithms and their underlying code as entities, scholars examine how stakeholders, particularly regulatory bodies, can effectively oversee or manage algorithms or their developers. Research within this domain concentrates on the ethical concerns surrounding algorithms, emphasizing the necessity for transparency, accountability, and fairness (e.g., Bellanova & De Goede, 2022; Coglianese &

Lehr, 2019; Katzenbach & Ulbricht, 2019). This perspective presupposes that certain algorithmic entities represent significant loci of agency, thereby warranting targeted regulatory attention. It discusses the challenges in regulating algorithmic decision-making processes. While there is an ongoing debate regarding the potential overemphasis on algorithms' agency (Introna, 2016), proponents of this viewpoint underscore the importance of mitigating risks and enhancing transparency to legitimize the role of algorithmic actors.

A mutual shaping perspective of algorithms and governance

While distinguishing governance by and of algorithms is a valuable framework for conceptual discussions, it presents certain limitations. First, this distinction could lead to what Eagle (2001) describes as "a spiral of regulation" (p. 914): a situation in which the growing number of mechanisms for algorithmic governance prompts the need for even more mechanisms used to regulate the former mechanisms. Second, it risks oversimplifying the complexities involved in practicing governance related to algorithms. The oversimplification of governance complexity arises from underestimating the intertwined nature of algorithms' materiality with governing bodies and overemphasizing the governing entity—algorithmic or human—without fully recognizing their integration in socio-technical practices (Introna, 2016).

Several scholars have sought to unify two prevailing threads by introducing diverse perspectives. For instance, Introna (2016) underscores the significance of governing practices and advocates for a Foucauldian perspective to comprehend the governance of algorithms, or through algorithms, viewing them "as practices of governmentality to understand the act of governance" (p. 30). Similarly, Campbell-Verduyn and colleagues (2017) present a continuum of governance concerning algorithms, distinguishing it by the level of human engagement and the degree of automation and independence in the roles of big data and algorithms. Their model seeks to delineate the various degrees of interaction between the informational and material properties of humans and artifacts (algorithms), thereby elucidating the complex entanglements of these transformations.

These studies imply a mutually shaping relationship between technology and human actors—a concept central to social informatics (Sawyer & Tyworth, 2006). This field regards Information and Communication Technology (ICT), including algorithms, as an inseparable network of technological artifacts, people, social norms, and practices. Scholars examine the interdependencies among these elements, acknowledging the integration of digital technologies into organizational and social contexts. Meyer (2014) stresses the importance of balancing social and technical aspects in socio-technical constructs, cautioning against prioritizing one dimension in research.

Social informatics draws on two key principles: a critical orientation (Day, 2007; Sawyer & Tyworth, 2006) and a focus on socio-technical networks (Lamb et al., 2000). The critical approach challenges prevailing assumptions about technology—promoting a nuanced understanding of its design, use, and societal impact—and steering clear of simplistic determinism. It allows researchers to explore the wide-ranging consequences of technological integration. Meanwhile, the concept of the socio-technical network underscores the inseparable intertwining of people, organizations, and technologies—recognizing that while technologies are essential, they are not the only components of networked social structures. This perspective enriches traditional socio-technical studies by emphasizing the multifaceted influence of technology on social organization. Therefore, social informatics provides critical insights, grounded in socio-technical theory, into the interplay between algorithms and governance, and offers a balanced view that considers both the societal and technological implications of ICT, including AI and algorithms.

Methodology

We employed a critical policy analysis approach to examine the nexus between algorithms and disinformation within the policy documents of China and the US. Our analytical framework draws upon Wijermars and Makhortykh's (2022) problem-solution-outcome model to dissect the language and discourse of policy documents. Additionally, the framework integrates Bacchi's (2009) critical policy analysis, a comprehensive and transformative framework that systematically deconstructs the representation of problems within policy discourse. As Trosow (2010) suggests, a critical perspective is vital yet often overlooked in the study of information policy. A critical approach enables us to challenge uncritically accepted assumptions and prompts the inquiry of essential questions.

The US federal government and the Chinese central government are selected as cases in this study because these two countries' distinct characteristics in political systems and policymaking processes make them two extreme cases of policy analysis, offering more opportunities for critical analysis. Our previous work has demonstrated how such extreme cases can offer a variety of factors/variables for further in-depth study and the potential for building substantive theoretical frameworks (Zhu & Yang, 2023a, 2023b).

Critical analytical framework

In a case study research analyzing algorithmic governance in the EU, Wijermars and Makhortykh (2022) identified three aspects of utilizing algorithmic governance: problem formulation, problem solution, and problem outcome. These aspects proved a useful analytical tool combined with Bacchi's (2009) critical examination of problem construction as delineated in her seminal work: *What's the Problem Represented to Be*. Focusing on the representation of problems within policy analysis, Bacchi (2009) proposed a six-step analytical framework (p. 7). She argued that how a problem is framed or represented in policy discourse shapes the range of possible solutions and policy intervention. Therefore, it is important to critically examine the assumptions underlying representations of problems in order to uncover potential biases and power dynamics in policymaking processes. This perspective is instrumental in critically assessing how policy documents construct and represent disinformation issues over time, focusing on their representation, underlying assumptions, and the consequential effects of such representations. It delves into the origins of these representations, the silences that they create, and the effects that they produce. Importantly, it considers how these representations of problems are produced, disseminated, and defended, and how they might be questioned and replaced. This approach is not merely analytical, but also transformative, aiming to uncover and challenge the power structures that define societal issues within policy contexts. Based on these works, we try to answer the overall research question—what is the role of algorithms in the governance of disinformation—by addressing the following specific questions that constitute our analytical framework:

1 How is disinformation characterized and depicted? What assumptions underlie its portrayal (such as implicit or explicit dichotomies, as well as other pertinent keywords or concepts), and how do these assumptions influence the conceptualization of the "problem?"
2 What array of techniques is employed to combat disinformation, with a particular focus on the role of algorithms within these methods?
3 What are the anticipated results of disinformation regulation, and how do these expectations incorporate the functioning of algorithms?
4 How is this problem of disinformation affected by algorithms? What effects are produced by this representation of the problem? That is to say, we examine the changes and constants in the broader societal discourse, the beneficiaries and those adversely affected by this portrayal, and the impact of attributing responsibility for the "problem" to targeted individuals and the community's perception of blame.

Document selection and analysis

In our previous work, we conducted an exhaustive search and analyses of policy documents regarding disinformation—especially those issues discussed by the Chinese central government and the US federal government during the COVID-19 pandemic—and identified 92 highly-relevant documents from the US and 47 from China between January 1, 2020, and December 31, 2021(Zhu & Yang, 2023a, 2023b; Zhu et al., 2022). This corpus includes bills, regulations, directives, orders, enacted laws, etc., which provide a starting point for data collection in this study. Based on the coding results from previous studies, we selected all documents that mentioned algorithms and/or AI. We use the term *policy documents* instead of *policies* because in the US context—unlike China, where laws and rules on disinformation have been enacted—most of the key documents are proposed bills that only represent the government's intent and legislative efforts.

Using the same approach, we collected policy documents on disinformation and algorithms issued between January 1, 2022, and December 31, 2023, relying on the US' govinfo.gov and China's official government document databases. After careful reading, tracing, and selection, we identified a total of 31 relevant policy documents for the purpose of this study: 14 from China and 17 from the US. The selected documents are listed in the next section, together with the corresponding analysis of algorithmic governance and governance of algorithms. Our document analysis follows a qualitative, critical approach, identifying the general patterns, contexts, ideologies, rationales, and the underlying dynamics among actors. Specifically, we focus on the questions laid out in the analytical framework.

The case of China

Algorithmic governance in content regulation

The governance of disinformation in China is a sophisticated amalgamation of manual oversight and algorithm-enabled solutions, offering a broad regulatory scope in which digital platforms assume a central role in the ecosystem. This multifaceted approach empowers platforms to engage in rigorous content mediation, employing both human expertise and advanced technology to maintain a healthy online discourse and uphold social values.

In 2012, China's online content regulation transitioned from development-oriented to security-oriented, leading to centralized regulatory efforts under a newly established central governmental agency: the Cyberspace Administration of China (CAC). A complex strategy—including centralized control, standardized campaign-style operations, and cooperation between government and technology companies—broadened the scope of online information governance (Zhu & Yang, 2023a). Following this pivot, the government introduced several key policies focused on online content and its creators, including:

- *Provisions on the Ecological Governance of Network Information Content* (PEG-2019)
- *Opinions on Further Consolidating the Primary Responsibility of Online Platforms for Information Content Management* (RPC-2021)
- *Provisions on the Administration of Public Account Information Services of Internet Users* (SMA-2021)
- *Administrative Provisions on Internet Live-Streaming Services* (ILSP-2016)
- *Measures for the Administration of Live-Streaming Marketing* (ISM-2021)
- *Provisions on the Administration of Information Services of Mobile Internet Apps* (MAP-2016, 2022)

- *Provisions on the Administration of Internet Comments Posting Services* (ICPP-2017, 2022)
- *Provisions for the Administration of Internet News Information Services* (INIS-2017)

PEG-2019 significantly enhanced China's control over online content by setting a comprehensive regulatory framework. This policy aims to foster an online "content ecosystem," tackle illegal and negative information, and promote Socialist Core Values. It classifies online content into three categories—illegal, unhealthy, and encouraged. It bans illegal content, combats unhealthy content, and endorses government-favored narratives. Detailed policies were also introduced to regulate social media, live-streaming, mobile apps, and online news services (ILSP-2016; ISM-2021; ICPP-2017, 2022; MAP-2016, 2022; INIS-2017). They include specific measures to regulate disinformation activities such as data traffic fraud and illegal account trading, emphasizing the government's dedication to maintaining a well-managed, positive online environment.

These regulations underscore the vital role of technology, including algorithmic interventions, for a "continuous high-pressure and strict management stance" to enhance the efficacy of rectification campaigns (RPC-2021). The government also established principles on managing content, behavior, and entities to guide the implementation of these regulations, with a particular emphasis on platforms and processes that tend to spread unhealthy information. Additionally, it calls for establishing a robust, regular governance mechanism to manage online content effectively, wherein algorithms are recognized as a tool that can support and enhance governmental objectives.

Under RPC-2021, digital platforms, as the primary sources of algorithms, have a responsibility to prevent the production and spread of illegal and harmful content. Under the government's oversight, digital platforms are instructed to enhance manual review processes and incorporate technological solutions to fulfill these mandates (Beijing CAC, 2023). Although the use of technology in the governance of false information is still in the exploratory stage, it represents a significant stride. Algorithm-related solutions constitute the "well-developed regular governance mechanism" for refuting rumors (RPC-2021). Such solutions include tracing the origins and pathways of false information dissemination, setting up dynamically updated databases, identifying and intercepting problematic content, and other measures as requested by a government initiative called "Clear and Bright: Combat Online Rumors and False Information." In response, platforms employed algorithms to better detect harmful information. One of China's largest Q&A platforms, Zhihu, for instance, launched its governance robot to provide real-time filtering of inappropriate comments and created a "Network Rumor Database" (People's Political Consultative Conference Network, 2023). Bilibili, a platform for user-created video content, employs an AI system in combination with user input and manual moderation for content regulation (Chen, 2021).

Governance of algorithms

Compared to the sophisticated governance of online content, regulating algorithms and their related activities in China is in an early stage. Between 2021 and 2023, China issued a series of key policies, summarized below, to regulate algorithm usage within its national security framework.

- *Guiding Opinions on Strengthening Overall Governance of Internet Information Service Algorithms* (OGA-2021)
- *Provisions on Administration of Algorithmic Recommendation in the Internet Information Service* (ARP-2022)
- *Provisions on the Administration of Deep Synthesis of Internet-based Information Services* (DSP-2022)
- *Interim Measures for the Management of Generative Artificial Intelligence Services* (MGAI-2023)
- *White Paper on Artificial Intelligence Security Standardization* (2023)
- *Interim Measures for the Management of Generative Artificial Intelligence Services*, published in July 2023 (MGAI-2023)

These policies try to balance the promotion of technological innovation for competitive advantage and the need to address ethical concerns and protect individual rights. In particular, they aim to ensure that: algorithm applications are fair, just, and transparent; their development is safe and controllable; and risks and hidden dangers associated with algorithm misuse can be effectively prevented. It is worth noting that algorithm regulations bolster the requirements of content regulation, which ensures that algorithms are "correctly oriented and full of positive energy" (OGA-2021). These regulations specifically address recommendation systems, AI, big data, and related technologies, providing detailed guidance.

The ARP-2022 is the first specific policy governing algorithms, and it applies to most platforms in China that use algorithmic recommendation technology. This policy introduces mechanisms to safeguard user rights in algorithm use, focusing on transparency, autonomy, interpretability, and accountability; it recognizes rights such as being informed, making independent choices, receiving explanations, and obtaining remedies. Moreover, the ARP-2022 explicitly forbids algorithmic recommendation services from creating or spreading fake news and manipulating digital interactions to ensure news content conforms to the state-defined parameters. Building on this foundation, the DSP-2022 provisions require developers and users of deep synthesis services not to generate or circulate false news. They advocate for establishing rumor-debunking mechanisms and applying sanctions for disinformation that range from warnings to account suspensions. These regulatory measures highlight China's proactive approach to algorithm governance, striving to secure digital safety and encourage the production of high-quality content via algorithmic recommendations.

The latest Chinese policy on algorithms, MGAI-2023, is China's first policy initiative on generative AI (GenAI). Unlike other policies primarily focused on security, this governance strategy adopts a relatively open attitude. It emphasizes that development and innovation are as prioritized as security. The policy advocates for a balanced approach, stressing: "*The nation insists on giving equal importance to development and security ... employing a tolerant and prudent regulatory strategy that is categorized and tiered for generative artificial intelligence services*" (MGAI-2023). As a provisional policy, it lacks detailed specifications but outlines essential principles concerning content. Instead, it emphasizes a few high-level principles related to the misuse of GenAI—content produced by GenAI must adhere to the Socialist Core Values and refrain from spreading false information. A silent practice guided by this policy is the introduction of the AIGC-Safe platform by the Internet Illegal Information Reporting Center under the Central Cyberspace Affairs Commission to tackle AI-generated disinformation using cutting-edge technology. This project, by utilizing algorithms to govern false information online, embodied the approach of "fighting magic with magic" (Xinhua Net, 2023).

Case summary

In summary, within the Chinese context, online disinformation encompasses not only legally defined false information, but also discourse not sanctioned by authorities. The perceived threat extends beyond economic implications to national security concerns. To tackle this issue, Chinese state-led regulatory efforts to address online disinformation span the governance of algorithms and algorithmic governance, with distinct focuses yet designed to be compatible and complementary. Policymakers aim to address efficiency and fairness—key aspects in algorithm governance—through these policies, believing that successful policy design and technological solutions will maintain a healthy ecosystem for both content and the algorithm industry. Because algorithms are viewed as both antidotes to and sources of disinformation, the policy discourse reveals an anticipation of utilizing more sophisticated algorithms to combat disinformation generated by algorithms themselves.

However, there is debate regarding the understanding of disinformation as well as the role and potential outcomes of algorithm-enhanced solutions within this state-led model. Firstly, while this state-led approach seeks to safeguard individual rights through stringent content regulations, it potentially neglects the value of diverse viewpoints and underestimates the effectiveness of grassroots or self-regulatory measures. The broadly defined scope of disinformation carries the underlying assumption that purifying online content is necessary due to the belief that diverse individual voices might cause social unrest. However, this approach might increase distrust and tension between the government and public rather than foster the expected harmony and stability.

Secondly, from a governance perspective, an overly comprehensive protection strategy that is top-down might undermine the strengths of other governing possibilities, such as social norms and market mechanisms. Existing Chinese strategy implies that neither individuals nor platforms are deemed sufficiently capable of identifying harmful content on their own. Since governance relies on the network and interaction among different actors, the effectiveness and sustainability of this imbalanced governing relationship include uncertainties.

Additionally, implementing detailed and comprehensive disinformation governance is labor-intensive and costly. Consequently, technological solutions, particularly sophisticated governance algorithms, are expected to play a crucial role. Platforms, as providers of these algorithms, are anticipated to be instrumental in implementing governance principles. While algorithms are seen as potentially effective in increasing governance efficiency, their reliance on manual verification and labor, as previously analyzed, necessitates significant investment from platforms in their implementation. The immaturity of algorithms implies a need for supplementary measures to ensure effective governance. When technological solutions become coercive rather than self-motivated, they impose an additional burden on corporations. As a result, under this model, companies focus on complying with the government's commands and requirements instead of achieving the desired outcomes.

The case of the US

Governance of algorithms regarding disinformation

Disinformation governance in the US has been challenging due to concerns about censorship of free speech as well as the traditional reliance on self-regulation of the industry and individual companies. However, the government's extensive regulatory attempts against disinformation started soon after the quick spread of a fake video of former US President Barack Obama in late 2018. Within a year, multiple bills against deepfake algorithms were introduced, as summarized below. Ranging from brief to highly detailed, these bills typically attempt to combat the spread of disinformation by regulating deep fake video alteration technology. As their titles indicate, they focus on the harm caused by deepfake videos and political disinformation related to American politicians, military members, politics, and especially elections.

- *To require the Secretary of Defense to conduct a study on cyberexploitation of members of the Armed Forces and their families, and for other purposes* (S.3786, 115th Cong., 2018)
- *Malicious Deep Fake Prohibition Act of 2018* (S.3805, 115th Cong., 2018)
- *Deepfakes Report Act of 2019* (S.2065, 116th Cong., 2019)
- *Deep Fake Detection Prize Competition Act* (H.R. 5532, 116th Cong., 2019)

- *DEEP FAKES Accountability Act* (H.R.3230, 116th Cong., 2019; H.R.2395, 117th Cong., 2021; H.R.5586, 118th Cong., 2023)
- *Deepfake Task Force Act* (S. 2559, 117th Cong., 2021)
- *Preventing Deep Fake Scams Act* (HR 5808, 118th Cong., 2023)

US legislation regarding disinformation has a strong concentration on political matters, particularly foreign interference in US elections (Zhu & Yang, 2023a). A close examination of the bills cited above reveals that the regulation of algorithms is often framed in a national security narrative. A typical example can be found in the *DEEP FAKES Accountability Act* (2019, 2021, 2023), which requires establishing a task force for deepfake detection to "advance efforts of the United States Government to combat the national security implications of deep fakes" (Sec 7(a)(1)). Although not all disinformation legislation introduced in recent years centered on deepfake technology (there are also bills such as the *COVID-19 Disinformation Research and Reporting Act* (2021) and *Health Misinformation Act* (2021)), likely because of the exacerbated disinformation problem during the pandemic, the legislative efforts to regulate deepfake algorithms in order to prevent political disinformation have been a dominant trend since 2018.

Although deepfake technology is the primary algorithm appearing in various disinformation legislation, in many other bills (listed below) that try to regulate content/disinformation, algorithms are often framed as a means of manipulating user data and user-generated content by or through social media platforms. One legislative focus is to hold social media platforms responsible for the content published on them, including disinformation. Multiple attempts have been made to limit the liability protections that internet platforms acquired due to Section 230, which is a part of the *Communications Decency Act* (1996) that gives immunity to online service providers from user-generated content.

- *Biased Algorithm Deterrence Act of 2018* (H.R.7363, 115th Cong., 2018)
- *Filter Bubble Transparency Act* (S.2763, 116th Cong., 2019; S.2024, 117th Cong., 2021.)
- *Protecting Americans from Dangerous Algorithms Act* (H.R. 8636, 116th Cong., 2020; S. 3029, 117th Cong., 2021)
- *Justice Against Malicious Algorithms Act of 2021* (H.R. 5596, 117th Cong., 2021)
- *Algorithmic Justice and Online Platform Transparency Act* (S.1896, 117 Cong., 2021; S.2325, 118th Cong. 2023)
- *Digital Platform Commission Act of 2022* (S.4201, 117th Cong., 2022; S.1671, 118th Cong., 2023)

The background of such bills is complex, and they often do not address disinformation issues explicitly, but if enacted, they could have a direct influence on content moderation and content availability. For example, the *Algorithmic Justice and Online Platform Transparency Act* (2021, 2023) requires transparency in the use of algorithmic processes for content manipulation and moderation in order to prevent discriminatory outcomes and protect voting rights. In a bill not directly targeted at *Section 230*, the *Filter Bubble Transparency Act* (2019, 2021) requires that the algorithmic ranking systems used by internet platforms give users options to see results not manipulated by algorithms driven by user-specific data; otherwise, it would be considered "an unfair or deceptive act or practice" (sec 4(a)). The most comprehensive bill that tries to regulate platforms, the *Digital Platform Commission Act* (2022, 2023), lists "disseminating disinformation and hate speech" as part of the "demonstrable harm" of unregulated digital platforms (Sec 2(a)(6)). It requires that the "recommendation systems and other algorithmic processes ... are fair, transparent, and without harmful, abusive, anticompetitive, or deceptive bias" (Sec 5(b)(2)).

Algorithmic governance of disinformation

Thus far, US legislatures have focused more on regulating algorithms than on algorithmic governance. The US government has remained cautious about using the algorithmic approach to solve the disinformation problem. Several bills cited above mention the adoption of technology to detect deepfake videos. For example, the *DEEP FAKES Accountability Act* (2019, 2021, 2023) asks the government and private sector to research and develop disinformation technology collaboratively (Sec 7). Additional bills below encourage research on and development of AI technologies to detect deepfakes and other types of disinformation.

- *Deep Fake Detection Prize Competition Act* (2019)
- *American Competitiveness Of a More Productive Emerging Tech Economy Act* (2020)
- *Countering Online Harms Act* (2020)
- *Deepfake Task Force Act* (2021, 2022)

As shown, US legislators recognize the harm of deepfake videos and ask government agencies to fund research on deepfake detection technology in the *Deep Fake Detection Prize Competition Act*. In the other three bills, legislators ask government agencies and researchers in the private sector and academia to enhance research on the harm and mechanisms of deepfake technology as well as develop plans to use AI and machine learning methods to detect deepfakes, among other types of disinformation and online harms. It is worth noting, though, that such provisions are vague and lack details about application approaches as well as methods for measuring outcomes.

Despite the caution of Congress, the US federal government has already been utilizing algorithmic governance in many areas. Two Presidential Executive Orders—*Promoting the Use of Trustworthy AI in the Federal Government* (Exec. Order No. 13,960, 2020) and *Safe, Secure, and Trustworthy Development and*

Use of Artificial Intelligence (Exec. Order No. 14,110, 2023)—recognize the potential benefits of AI in identifying information security threats and tackling disinformation. However, among hundreds of AI use cases listed on AI.gov, we found only two cases related to disinformation, both of which illustrate how the Department of State used AI to detect deepfakes and foreign disinformation / propaganda.

Case summary

The analysis of related US policy documents—i.e., the aforementioned unenacted bills—shows a primarily market-driven approach with an attempt to increase the government's role in disinformation governance through regulating algorithms. Algorithmic governance has a weak, if it exists at all, presence.

The disinformation problem in the US context has a political emphasis, and the problem has been framed around American democracy and national security. Legislators stress the harm of disinformation on democracy and national security, emphasizing foreign propaganda and disinformation campaigns as tools of foreign interference, which fits well within current political narratives. Deepfake content, therefore, has been framed as the primary form of disinformation and one of the major targets of legislative efforts. The role of platforms in disinformation dissemination and their responsibilities were acknowledged implicitly within the context of regulating algorithms in content moderation, likely indicating the power of platforms and the lingering dominance of self-regulation.

In terms of the problem's solution, Congress has mainly tried to regulate algorithms that generate disinformation—e.g., deepfake algorithms—to prevent or control the generation of political disinformation. Regulating algorithms used for with content moderation and user manipulation by social media platforms is framed within a user rights and social justice framework, with the disinformation problem implied. Algorithmic governance may have been used by the government, but this aspect has only been briefly mentioned in policy documents, typically encouraging research and development on deepfake detectors. In other words, algorithmic governance is only loosely embedded in the government's attempt to regulate algorithms.

Since none of these bills have been enacted (even though multiple bills have been introduced several times), this analysis can only indicate the expected outcomes. On the surface level, the expected outcomes of such legislative attempts are: the prevention of disinformation creation and dissemination, holding social media platforms responsible for user-created content, the reduction of harm of disinformation in elections and politics, and the prevention of foreign propaganda/interference with American democracy. On a deeper level, the problematization of disinformation and algorithms demonstrates certain US government members' attempt to change the current market-driven, self-regulation approach to platform governance and play a more active role in governing information, algorithms, and AI.

Discussion and conclusion

In this chapter, we examine the disinformation problem in policy documents to understand the roles of algorithms in the governance of disinformation. By examining two cases, we also unpack the relationship between algorithmic governance and governance of algorithms in the policy landscape. The analytical framework, composed of four critical questions, represents a multifaceted approach that intertwines the definition and implications of disinformation with the nuanced roles of algorithms. Table 4.1 summarizes the key findings from the two cases side by side.

TABLE 4.1 Comparisons of China and the US using the critical analytical framework

Analytical questions	China	US
Formulation of disinformation problem	False information and unhealthy content as a threat to national security, social stability, and the moral fabric of society; implying diverse viewpoints and unsanctioned discourse are inherently harmful.	Disinformation as a significant threat to American democracy and national security; emphasizing the malicious intent behind disinformation and its potential to cause harm, especially in political contexts.
Technologies (algorithms) employed as solutions	*Enacted*, integrated algorithmic governance and governance of algorithms: algorithms play a crucial role in detecting, tracing, and intercepting false information; platforms are required to implement technological solutions, such as AI systems for content moderation.	Algorithmic governance is loosely embedded in the *intended* governance of algorithms: trying to establish task forces for deepfake detection, promote research on AI to identify disinformation, and increase transparency in algorithmic processes.
Expected outcome of using Technologies (algorithms)	Prevention of the spread of false and harmful content, promotion of government-favored narratives, and maintenance of a positive online environment. Algorithms are transparent, fair, and aligned with state-defined parameters.	Holding social media platforms accountable for user-generated content and reducing the impact of disinformation on elections and politics.
Broader social impact	Reinforcing the government's control over online content and limiting the diversity of viewpoints.	Reshaping the governance of (dis) information by moving from a market-driven, self-regulatory approach to more active government involvement.

In the United States, disinformation governance is primarily driven by legislative efforts that focus on regulating specific technologies like deepfake algorithms and the role of social media platforms. The existing market-driven approach and the interest of these stakeholders have made it difficult to enact any law regulating disinformation, and algorithms are not the central focus of disinformation governance. The US legislation attempts regarding algorithms are fragmented, primarily targeting the detection and prevention of deepfake videos and other forms of disinformation through research and development initiatives. These efforts are supplemented by broader attempts to regulate social media algorithms that manipulate content and user data, often framed within user rights and social justice contexts.

In contrast, China employs a more centralized and state-driven approach and places a strong emphasis on algorithmic governance as part of its broader content regulation strategy. The regulatory framework is already comprehensive, covering a wide range of online activities and content. Policies aim to foster a controlled online environment that promotes Socialist Core Values. As a major component of disinformation governance, algorithmic solutions are fully integrated into manual oversight, both in terms of the government's overall management and platforms' content moderation activities. China's approach showcases how algorithmic governance and governance of algorithms can work together by integrating stringent regulations on the development and use of algorithms (governance of algorithms) with the application of these algorithms to control and moderate online content (algorithmic governance). This approach ensures that the algorithms used for content moderation adhere to state-defined standards while leveraging technological solutions to enhance the effectiveness and efficiency of content regulation.

The policies scrutinized in this research recognize disinformation as a dual-faceted phenomenon, presenting both challenges and opportunities, particularly in how digital algorithms can amplify or mitigate its spread. Solutions proposed within these frameworks are diverse, ranging from the deployment of sophisticated algorithmic adjustments aimed at curtailing the dissemination of false narratives to more traditional methods such as public education and legal reforms. Notably, these policies also posit algorithms as part of the solution, leveraging artificial intelligence for the detection and mitigation of misinformation, thereby embodying a tech-centric approach to restoring informational integrity. The envisioned outcomes of these strategies underscore a desire to not only counteract disinformation, but also to foster an information ecosystem where truth prevails, facilitated by algorithmic transparency and ethical governance. This analysis underscores the critical interplay between technology and policy in tackling the pervasive issue of disinformation, highlighting the need for ongoing adaptation and evaluation to address the complex dynamics of the digital information landscape effectively.

Our analysis centers on the framing of problems and the implications of specific policies, moving beyond merely identifying assumed "problems" to critically analyzing the formation and characteristics of these problematizations. Critical policy analysis focuses on the practices of policy formulation and evaluation, scrutinizing the purported realities presented by policies, which may reflect political rhetoric rather than objective realities. It unveils the inequitable distribution of knowledge, power, and resources, and how policies—intentionally or not— perpetuate stratified social relations and institutionalize biases (Fischer et al., 2015; Diem et al., 2014). Drawing from Bacchi's (2012) critical perspective for discourse analysis within policy documents, we attempt to demonstrate the importance of studying problematizations by examining the representations that they encompass rather than taking the "problems" at face value.

This study employed a social informatics perspective of the mutual shaping relationship between technology and human activities (Meyer, 2014; Sawyer & Tyworth, 2006) to discuss the interplay between algorithms and governance as suggested by Campbell-Verduyn et al. (2017) and Introna (2016). To demonstrate this complex intertwinement empirically, this chapter explores the governance practices addressing the disinformation problem, focusing on both algorithmic governance and the governance of algorithms in two distinct contexts. This approach can be applied to other emerging social issues such as privacy concerns and data sovereignty, revealing further complexities surrounding AI and algorithms. While multilingual policy analysis poses challenges that require deep cultural understanding and contextual awareness, the comparison of cases from various contexts can be highly insightful and productive, as it can provide a comprehensive view of how various factors and approaches interact and impact society, leading to deeper understanding and more informed decision-making and policy development.

Algorithmic governance is deeply integrated into various aspects of society, and this concept has been discussed by many scholars of diverse disciplines who are interested in the interplay of people, information, technology, and society. The agency, power, and politics of technology can be traced back to the classic works of Bruno Latour and Langdon Winner in the 1980s, when AI was not a real issue. Concerned about the impact of algorithmic governance, information scientists and scholars are increasingly interested in ethical and responsible AI, often using critical views and bringing new insights to social informatics research. However, such discussions will not be complete and applicable without looking into the governance of algorithms, an area often avoided by library and information science (LIS) researchers. We hope that our exploration of algorithmic governance and the governance of algorithms through the information policy lens provides a bridge between social informatics research and other disciplines as well as inspires the development of substantive theories and models to address the evolving relationships between technology, information policies, and various social actors.

References

Ames, M. G. (2018). Editorial: Deconstructing the algorithmic sublime. *Big Data & Society, 5*(1). https://doi.org/10.1177/2053951718779194

Bacchi, C. (2009). *Analysing policy: What's the problem represented to be?* Pearson Higher Education AU.

Bacchi, C. (2012). Why study problematizations? Making politics visible. *Open Journal of Political Science, 2*(1), 1–8.

Beer, D. (2009). Power through the algorithm? Participatory web cultures and the technological unconscious. *New Media & Society, 11*(6), 985–1002. https://doi.org/10.1177/1461444809336551

Beijing CAC. (2023, September 13). *The Beijing Municipal Cyberspace Administration guides key local websites and platforms to set fixed positions for rumor refutation in trending searches and hot lists*. Weixin. http://mp.weixin.qq.com/s?__biz=MzIwMTU5MzM0OQ==&mid=2653758434&idx=1&sn=fb8e9eb39453955004d0d876fd9cc51e&chksm=8d320488ba458d9e46c7e32443fa70b98666bc3a50586a6e6cfc484d64e8d2cbc34e263a1089#rd

Bellanova, R., & De Goede, M. (2022). The algorithmic regulation of security: An infrastructural perspective. *Regulation & Governance, 16*, 102–118.

Black, J. (2001). Decentring regulation: Understanding the role of regulation and self-regulation in a 'post-regulatory' world. *Current Legal Problems, 54*(1), 103–146.

Campbell-Verduyn, M., Goguen, M., & Porter, T. (2017). Big Data and algorithmic governance: The case of financial practices. *New Political Economy, 22*(2), 219–236. https://doi.org/10.1080/13563467.2016.1216533

Cath, C. (2018). Governing artificial intelligence: Ethical, legal and technical opportunities and challenges. *Philosophical Transactions of the Royal Society A: Mathematical, Physical and Engineering Sciences, 376*(2133), 20180080. https://doi.org/10.1098/rsta.2018.0080

Chen, R. (2021, June 26). *12th Anniversary Keynote Speech*. BILIBILI 12th Anniversary Keynote Speech. www.bilibili.com/video/BV1CV411s7jd?p=2

Coglianese, C., & Lehr, D. (2019). Transparency and algorithmic governance. *Administrative Law Review, 71*, 1–56.

Danaher, J., Hogan, M.J., & Noone, C. (2017). Algorithmic governance: Developing a research agenda through the power of collective intelligence. *Big Data & Society, 4*(2), 1–21.

Day, R. E. (2007). Kling and the "critical": Social informatics and critical informatics. *Journal of the American Society for Information Science and Technology, 58*(4), 575–582. https://doi.org/10.1002/asi.20546

De Gregorio, G., & Stremlau, N. (2021). Information interventions and social media. *Internet Policy Review, 10*(2), 1–25. https://doi.org/10.14763/2021.2.1567

Diem, S., Young, M. D., Welton, A. D., Mansfield, K. C., & Lee, P.-L. (2014). The intellectual landscape of critical policy analysis. *International Journal of Qualitative Studies in Education, 27*(9), 1068–1090. https://doi.org/10.1080/09518398.2014.916007

Dourish, P. (2016). Algorithms and their others: Algorithmic culture in context. *Big Data & Society, 3*(2), 1–11.

Eagle, S. J. (2001). The regulatory takings notice rule symposium: Property rights after palazzolo. *University of Hawai'i Law Review, 24*(2), 533–588.

Fischer, F., Torgerson, D., Durnová, A., & Orsini, M. (Eds.). (2015). *Handbook of critical policy studies*. Edward Elgar Publishing.

Gibbons, A., & Carson, A. (2022). What is misinformation and disinformation? Understanding multi-stakeholders' perspectives in the Asia Pacific. *Australian Journal of Political Science, 57*(3), 231–247. https://doi.org/10.1080/10361146.2022.2122776

Gillespie, T. (2014). The relevance of algorithms. In T. Gillespie, P. J. Boczkowski, & K. A. Foot (Eds.), *Media technologies* (pp. 167–194). The MIT Press.

Gorwa, R. (2019). What is platform governance? *Information, Communication & Society, 22*(6), 854–871. https://doi.org/10.1080/1369118X.2019.1573914

Gorwa, R., Binns, R., & Katzenbach, C. (2020). Algorithmic content moderation: Technical and political challenges in the automation of platform governance. *Big Data & Society, 7*(1), 2053951719897945.

Graves, L. (2018). *Understanding the promise and limits of automated fact-checking*. Reuters Institute for the Study of Journalism. https://doi.org/10.60625/RISJ-NQNX-BG89

Gritsenko, D., & Wood, M. (2022). Algorithmic governance: A modes of governance approach. *Regulation & Governance, 16*(1), 45–62.

Hill, R. K. (2016). What an algorithm is. *Philosophy & Technology, 29*(1), 35–59.

Hofmann, J., Katzenbach, C., & Gollatz, K. (2017). Between coordination and regulation: Finding the governance in Internet governance. *New Media & Society, 19*(9), 1406–1423.

Introna, L. D. (2016). Algorithms, governance, and governmentality: On governing academic writing. *Science, Technology, & Human Values, 41*(1), 17–49.

Jobin, A., Ienca, M., & Vayena, E. (2019). Artificial Intelligence: The global landscape of ethics guidelines. *Nature Machine Intelligence, 1*(9), 389–399.

Just, N., & Latzer, M. (2017). Governance by algorithms: Reality construction by algorithmic selection on the Internet. *Media, Culture & Society, 39*(2), 238–258.

Katzenbach, C., & Ulbricht, L. (2019). Algorithmic governance. *Internet Policy Review, 8*(4), 1–18.

Lamb, R., Sawyer, S., & Kling, R. (2000). A social informatics perspective on socio-technical networks. In *AMCIS 2000 Proceedings* (Vol. 1). AMCIS. http://aisel.aisnet.org/amcis2000/1

Lash, S. (2007). Power after hegemony: Cultural studies in mutation? *Theory, Culture & Society, 24*(3), 55–78.

Latzer, M., & Festic, N. (2019). A guideline for understanding and measuring algorithmic governance in everyday life. *Internet Policy Review, 8*(2), 1–19.

Latzer, M., Hollnbuchner, K., Just, N., & Saurwein, F. (2016). The economics of algorithmic selection on the Internet. In J. Bauer & M. Latzer (Eds.), *Handbook on the economics of the internet* (pp. 395–425). Edward Elgar.

Lessig, L. (1999). *Code: And other laws of cyberspace*. Basic Books.

Manovich, L. (2013). *Software takes command*. Bloomsbury Publishing USA.

Marsden, C., & Meyer, T. (2019). *Regulating disinformation with artificial intelligence: Effects of disinformation initiatives on freedom of expression and media pluralism*. Publications Office of the European Union. https://data.europa.eu/doi/10.2861/003689

Meyer, E. T. (2014). Examining the hyphen: The value of social informatics for research and teaching. In P. Fichman & H. Rosenbaum (Eds.), *Social informatics: Past, present and future* (pp. 57–74). Cambridge Scholarly Publishers.

Musiani, F. (2013). Governance by algorithms. *Internet Policy Review, 2*. https://doi.org/10.14763/2013.3.188

Napoli, P. M. (2013). *The algorithm as institution: Toward a theoretical framework for automated media production and consumption.* McGannon Center Working Paper Series. 26. https://fordham.bepress.com/mcgannon_working_papers/26

Pasquale, F. (2015). *The black box society.* Harvard University Press.

People's Political Consultative Conference Network. (2023, December 28). *Zhihu releases 2023 annual governance report.* RMZXB. https://mobile.rmzxb.com.cn/tranm/index/url/www.rmzxb.com.cn/c/2023-12-28/3468397.shtml

Rhodes, R. A. W. (2007). Understanding governance: Ten years on. *Organization Studies, 28*(8), 1243–1264.

Sastry, G., Heim, L., Belfield, H., Anderljung, M., Brundage, M., Hazell, J., ... & Coyle, D. (2024). *Computing power and the governance of artificial intelligence.* arxiv:2402.08797. https://arxiv.org/abs/2402.08797

Saurwein, F., Just, N., & Latzer, M. (2015). Governance of algorithms: Options and limitations. *Info, 17*(6), 35–49. https://doi.org/10.1108/info-05-2015-0025

Sawyer, S., & Tyworth, M. (2006). Social informatics: Principles, theory, and practice. In T. Berleur, M. I. Numinen, & J. Impagliazzo (Eds.), *Social informatics: An information society for all? In remembrance of Rob Kling* (IFIP International Federation for Information Processing, Vol. 223) (pp. 49–62). Springer.

Stoker, G. (1998). Governance as theory: Five propositions. *International Social Science Journal, 50*(155), 17–28.

Tandoc, E. C., Lim, Z. W., & Ling, R. (2018). Defining "Fake News": A typology of scholarly definitions. *Digital Journalism, 6*(2), 137–153. https://doi.org/10.1080/21670811.2017.1360143

Trosow, S. (2010). A holistic model for information policy, *Feliciter, 56*(2), 46–48.

Villasenor, J. (2020, November 23). *How to deal with AI-enabled disinformation.* Brookings. www.brookings.edu/research/how-to-deal-with-ai-enabled-disinformation/

Wardle, C., & Derakhshan, H. (2017). *Information disorder: Toward an interdisciplinary framework for research and policy making.* Ref. 162317GBR. Council of Europe. https://edoc.coe.int/en/media/7495-information-disorder-toward-an-interdisciplinary-framework-for-research-and-policy-making.html

Wijermars, M., & Makhortykh, M. (2022). Socio-technical imaginaries of algorithmic governance in EU policy on online disinformation and FinTech. *New Media & Society, 24*(4), 942–963.

Xinhua Net. (2023, July 16). *Xinhua Net tests release of AIGC-Safe: Exploring solutions to the pain points of AIGC security governance.* Xinhua Net. Retrieved from www.news.cn/2023-07/16/c_1212244992.html

Yeung, K. (2018). Algorithmic regulation: A critical interrogation. *Regulation & Governance, 12*(4), 505–523.

Yeung, K., & Bygrave, L. A. (2022). Demystifying the modernized European data protection regime: Cross-disciplinary insights from legal and regulatory governance scholarship. *Regulation & Governance, 16*(1), 137–155. https://doi.org/10.1111/rego.12401

Zhu, X., & Yang, S. (2023a). Towards a sociotechnical framework for misinformation policy analysis. In S. Yang, X. Zhu, & P. Fichman (Eds.), *The usage and impact of ICTs during the COVID-19 pandemic* (pp. 11–45). Routledge.

Zhu, X., & Yang, S. (2023b). Battling disinformation intermediaries: An analysis of information policies. *Proceedings of the Americas Conference on Information Systems (AMCIS) 2023 Conference*, Panama City, Panama, August 10–12, 2023.

Zhu, X., Yang, S., & Summer, A. (2022). A comparison of false-information policies in five countries before and during the COVID-19 pandemic. *Proceedings of the Hawaii International Conference on System Sciences 2022*, Maui, HI, January 4– 7, 2022.

Ziewitz, M. (2016). Special issue introduction: Governing algorithms: Myth, mess, and methods. *Science, Technology, & Human Values, 41*(1), 3–16.

5

NEUTRALITY OR CONTEXTUALITY

Challenges for sociotechnical data governance

Kyra Milan Abrams and Madelyn Rose Sanfilippo

Introduction

Government processes, services, and public infrastructure generate staggering volumes of data with significant value. Open government has grown significantly over the past five years, accounting for data valued at 0.5%–1.5% of GDP (World Bank, 2021). For example, since 2018, the total number of nations with open government data has increased over 50% (Wirtz et al., 2022). While this data offers significant opportunities and insights, it is neither autonomous nor simply managed.

Rather, data governance in the public sector raises numerous challenges regarding just treatment of data subjects as members of the public, ethical tensions, and conflicting policies. This complexity holds true for public interest technology—information and technology that significantly impact nearly every facet of social and public lives—to say nothing of how individuals engage with them personally. From issues of datafication and surveillance—to mechanisms for control or risks to security on the end of the spectrum that points to adverse impacts for those that offer benefits to sustainability, accuracy, or public safety—data and emerging technologies transform interactions, experiences, services, and processes. The specific case of public sector data governance intersects with issues of innovation and structural inequalities, raising concerns about who the winners and losers of such changes might be.

These concerns echo longstanding debates about neutrality and contextuality of technologies and their uses. A pervasive assumption about technology—often associated with techno-optimism and the paradigm of technological determinism, yet soundly rejected by social informatics and socially constructivist scholarship (Fichman et al., 2015; Wyatt, 2008)—is that it is neutral, with all connotations of impartiality, objectivity, and dissociation from values implied (Miller, 2021; Polgar,

DOI: 10.4324/9781032678542-8

2010). Such an assumption overlooks the significant evidence that embedded values shape the design and use of systems (Friedman & Hendry, 2019), as well as the contextuality of data relative to where it was collected and how it is used (Nissenbaum, 2019). Beliefs in neutrality drive efforts to re-engineer humanity via innovation (Frischmann & Selinger, 2018) and the adoption of technocratic and automated governance (Sætra, 2020), which iteratively lead to unanticipated and unequal outcomes in sociotechnical systems that present significant social challenges alongside or in place of the anticipated outcomes.

In this chapter, we explore the intersection of data governance and social informatics in the context of the public sector, critically examining court records, election data, and transportation data from California and Illinois. We aim to comparatively understand complexity and variation in outcomes associated with data governance, as well as how social informatics can better inform data governance.

Background

Sociotechnical data governance

Data governance is much more than the management of data. It involves who is able to make decisions about data and what effects are felt from those decisions (Micheli et al., 2020). This chapter explores that dynamic through a sociotechnical conceptualization of data governance in terms of an assemblage. This chapter also explores the relationship between privacy and data governance. Privacy laws provide exogenous supports and constraints upon how data can be governed in individual agencies and firms, such as how identifiable and unidentifiable data can be used (Iacovino & Todd, 2007), but are only one of many forces shaping outcomes. Centring a social informatics perspective, while often part of pragmatic governance by experienced professionals, is often missing from or implicit in the literature, despite the importance of engaging with alignment between values and data governance.

Principles of social informatics

Social informatics reflects a sociotechnical paradigm, recognizing the complexity and dynamics of interactions between people and technology in context (Kling et al., 2005). It is defined not by a single theory or framework, nor by particular methods, but rather by a set of principles and concepts that iteratively emerge from empirical research across domains, places, and time (Fichman et al., 2015). Among those key social informatics principles are key assertions that align with data governance: reciprocal shaping, transparency, embedded values, paradoxical uptake outcomes, and non-neutrality.

First, information and communication technologies (ICTs) have a reciprocal relationship with sociotechnical context. ICTs have an effect on the group, while the group shapes the development of the ICTs. While the same type of group may use the same technology, there is no guarantee that they will use it the same way. For example, different organizations in the same domain may use the exact same platform differently (Kling, 2007). Reciprocal shaping also factors into how governments react to laws or directives concerning privacy (Iacovino & Todd, 2007). In relation to reciprocal shaping, how we govern data impacts how the design, usage, and implementation of technology is built upon that data (Micheli et al., 2020). What is important in specific contexts may not be as valued in others, which in turn shapes how technology is developed and used in relation to public sector data.

A second key concept of social informatics surrounds transparency. Transparency pertains to the availability of information, often via ICTs as well as about them. This element builds on reciprocity, as peoples' knowledge of the ICTs influence the development of the ICTs and their usage or implementation. The lack of transparency can benefit certain groups of people more than others, as those with more information can use the ICTs to their advantage; using ICTs to control flows of information prevents transparency, via information asymmetry, with respect to many domains. This reality presents a disadvantage to those without access to information (Sawyer & Eschenfelder, 2002). In relation to transparency, data governance can suffer from a lack of communication with those who are governed. This deficiency can result in technology that is not beneficial to its users or unknowingly harmful (Oostveen & Van den Besselaar, 2004). Transparency arises throughout the accessibility of public sector data, as there is often a lack of it. However, certain laws that govern public sector datasets may provide explanations for why things may or may not be available.

A third key principle of social informatics is that technology is shaped by and embedded with values by design. Embedded values stem both from individuals and communities or cultures. Human values are not solely psychological or sociological. They represent the intersection of the two aspects (Fleischmann, 2007). Social informatics literature also contrasts the typical analysis of values that consist of individuality by emphasizing the importance of the psychological and sociological intersection and design (Fleischmann, 2014). Embedded values can be related to the different biases that exist within technology, such as pre-existing, technical, and emergent biases (Friedman & Nissenbaum, 1996). For example, pre-existing biases are developed from societal biases, but are often implemented into technology at the individual level. Values are embedded in data governance, directly influencing what data is available for algorithm usage. For example, algorithms are not neutral but instead are value-laden (Rosenbaum & Fichman, 2019). The knowledge that algorithms contain embedded values provides guidance as to why the impacts of misuse of public sector data are felt by specific communities.

Paradoxical uptakes and outcomes in social informatics pertain to technological impacts on different groups. Paradoxical uptake outcomes reinforce the non-neutrality of technology (Sanfilippo & Fichman, 2014). These outcomes can result from differences in knowledge levels, as one person using technology with little knowledge in the domain will have a much different experience than a person with substantial knowledge (Oltmann et al., 2006). Such outcomes, when not anticipated by designers due to embedded values, can perpetuate existing inequalities exacerbated by the digital divide. Other factors that contribute to paradoxical uptake outcomes include organization structure and pre-existing rules and regulations. These factors can control what technology is used for, what types of information can be disseminated, and who is allowed access to specific types of technology (Oltmann et al., 2006). The methods used to govern data will have an impact on the multiple different outcomes that arise. For example, capitalist society demands exploitation for profit and has a great impact on how data is governed (Bradley, 2013). With algorithms, marginalized communities are often exploited to maximize profit. The algorithms created from these public sector datasets could be used to harm marginalized communities.

Non-neutrality is a critical concept of social informatics. Social informatics challenges the paradigm of technological determinism through non-neutrality. Technological determinism conceptualizes technology as the sole factor shaping societal outcomes. This model drives broader assumptions that: the only way to achieve economic progress or development is via technological innovation and adoption, technology operates outside of social control, and technology is a value-neutral tool or force for progress. The association between technology and progress serves to diminish responsibility when technology harms social groups (Wyatt, 2008). The sociotechnical principle of non-neutrality asserts that technology is neither objective, nor independent of social values. If there is an assertion that technology is non-neutral in the developmental stage, it ensures accountability and can reduce harm.

As aligned with the social informatics principle of non-neutrality, how we govern data is not neutral. For example, there are different groups at play when it comes to crisis intervention in relation to natural disasters. This variability includes the state's view of the problem and the perspectives from the knowledge of professionals in engineering and physical science backgrounds (Soden & Palen, 2018). As the ways in which technology is used by different groups are non-neutral, this variation is often not reflected in the design choices by developers. These design choices have a huge impact on data governance. Marginalized communities' ways of using technologies that differ from predominately western uses of technology are often not reflected in design and data governance choices. Simultaneously, companies and developers may implement design and data governance choices that exist to their economic benefit disguised as neutral features, but that present potential harm to their employees (Levy, 2015; Nemer, 2016; Rosenblat et al., 2017). This chapter not only concurs that technology is non-neutral, but also explores the relationship that data governance has in emphasizing that non-neutrality. Public sector data is utilized by many different groups of people for different reasons, and the design of how that data is disseminated is not neutral and it should not be.

Ethics, justice principles, and public interest technology

Recent developments regarding public interest technology have greatly influenced technological development, adoption, and use. Emerging public interest technology research emphasizes the need for democratic governance with meaningful community participation and support (Züger & Asghari, 2023). However, significantly more research on public interest technology is warranted to empirically support governance and design. For example, research has only just begun to analyze smart cities from a sociotechnical point of view. Findings indicate that a focus on human and moral elements is needed, emphasizing the value of transparency (Kitchin et al., 2017). By critically evaluating the systems that already exist, clear investigations of public interest technology can highlight how developers may be upholding systemic oppression through public interest technology that was meant to counter it (Sweeney & Brock, 2014; Washington & Kuo, 2020). These investigations need to be designed with attributes that are based in justice principles that serve those who are at risk of being harmed (Metcalf et al., 2021).

When societal norms and expectations are violated, the appropriate methods for justice and their perceived legitimacy are questioned. Justice is often decided and constructed by institutions, even if those who are harmed would prefer an alternative to the status quo (McPhail et al., 2012). This disconnect grows as algorithms are increasingly in usage, as they can cause harm to specific groups. Providing justice to these groups becomes difficult, as there is not one person to hold accountable. However, justice is not impossible (Rosenbaum & Fichman, 2019). This chapter emphasizes the importance of equity and justice, as the non-neutrality of data governance calls for equitable solutions grounded in justice principles that do not solely exist to protect institutions.

Public sector data in context

Public sector data is a valuable resource (Munné, 2016) as well as a mechanism for transparency and accountability across domains of public interest (Biancone et al., 2018). While election data is helpful to ensure free and fair elections and engender trust and legitimacy (Gorwa & Ash, 2020), the usage of public court records and transportation data are important for both public and private sector organizations (Akman & Mishra, 2009). It is imperative that public records have strong data governance and that there is more dialogue between public and private sector organizations in order to ensure that available data meets public needs and has sufficient documentation and quality standards to ensure appropriate use. Additionally, privacy is often sacrificed as more public data is generated (Kitchin, 2017). Robust data governance can work as a preventive measure against immediate relinquishing of privacy, in tandem with efforts regarding transparency, access, usability, data quality, and robust documentation.

Robust conceptualization of data throughout its lifecycle is key to understanding the impact of public data and social expectations regarding appropriate governance of data. We utilize the contextual integrity (CI) framework throughout our analysis, which defines privacy in terms of the appropriate flow of personal information in context (Nissenbaum, 2009). Within this framework, information flows are structurally defined via five parameters: (1) information senders, (2) subjects, (3) recipients, and (4) types, as well as (5) transmission principles. The CI framework conceptually structures analysis of data flows and lifecycles, and provides guidance on cross-contextual comparisons, considering both domains and places as contexts. CI may be violated in some cases in which algorithms are trained on data in inappropriate contexts (Nissenbaum, 2018), and it is useful to support critical qualitative inquiry of privacy and data (Kumar et al., 2024), as explained in Section "Methods".

Methods

Analysis in this chapter depends on an intersectional design, considering the geographic contexts of California and Illinois, as well as the domains of court records, election data, and transportation data, as summarized in Figure 5.1. This design allows for comparisons between agencies that must comply with the same state requirements regarding open and public data governance, as well as how specific domain attributes shape governance, by comparing across states, reflecting multiple dimensions of context under the CI framework (Abrams & Sanfilippo, 2023). These locations were selected given adoption of open records and transparency laws on similar timelines, and as they were shaped by the same

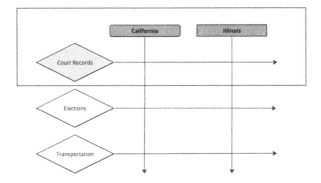

FIGURE 5.1   Comparative research design.

political party (Stewart, 2010). The three domains were selected because they include similar breadth and depth of datasets across states, as well as similar personally identifiable information; in contrast, educational or policing data are not comparable across states.

To make contextual comparisons across places and within domains, as well as within places and across domains, a dataset was compiled including: primary documents, such as state laws and agency policies; data portal documentation; and open data sets and public data access portals. Transportation data was centralized for both states, excluding data duplication from individual transit authorities; Chicago Transit Authority (CTA) data was the only localized open data that was not replicated by the centralized Illinois data.gov. Election data was centralized for California and distributed across Illinois' 108 election authorities (100 county clerks, 2 county election commissions, and 6 municipal election commissions).

TABLE 5.1 Data and policy documents analyzed

	California	*Illinois*
Law and policies considered	California Constitution California Department of Technology—Technology Letter (TL) 19-01 California State Administrative Manual (SAM) Open Data Policy Megan's Law Public Records Act	20 ILCS 45/Open Operating Standards Act—Illinois Open Data Chicago Open Data Executive Order (No. 2012-2) Freedom of Information Act, 5 ILCS 140/1 to 11 Illinois Constitution
Election data	Election Data Sandbox Open Data—Election Data Secretary of State—Election Statistics	Illinois Election Open Data Illinois State Board of Elections Records + Open Records and Data from all 108 Election Authorities
Public court records	California Courts Records California Supreme Court Public Records Department of Justice Public Records Open and Public Records from 58 County Courts	E-Services Cook County Clerk of Courts Electronic Access for Circuit Court Records Illinois Courts Supreme Court Data Open and Public Records from 102 County Courts
Transportation data	Cal-ITP Caltran Live Traffic Cameras Caltrans GIS Data Open Data—Transportation Traffic Census Program	Data—Transportation I-DOT Travel Statistics Illinois Transit Data Illinois Transit Database—County & City (union of 60 datasets) Open Data from the CTA

Court records and access to public data about legal proceedings were available at the state and county levels, with 102 counties in Illinois and 58 counties in California. A summary of policy documents and datasets evaluated in this research is presented in Table 5.1. In the end, 348 of the datasets and their individual associated documentation were considered relative to the requirements stipulated in nine laws or standards.

Qualitatively, policy analysis of state laws or standards and agency policies was conducted via a combination of thematic coding and structured content analysis. This approach is grounded in the governing knowledge commons (GKC) framework tradition, which leverages a structured descriptive framework to deeply understand the background, attributes, governance processes, patterns, and outcomes regarding data and information resources (Sanfilippo et al., 2021), as well as facilitate comparisons between cases without imposing normative judgment. The structured coding leveraged broadly validated institutional grammar (Crawford & Ostrom, 1995) to understand the hierarchy of strategies, norms, and rules as applied to information (e.g., Sanfilippo et al., 2021). Specifically, codes were applied at the level of attributes, aims, conditions, deontic or modal logic, and consequences. This approach is compatible with the CI framework (Shvartzshnaider et al., 2021); when applied in tandem, institutional attributes can be further deconstructed into the actors (information senders, subjects, and recipients) and information types within information flows, as defined by CI, while the aims, conditions, modalities, and consequences comprise transmission principles (Shvartzshnaider et al., 2022). In addition, thematic coding was applied to surface-specific action arenas and data governance responsibilities as intersected with identified institutions and roles.

Quantitatively, computational linguistic analysis was performed on text extracted with Python from the same documents to identify tentativeness as a measure of uncertainty, via sentiment models (Liu, 2010), and hedging language, via an ontology of modal logic (White, 2003), to determine where ambiguity regarding operationalization and implementation might occur. Computational analysis of tentativeness and hedging was conducted via R and compared with results from qualitative coding to identify overlap between ambiguities and structures, as well as within specific action arenas or governance aims.

Evaluation of access and auditing of compliance relative to both portal documentation and the open public datasets or public data access portals themselves was modeled after the approach developed for EFOIA compliance audits (Oltmann et al., 2006). While Oltmann et al.'s (2006) method is built on Gordon-Murnane's (1999) study to specifically apply to data collection via EFOIA, they offered a more generalizable model to identify legal and regulatory mandates regarding information and determine the absence or presence of such information through content analysis, along with related accessibility and usability metrics. Based upon legal requirements regarding open data and dataset documentation, prompts were developed to ascertain whether what was required (law, policy, or standard) has actually been implemented, as well as whether what the agency in

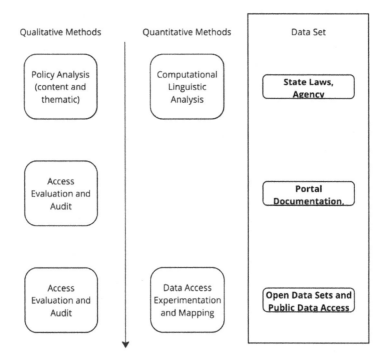

Qualitative Methods   Quantitative Methods   Data Set

Policy Analysis   Computational   State Laws,
(content and   Linguistic   Agency
thematic)   Analysis

Access   Portal
Evaluation and   Documentation.
Audit

Access   Data Access   Open Data Sets and
Evaluation and   Experimentation   Public Data Access
Audit   and Mapping

FIGURE 5.2   Multi-method research design flow chart.

question said was possible mapped to the reality of the system or dataset. This facilitated identification of gaps between policy and practice, as well as served as a mechanism to test assertions based on social informatics principles. Figure 5.2 synthesizes the multi-method research design employed in this chapter.

Results

Transportation

Transportation datasets are multifaceted and diverse, drawing on state Department of Transportation processes and services, as well as surveillance in public-private partnerships through tolling and mass transit. The transit agencies in Illinois that have more than two million boardings per year are Connect Transit in Bloomington, Champaign-Urbana MTD in Champaign, Chicago TA, METRA, PACE Suburban Bus in Chicago, CityLink in Peoria, MetroLink in Rock Island, and Madison County Transit and St. Louis Metro in St. Louis. By comparison, there are 45 transit agencies in California that have more than two million boardings per year. These agencies are divided between 12 cities. In deeper analysis evaluating the data governance of a subset of ten transit agencies, five each in California and Illinois, three distinct attributes were used to analyze their digital environments: usability of the site, transparency of governance, and accessibility of the data set. Usability of the site refers to the functionality of the site, such as the UI/UX, efficiency of links, and availability of translation. Transparency of governance indicates which specific types of data are available. While some sites may include information on ridership reports or performance metrics, others may not. Accessibility of the data set concerns the methods in which the data can be obtained. This aspect can differ by category depending on the site.

Beyond transparency, usability, and accessibility of specific transportation and transit datasets, there are various governance action arenas in flux. For example, numerous transportation datasets were not initially generated with public purposes in mind, but rather resulted from quantification of basic ridership statistics to determine scheduling needs; over time this morphed and extended to justifications for additional investments and infrastructure upgrades, transparency and equity efforts, and a commodity of interest to private sector development.

California transportation data reflected diversity of data types and evolution in uses overtime. Beyond the ridership statistics for public transit or licensure, GIS data and video collected from every traffic camera in the state are publicly available, including real-time video feeds. The use of these video streams to train commercial facial recognition and automated license plate readers (ALPR) is far outside the intended use cases proposed or planned for either by lawmakers regarding California's open data laws, or by Department of Transportation officials seeking to implement and comply with such laws for transparency and accountability. While the data can support innovation, such uses are outside the scope of the California Consumer Privacy Act's (CCPA) provisions.

Illinois transportation datasets are more diverse in provenance than those offered by California. Some, for example, intersect with other public agencies, including the Department of Natural Resources, to provide details regarding deer-vehicle accidents. Compilations of transportation data in Illinois raised multiple consequences of such distribution and plurality; these datasets and associated documentation highlighted conflicts between local and state transportation authorities regarding what to document and make available, as well as the diversity of interpretations of generalized state rules regarding open data, rather than specific guidelines for individual domains. Further, other records pit public interests in disclosure against privacy concerns, as with data regarding DUIs. While individual records can be searched with sufficient detail to identify a specific record, most of the data is in anonymized summary form, in comparison to Illinois' deer-vehicle accident data, which variously includes details like license plates and drivers' license numbers. Sensitive and identifiable data is available throughout multiple transportation data sets.

Elections

Election data and access to these datasets differed significantly across the two states. While California offered a model with respect to documentation, data, quality, and usability, Illinois did not offer a centralized or usable digital platform to engage with election data for the state in one place. Rather, Illinois maintained summary Board of Elections data and a centralized repository regarding statewide elections only, without details regarding local elections or voters. Data pertaining to local elections and voters, along with local data for statewide elections, could be obtained from 108 different election authorities, directly or via non-profit efforts, to compensate for the public records failures in the domain. Scrutiny of local election data raised various non-compliance issues: missing elections, incomplete data, unlabelled data, unstructured data, proprietary data formats, and non-digital access. In our assessment, and in alignment with non-profit scrutiny of Illinois election data, granular statewide comparisons with this data would not be meaningful due to irregularities, incompleteness, and quality issues; the data in aggregate cannot be considered objective.

Election data in both states, while initially collected for election integrity purposes, was expanded in scope over time. Documentation from both states details how historic election results and population changes need to be accounted for, specifically in maintaining and updating electoral maps, and in California by emphasizing the role of this transparency effort concerning maintaining election integrity and trust. Further, in integrating this data with details about demographics and population distributions, state-level data is integrated with federal records from the US Census Bureau. Of all of the datasets considered in this study, California election data was the most usable and mapped most clearly onto regulatory and policy document objectives and requirements regarding metadata, openness, accessibility, documentation, and availability.

Illinois took a decentralized approach to election data collection and further complicated subsequent empirical analysis or public access by also decentralizing dissemination of the data; non-profit efforts to compile the data are limited in that reporting is so non-standardized that they are of comparatively limited use. This reflected a significant gap between the rules on the books and those in effect, indicating incomplete compliance; public records and open data requirements that apply to this data in Illinois stipulate that state transparency and accountability portals or local platforms must provide "easily accessible data to the general public" (Exec. Order No. 15-10, 2015) and that it needs to be "readily available to the general public" (Illinois Transparency and Accountability Act, 2013). Local authorities did not leverage the Open Data Portal built upon the Comprehensive Knowledge Archive Network (CKAN), which could have addressed accessibility and availability, and enhanced usability and findability. The ambiguity of such requirements likely leads to such outcomes.

Courts

While the implementation of open data and public records laws reflects the most nuance regarding court data—treating family law distinct from traffic court and classes of criminal proceedings in different ways to protect the privacy of specific subsets of individuals, such as children, victims, and witnesses—it also highlights embedded biases along racial, ethic, and socioeconomic lines. The latter is notable interpedently, despite its alignment with issues of race and ethnicity, particularly considering fees to access specific courts data in California. Data about financial crimes, for example, are less detailed and identifying than records around petty theft, burglary, or armed robbery, reflecting inequities. California county court datasets offer a strong parallel to Illinois elections, crossing domain and state, but are even more limited in that much data is available case-by-case or only at a high-level summary, providing wildly different granularity or preventing aggregation.

Illinois court records, by comparison, highlight how a complex hierarchy produces dysfunction and inconsistencies in implementation, as well as mismatches between governance and practice. For example, the datasets from the Cook County Clerk of Courts highlight specific issues regarding reidentification and non-anonymization, forcing a trade-off between transparency and privacy, in addition to regulatory conflicts. Unequal equivalencies are also made in the development of bespoke classifications and controlled vocabularies in the absences of coordination or standardization at the state level. Non-standard treatment of family law and criminal trial data statewide limits the utility of such data.

Discussion

The results of this research indicate that while open and public data governance is rooted in democratic values—such as transparency, accountability, and openness—there are significant challenges for data governance within modern sociotechnical systems. Each of these challenges map onto recognized patterns regarding the complexity associated with ICT and data in society via a social informatics lens.

Sociotechnical challenges for data governance

This subsection explores five key challenges for data governance, comparing results to established concepts in the literature.

Function creep—as the broadening of use or repurposing of information or technology (Frischmann & Selinger, 2018)—was recognizable in all three domains and both states. The original purposes of data sets or public records did not map onto the current uses or the open or public data set aims. Transportation and election datasets in both states reflected shifts and expansions in functions of data collection and use. Governance, broadly in the form of state laws and standards, did not acknowledge these conflicts in aims; governance—narrowly in the form of data set documentation—and agency policy only occasionally acknowledged, and sought to reconcile, these cross purposes.

The *intersection of privacy and equity concerns* presents another major data governance challenge. Who is covered in the data, in terms of representation versus targeting via scope of collection or curation, matters significantly to the subdomains of privacy and equity in data governance. Court records, and access to individual records or data about court proceedings, across both states best illustrate these challenges. A parallel is provided with respect to the discrepancies between transportation datasets regarding DUIs versus deer-vehicle accidents in Illinois; however, it is the DUIs that offer less identifiers to the public. The level of personally identifiable information (PII) available by case type easily raises equity issues—in addition to the privacy concerns regarding identifiability and reidentification—by combining open and public datasets or with information easily obtained in Google searches, such as names and addresses of homeowners. The challenge becomes coordination across agencies in order to determine that one dataset does not become the key to another. The equity and justice implications align with recent social informatics literature in connecting them to the unintended consequences regarding technology and data (Rosenbaum & Fichman, 2019).

Results regarding Illinois election and transportation data and California county court records also echoed broader scholarship regarding *dysfunctional polycentricity*, highlighting how multiple centers of decision-making regarding the same process, service, or data resource produce significant challenges for the public when they do not coordinate. This finding not only echoes earlier social informatics scrutiny of government information systems, but illustrates that in some ways, despite significant technological advancement, not much has changed in two decades (Tyworth & Sawyer, 2006). While the data may be open or public, it can be impractical to use—or even entirely impossible to meaningfully compare or analyze—given data governance choices, including those concerning what to record and how to structure it. Low quality and incomplete or inconsistent data does not support transparency or accountability as intended or lend itself as a resource for informed decision-making. Dysfunctional polycentricity regarding public data has potential to undermine entire domains.

Another major challenge highlighted by this analysis centered the distinct *differences in governance needs when considering data type*; evidence regarding significant differences in reidentification, privacy harms, and unintended consequences of identical data governance rules and implementation choices revealed how different tabular textual data and video data really are. California traffic camera data offered one of the most unexpected open public data sets and one of the clearest instances of how uses of open data can undermine the original intent and cause harm. Challenges regarding the nuance of data domain and type align with prior social informatics scholarship concerning data governance (Winter & Davidson, 2019).

The spectrum of *compliance* possibilities is also a challenge to consistency and efficacy of governance. From malicious compliance to compliance in name only, wherein data is available but not accessible or usable, there were numerous examples in the dataset that highlight how legal obligations toward openness can be undermined in practice by public officials or offices that either disagreed with open data or were unwilling or unable to compromise other responsibilities to appropriately implement such requirements. While there were certainly several examples of usable data in compliance with the law and without major externalities, such as California election data, even many conscientious compliance efforts concerning openness were compromised by externalities. For example, transportation datasets in both states raised questions beyond those already discussed regarding commercialization and tensions between private data and open data. Enforcement and compliance evaluation are necessary to promote fairness in line with recent research regarding data and system (e.g., Green, 2021; Selbst et al., 2019).

Evidence for social informatics principles

This subsection discusses the evidence from this case regarding social informatics principles, connecting them to key data governance challenges and practices, and exploring the ways in which the cases of public data governance analyzed in this chapter build on these assertions and concepts: non-neutrality, reciprocal shaping, transparency, embedded values, and paradoxical uptake outcomes.

Non-neutrality of data governance is evident both in the forms of bias that manifest due to decisions made and relative to externalities for particular groups. Assumptions about neutrality imply both objectiveness and relative consistency, yet neither of those are apparent upon examination of open and public data in the domains of transportation, elections, and public court records within the states of Illinois and California. Technologies and data, even when constructed around pro-social values, can cause harm and are decidedly non-neutral (Oostveen & Van den Besselaar, 2004). California court records regarding criminal proceedings, bail, and pre-trial release offer an example of non-neutrality of data. From the contentious nature of the concepts quantified themselves, to the intersections with historic and instructional inequalities and biases, court records are demonstrably non-neutral, aligning this insight with work by Marcinkowski (2016) regarding social informatics approaches to the treatment of data that are premised by the inherently political nature of data, rejecting assertions of neutrality and reification that are prominent in data science.

Evidence for reciprocal shaping between technology and people (Kling, 2007) was observable in the form of evolution in scope of data as collected and disseminated over time. As demands and uses shifted, value was identified regarding new data points changing scope. Further, as uses shifted beyond those initially envisioned by public administrators and data experts, so too did interfaces and systems.

Transparency was a key value motivating public data openness and availability in the first place, as well as evidently in tension with other meaningful concerns, such as privacy. While social informatics traditionally highlights the importance of transparency to the success of technological implementation or adoption (Sawyer & Eschenfelder, 2002), these results highlight that there is nuance to this significance. There is no one-size-fits-all transparency solution, and transparency is not the panacea to success.

Transparency is but one component of developing trust and accountability in public information systems (Selbst et al., 2019). It must be balanced with privacy and other design objectives. While the trade-offs with privacy are intuitive, particularly around issues of identification from court records and data, other relationships between values are more complex, as with openness and innovation. The expectation was that innovation based on valuable public data would yield social benefits; the reality is that much of the data goes unused and instances in which it is training systems, as with ALPR and facial recognition from California transportation video data, tend to cause significant social harms and may violate state privacy laws. As it is, values are embedded deeply in data collection, sharing, and use (Miller, 2021).

Paradoxical uptake of new technology and outcomes associated with data and systems reflect another key social informatics tenet (Sanfilippo & Fichman, 2014) evident in this study. In addition to the unintended consequences of data availability and retention with respect to court cases or with respect to governance choices regarding transportation data embedded with PII, such as license plates or driver's license numbers, the principles of technology reinforcing the status quo and the axiom that there will be winners and losers in the adoption of new technologies proved true. In this case, part of these patterns stem from the contextual nuances of domains and states, while resistance to change, resulting in malicious compliance and non-compliance, led to other paradoxical instances.

Conclusion

Comparative analysis of data governance across domains and states highlights both models for how approaches to managing public data through its life cycle can succeed, as well as where efforts to increase accountability and transparency via access to and openness of public records are likely to be challenged. While California offers a strong model around consistency and documentation, Illinois offers a model for how nuance can be provided regarding sensitive data sets like court records. On the other hand, governance gaps and failures are evident regarding: function creep, privacy and equity, polycentricity, oversimplification of data nuance, and enforcement and compliance.

These results can be synthesized in a number of practical implications. First, resources need to accompany mandates for public and open data. Support for centralized repositories, expertise in documentation, and overall usability are necessary for data to be meaningfully open to the public. Second, open data need not be one-size-fits-all. Contextualization of governance by domain is important, given the variations and sensitivity of the data and potential harm to individuals in contrast with the overall value or utility of the aggregate data. Third, pure and unlimited openness need not be the default legal status of data resources. Monetization of open and public data—supporting not just innovation but also profiteering at the expense of individual citizens—is not in alignment with the aim of openness and access. Fourth, Freedom of Information requests can supplement open data in ways that are meaningful, while still protecting individuals with respect to privacy and equity.

Research implications also emerge, both as an agenda for future research applying social informatics to data governance and public interest technology, and in the form of conceptual and epistemological contributions. Application of an interdisciplinary sociotechnical lens to issues of data governance better aligns with the multidimensionality of such practices, in comparison to legally oriented or information systems management approaches. Additional research exploring what leads to unintended consequences and the non-neutrality of data governance in other contexts is warranted, as is future research to scrutinize public interest technologies and their mutual shaping with society, expanding earlier scholarship on public infrastructure (Bishop & Star, 1996). Such research would build upon this chapter and other works exploring fairness and data or algorithms (e.g., Dolata et al., 2022) to center social informatics in approaching responsible data and AI. Finally, the new baseline assumption about technology and data, in light of insights from this chapter and decades of other social informatics scholarship, must be that information and systems are contextual, not neutral.

References

Abrams, K. M., & Sanfilippo, M. R. (2023, May). Governance conflicts and public court records. *International Conference on Computer Ethics, 1*(1), 1–15.

Akman, I., & Mishra, A. (2009). Ethical behavior issues in software use: An analysis of public and private sectors. *Computers in Human Behavior, 25*(6), 1251–1257.

Biancone, P., Secinaro, S., & Brescia, V. (2018). The innovation of local public-sector companies: Processing big data for transparency and accountability. *African Journal of Business Management, 12*(15), 486–500.

Bishop, A. P., & Star, S. L. (1996). Social informatics of digital library use and infrastructure. *Annual Review of Information Science and Technology (ARIST), 31*, 301–401.

Bradley, G. (2013). Social informatics and ethics: Towards the good information and communication society. In C. Fuchs & M. Sandoval (Eds.), *Critique, social media and the information society* (pp. 103–118). Routledge.

Crawford, S. E., & Ostrom, E. (1995). A grammar of institutions. *American Political Science Review, 89*(3), 582–600.

Dolata, M., Feuerriegel, S., & Schwabe, G. (2022). A sociotechnical view of algorithmic fairness. *Information Systems Journal, 32*(4), 754–818.

Exec. Order No. 15-10 (2015). *State of Illinois Executive Order Requiring Transparency within State and Local Government.* www.illinois.gov/government/executive-orders/executive-order.executive-order-number-10.2015.html

Fichman, P., Sanfilippo, M. R., & Rosenbaum, H. (2015). Social informatics evolving. *Synthesis Lectures on Information Concepts, Retrieval, and Services, 7*(5), 1–108.

Fleischmann, K. R. (2007). Digital libraries and human values: Human-computer interaction meets social informatics. *Proceedings of the American Society for Information Science and Technology, 44*(1), 1–17.

Fleischmann, K. R. (2014). Approaches to understanding values. In *Information and human values* (pp. 7–30). Springer International Publishing.

Friedman, B., & Hendry, D. G. (2019). *Value sensitive design: Shaping technology with moral imagination.* MIT Press.

Friedman, B., & Nissenbaum, H. (1996). Bias in computer systems. *ACM Transactions on Information Systems (TOIS), 14*(3), 330–347.

Frischmann, B., & Selinger, E. (2018). *Re-engineering humanity.* Cambridge University Press.

Gordon-Murnane, L. (1999). The Electronic Freedom of Information Act: The promise remains unfulfilled. *Searcher, 7*(4), 34–49.

Gorwa, R., & Ash, T. G. (2020). Democratic transparency in the platform society. In J. A. Tucker & N. Persily (Eds.), *Social media and democracy: The state of the field and prospects for reform* (pp. 286–312). Cambridge University Press.

Green, B. (2021). The contestation of tech ethics: A sociotechnical approach to technology ethics in practice. *Journal of Social Computing, 2*(3), 209–225.

Iacovino, L., & Todd, M. (2007). The long-term preservation of identifiable personal data: A comparative archival perspective on privacy regulatory models in the European Union, Australia, Canada and the United States. *Archival Science, 7*, 107–127.

Illinois Transparency and Accountability Act, Illinois Public Act 098-0627. (2013). www.ilga.gov/legislation/publicacts/98/098-0627.htm

Kitchin, R. (2017). Data-driven urbanism. In R. Kitchin, T. P. Lauriault, & G. McArdle (Eds.), *Data and the city* (pp. 44–56). Routledge.

Kitchin, R., Coletta, C., Evans, L., Heaphy, L., & MacDonncha, D. (2017). Smart cities, epistemic communities, advocacy coalitions and the 'last mile' problem. *It-Information Technology, 59*(6), 275–284.

Kling, R. (2007). What is social informatics and why does it matter? *The Information Society, 23*(4), 205–220.

Kling, R., Rosenbaum, H., & Sawyer, S. (2005). *Understanding and communicating social informatics: A framework for studying and teaching the human contexts of information and communication technologies.* Information Today, Inc.

Kumar, P. C., Zimmer, M., & Vitak, J. (2024). A roadmap for applying the Contextual Integrity Framework in qualitative privacy research. *Proceedings of the ACM on Human-Computer Interaction, 8*(CSCW1), 1–29.

Levy, K. E. (2015). The contexts of control: Information, power, and truck-driving work. *The Information Society, 31*(2), 160–174.

Liu, B. (2010). Sentiment analysis and subjectivity. *Handbook of Natural Language Processing, 2*(2010), 627–666.

Marcinkowski, M. (2016). Data, ideology, and the developing critical program of social informatics. *Journal of the Association for Information Science and Technology, 67*(5), 1266–1275.

McPhail, M. L., Lyon, R., & Harris, D. (2012). Digital divisions: Racial (in) justice and the limits of social informatics in the State of Georgia vs. Troy Anthony Davis. *Northern Kentucky Law Review, 39*, 137.

Metcalf, J., Moss, E., Watkins, E. A., Singh, R., & Elish, M. C. (2021, March). Algorithmic impact assessments and accountability: The co-construction of impacts. In *Proceedings of the 2021 ACM Conference on Fairness, Accountability, and Transparency* (pp. 735–746). ACM.

Micheli, M., Ponti, M., Craglia, M., & Berti Suman, A. (2020). Emerging models of data governance in the age of datafication. *Big Data & Society, 7*(2), 2053951720948087.

Miller, B. (2021). Is technology value-neutral? *Science, Technology, & Human Values, 46*(1), 53–80.

Munné, R. (2016). Big data in the public sector. In J. M. Cavanillas, E. Curry, & W. Wahlster (Eds.), *New horizons for a data-driven economy: A roadmap for usage and exploitation of big Data in Europe* (pp. 195–208). Springer.

Nemer, D. (2016). Rethinking social change: The promises of Web 2.0 for the marginalized. *First Monday.* http://dx.doi.org/10.5210/fm.v21i6.6786

Nissenbaum, H. (2009). *Privacy in context.* Stanford University Press.

Nissenbaum, H. (2018). Respecting context to protect privacy: Why meaning matters. *Science and Engineering Ethics, 24*(3), 831–852.

Nissenbaum, H. (2019). Contextual integrity up and down the data food chain. *Theoretical Inquiries in Law, 20*(1), 221–256.

Oltmann, S. M., Rosenbaum, H., & Hara, N. (2006). Digital access to government information: To what extent are agencies in compliance with EFOIA? *Proceedings of the American Society for Information Science and Technology, 43*(1), 1–14.

Oostveen, A. M., & Van den Besselaar, P. (2004, July). From small scale to large scale user participation: A case study of participatory design in e-government systems. In *Proceedings of the Eighth Conference on Participatory Design: Artful Integration: Interweaving Media, Materials and Practices* (Vol. 1, pp. 173–182). PDC.

Polgar, J. M. (2010). The myth of neutral technology. In *Design and use of assistive technology: Social, technical, ethical, and economic challenges* (pp. 17–23). Springer New York.

Rosenbaum, H., & Fichman, P. (2019). Algorithmic accountability and digital justice: A critical assessment of technical and sociotechnical approaches. *Proceedings of the Association for Information Science and Technology, 56*(1), 237–244.

Rosenblat, A., Levy, K. E., Barocas, S., & Hwang, T. (2017). Discriminating tastes: Uber's customer ratings as vehicles for workplace discrimination. *Policy & Internet, 9*(3), 256–279.

Sætra, H. S. (2020). A shallow defence of a technocracy of artificial intelligence: Examining the political harms of algorithmic governance in the domain of government. *Technology in Society, 62*, 101283.

Sanfilippo, M., & Fichman, P. (2014). The evolution of social informatics research (1984-2013): Challenges and opportunities. In P. Fichman & H. Rosenbaum (Eds.), *Social informatics: Past, present and future* (pp. 29–53). Cambridge Scholars Publishing.

Sanfilippo, M. R., Frischmann, B. M., & Strandburg, K. J. (Eds.). (2021). *Governing privacy in knowledge commons.* Cambridge University Press.

Sawyer, S., & Eschenfelder, K. R. (2002). Social informatics: Perspectives, examples, and trends. *Annual Review of Information Science and Technology, 36*(1), 427–465.

Selbst, A. D., Boyd, D., Friedler, S. A., Venkatasubramanian, S., & Vertesi, J. (2019, January). Fairness and abstraction in sociotechnical systems. In *Proceedings of the Conference on Fairness, Accountability, and Transparency* (pp. 59–68). ACM.

Shvartzshnaider, Y., Sanfilippo, M. R., & Apthorpe, N. (2021). Contextual integrity as a gauge for governing knowledge commons. In M. R. Sanfilippo, B. M. Frischmann, & K. J. Strandburg (Eds.), *Governing Privacy in Knowledge Commons*, (pp. 220–244). Cambridge University Press.

Shvartzshnaider, Y., Sanfilippo, M. R., & Apthorpe, N. (2022). GKC-CI: A unifying framework for contextual norms and information governance. *Journal of the Association for Information Science and Technology, 73*(9), 1297–1313.

Soden, R., & Palen, L. (2018). Informing crisis: Expanding critical perspectives in crisis informatics. *Proceedings of the ACM on Human-Computer Interaction, 2*(CSCW), 1–22.

Stewart, D. R. C. (2010). Let the sunshine in, or else: An examination of the "teeth" of state and federal open meetings and open records laws. *Communication Law and Policy, 15*(3), 265–310.

Sweeney, M. E., & Brock, A. (2014). Critical informatics: New methods and practices. *Proceedings of the American Society for Information Science and Technology, 51*(1), 1–8.

Tyworth, M., & Sawyer, S. (2006, May). Organic development: A top-down and bottom-up approach to design of public sector information systems. In *Proceedings of the 2006 International Conference on Digital Government Research* (pp. 105–112). ACM.

Washington, A. L., & Kuo, R. (2020, January). Whose side are ethics codes on? Power, responsibility and the social good. In *Proceedings of the 2020 Conference on Fairness, Accountability, and Transparency* (pp. 230–240). ACM.

White, P. R. (2003). Beyond modality and hedging: A dialogic view of the language of intersubjective stance. *Text & Talk, 23*(2), 259–284.

Winter, J. S., & Davidson, E. (2019). Big data governance of personal health information and challenges to contextual integrity. *The Information Society, 35*(1), 36–51.

Wirtz, B. W., Weyerer, J. C., Becker, M., & Müller, W. M. (2022). Open government data: A systematic literature review of empirical research. *Electronic Markets, 32*(4), 2381–2404.

World Bank. (2021). *The potential of open data to help businesses.* World Development Report 2021: Data for Better Lives. https://wdr2021.worldbank.org/spotlights/the-potent ial-of-open-data-to-help-businesses/

Wyatt, S. (2008). Technological determinism is dead; long live technological determinism. In E. J. Hackett, O. Amsterdamska, M. Lynch, & J. Wajcman (Eds.), *The handbook of science and technology studies* (Vol. 3, pp. 165–180). MIT Press.

Züger, T., & Asghari, H. (2023). AI for the public. How public interest theory shifts the discourse on AI. *AI & Society, 38*(2), 815–828.

Social informatics perspectives on ethics and social justice

6

SMART GOVERNMENTS

The pitfalls of big data in public administration

Bárbara da Rosa Lazarotto

Introduction

The adoption of technology by the public sector and the consequent digitalization of administrative practices are movements that have gained momentum since the start of the twenty-first century, posing as a solution that addresses multiple bureaucratic failures such as slow public service, biased decision-making, and general inefficiency. These digitalization projects are one of the largest public investment sources in all governmental spheres, a testament to the blind enthusiasm for adopting technologies and their transformative capacities (McLoughlin & Wilson, 2013; Gauld & Goldfinch, 2006). As a part of these digitalization efforts, the concept of "smart governments" has emerged as a trendy concept in the last decade, defending the use of technology to achieve a more efficient and less costly public administration. However, this technological trend does not come without perils. The high demand for data collection brings a series of consequences, especially for citizens who have their movements, activities, past behavior, and preferences tracked for later use to make inferences and predictions about their future behaviors.

This chapter aims to analyze the digitalization of public administration practices in this context by focusing on "smart governments," exploring how they operate and their potential impacts. This analysis will take a social informatics perspective, which offers an approach that challenges the traditional techno-solutionist perspective of digitalization of public administration, replacing it with an "interdisciplinary study of design, uses and consequences of technological adoption, and their interaction with institutional and cultural contexts" allowing, a more comprehensive and complete analysis of the topic (Kling et al., 2000).

DOI: 10.4324/9781032678542-10

This chapter will proceed as follows. "The birth of evidence-based decision-making in public administration" section will explore the emergence of evidence-based decision-making in public administration, followed by a study of the "smart governments" concept in the "Defining 'smart governments'" subsection, which will explore what "smart governments" consist of and the influences of philosophy, political science, and administrative theories. The third part of this chapter (the "Examining the harmful effects of smart governments" section) will focus on the dangers posed by "smart governments"—how the process of datafication and its outcomes have the potential to impact public administration internally and externally, interfering in citizens' due process rights. The fourth and last part of this chapter (the "Concluding remarks and the path forward" section) will summarize the analysis, closing remarks, and the path forward for adopting technology in the public sector.

The birth of evidence-based decision-making in public administration

Over the past few decades, technological developments have increased the use of data for evidence-based decision-making. The adoption of technology by public administration was not immediate, but rather resulted from economic, political, and social factors that developed over time. This process is often overlooked in legal analyses of the consequences of digitalizing the state. Therefore, this section will provide a general analysis of technology adoption by the public sector. The use of data for government decision-making dates back to ancient Egypt and was essential for tracking agricultural practices (Cappers, 2006). In the Roman Empire, data collection was used for managing private property and tracking populations and soldiers. This early use of data became more sophisticated with the adoption of new technologies such as accounting techniques (Frank, 1924).

During the Industrial Revolution, which lasted from the mid-eighteenth to the nineteenth century, optimizing labor and resources became crucial. New work methods like Taylorism emerged to increase efficiency (Rabinbach, 1992). Data became important for decision-making, leading to the development of bureaucratic systems. Companies like Burroughs and Hollerith developed machines for automated data collection, making public sector data processing more efficient. This process created fertile soil for developing a robust bureaucratic apparatus that philosopher Alasdair MacIntyre calls "the culture of bureaucratic individualism" (MacIntyre, 2007; Van Zoonen, 2016; Breckenridge & Szreter, 2012). The concept of optimization gained momentum during and after World War I and World War II, both of which led to increased demand for resources and solutions for military purposes (Halpern et al., 2017). Advanced encryption methods, such as "The Enigma," were developed during this period, and the public sector gradually adopted technological advancements for various purposes including the creation of the Electronic Numerical Integrator and Computer (ENIAC) for large-scale numerical processing tasks (Ellis, 2005; Bellamy & Taylor, 1998; Lips, 2019).

During the mid-90s and early 2000s, the Clinton-Gore administration launched the 'National Partnership for Reinventing Government' (NPR) to modernize public administration using technology (Gore, 1996; McLoughlin & Wilson, 2013). This initiative continued with subsequent administrations that emphasized digitalization and the importance of efficiency and effectiveness in the public sector (Fountain, 2004). The concept also led to the replacement of outdated governmental procedures with technological solutions to provide better public services. This movement was influenced by "New Public Management" (NPM) and led to reforms known as "New Public Analytics" (NPA), which advocates for technologies and data to drive government changes and outcomes (Hood, 1995; Harlow, 1997; Yeung, 2023; Citron, 2007).

The digitization of public administration practices gained momentum after the September 11 terrorist attacks and the 2008 global financial crisis. These events led to technological advancements including: massive data collection, profiling, mapping, modeling, and simulations (Haggerty et al., 2011). Public administration has since collected data for decision-making and feeding simulation models. This process is known as "governance by data" (Matheus et al., 2020). Various terms have emerged to define the use of technology by governments, such as "government 2.0," "digital government," and "e-government" (Chun et al., 2010; Budi et al., 2020; Tapscott et al., 2008; Ranchordás & Scarcella, 2021; Schelin, 2007; Reitz, 2006; Lee-Archer, 2023).

Defining "smart governments"

Various terminologies have been developed aiming to describe governments' use of technology in a quest for efficiency and optimization. Some were more successful than others, and this is a movement still happening today. The first to emerge was "electronic government" shortly after the arrival of the public internet in the early 1990s (Janssen et al., 2004; Curthoys & Crabtree, 2003). At that time, the United States Federal Government put into action a vision of e-government revolutionizing citizens' access to information and public service by being available 24/7, taking a customer orientation to public service delivery. The term was also adopted in Europe with the "eEurope" program in 1999, which aimed to support a socially inclusive Europe through technology (European Council of Lisbon, 2000). Also, in 1999, the term "digital government"—a broader concept that aims to encompass all the uses of digital technologies to provide public services, support public policies, and improve government operations—was adopted by the US National Science Foundation (Lips, 2019). In the early 2000s, the term "i-Government" was coined, focusing on informational flows within the government and putting technology that allows these flows in second place (Prins et al., 2012). Since then, other terms have emerged—among them "smart governments," which is the focus of the present study.

Scholars have approached the concept of "smart governments" in different ways. Mellouli et al. (2014) and Cellary (2013) use the term to refer to the use of ubiquitous technology by governments to perform governmental tasks. Gil-Garcia and Aldama-Nalda (2013) use it to denote the use of technology as a medium for increasing the efficiency and effectiveness of the public sector (Anthopoulos & Reddick, 2016; Mellouli et al., 2014; Cellary, 2013; Gil-Garcia & Aldama-Nalda, 2013).

While I believe that these definitions encompass crucial aspects of smart governments, this study aims to explore a broader concept. The Cambridge Dictionary defines "smart" as an adjective meaning "intelligent, or able to think quickly or intelligently in difficult situations." Nevertheless, the term has become a buzzword that goes beyond this description, often having an underlying connotation of intelligent, wired, connected, efficient, sustainable, and digital (Anthopoulos & Reddick, 2016; Melgaço & van Brakel, 2021). Due to its different connotations, the term is flexible enough to refer to the latest technology available; at the same time, it remains recognizable, which allows people to adapt to different niches (Bensaude Vincent, 2014; Abdoullaev, 2011; Nam & Pardo, 2011). Besides its form as a buzzword, "smart" may also refer to the acronym "SMART"—which may correspond to multiple terms in law, life sciences, or social sciences—referring to "sustainable," "mobility," "accountability," "resilience," and "technology in the area of failure prediction in software" (Kaczorowski, 2014). It additionally refers to "self-monitoring," "analysis," and "reporting technology" (Yeung, 2023).

In this context, my proposed definition is that "smart governments" are a form of public governance heavily influenced by the New Public Management philosophy and are considerably different from previous forms of government. Traditionally, governmental agencies relied upon small, concrete, structured datasets such as official statistics, census data, and population data (Pentland, 2014; Janssen et al., 2004; Elkin-Koren & Gal, 2019). Smart governments, however, are grounded in the collection and use of large volumes, variety, and granularity of data collected with the objective of making public services efficient, seamless, and integrated—working with little bureaucratic burden and allowing a better connection with citizens (Anthopoulos & Reddick, 2016; Bensaude Vincent, 2014; Nam & Pardo, 2011; Lips, 2019; Harsh & Ichalkaranje, 2015). Thus, the mass collection of data is one of smart governments' main aspects, grounded in the ideology that data can provide more accurate and nuanced information in a neutral, non-biased form, allowing the prediction of all future human activities (Van Dijck, 2014; Andreassen et al., 2021).

Once the public sector has access to collected data, it can be inserted into government databases for inference purposes. It is essential, however, for an efficient and smooth-running public administration that data be interoperable, which means that all sectors and systems of public administration must "talk to one another" for the government to function well. Thus, the second pillar of smart governments is the integration of multi-agency datasets. The 9/11 terrorist attacks in the United States were the catalyst of this movement. Following the attacks, the 9/11 Commission recommended the creation of "fusion centers" to serve as a hub for internal information sharing and coordination, filling existent informational gaps in the public sector's databases (Roth et al., 2004). Consequently, governments proceeded to enact reforms that aimed to break the traditional Weberian model of governmental bureaucracy that structured the public sector in a vertical format with compartmentalization of public records, files, and data by functional areas. Hence, smart governments proceeded with vertical and horizontal integration of data. First, "vertical integration" allows the integration of data from different sectors, while "horizontal integration" comprises sharing standard services across different agencies—such as finance, procurement, and human resources management— implying the sharing of internal data from multiple areas with standard services (Lips, 2019).

A great example of smart government is the Chinese government's use of the WeChat application. Despite the political influences of the Chinese Communist Party (CCP) in the development of surveillance applications in the country—which are outside of the scope of this study—China remains a great example of a smart government due to the heavy reliance on data collection for public management, which is centralized on the WeChat app. This multipurpose app combines multiple functions—such as instant messaging between individuals, social media, e-commerce, payment services, and mini programs—which are "add-ons" to the app and allow users to integrate other functions (such as booking a taxi through the app), besides other services such as games and news articles (Lemke et al., 2020). Additionally, WeChat offers "public accounts," which are direct channels used by organizations (such as enterprises, universities, and governments) to disseminate information to users. Currently, there are over one billion active users of WeChat, making it one of the world's most popular apps and a great medium for data collection. Thus, the app acts as a two-way medium for the smart government, a data collection hub, and a platform for citizens to engage with the government easily and seamlessly (Montag et al., 2018). Taking into consideration the amount of data collected by apps, in 2014, the Chinese government launched the National Social Score: a vast national database encompassing both private and public data that covers citizens' individual activities, online behaviors, purchases, and traffic violations. All of the data from each citizen is processed and translated into a ranking with the objective of enhancing the market economy and social governance. In 2015, the Chinese government identified different companies that would share data for this scoring project; WeChat was one of them.

Since then, WeChat users are scored depending on the way that they use and interact with the app, an action that has multiple consequences for the fabric of society. Since 2013, around 7 million individuals have been banned from tracking flights overseas, and 3 million have been banned from riding in high-speed trains as a punishment for dishonest behavior tracked via these digital channels. The scoring punishment is not only restricted to the individual who did the "wrongdoing." Punitive measures can be extended to family members, such as not allowing the individual's child to attend a good school. Other technologies have been integrated into the system, such as facial recognition technologies. Cities such as Shenzhen and Fuzhou use this method to track and identify individuals who jaywalk, publishing their names in local media as a public shaming method. Facial recognition technology is also used by the private sector, such as hotels and banks, to identify potential troublemakers (Wong & Dobson, 2019). During the COVID-19 pandemic, this system was used to nudge individuals to behave as the government wanted. Individuals who hid their travel or medical history to conceal potential exposure to the virus, or who hoarded products such as toilet paper, were put on a blacklist and had their social score deducted (Yu, 2020).

One may argue that this example is extreme due to the political environment of China, which allows the development of such a widespread system. Although we do not have such a system in Western countries, we are not exempt from smart government practices. Cross-government data sharing became crucial to the EU's digital regulation in 2004 through the "European Interoperability Framework" and "The Hague Programme on Interoperability." In 2022, it was rebranded as "Interoperable Europe." The "Prüm Convention" in 2008 aimed to improve police cooperation in the EU. These processes allowed governments to create digital dossiers of citizens' data, facilitating data-driven predictions (Kalogirou & Charalabidis, 2019; Pflücke, 2023; Lips, 2019).

An example of this practice in Europe was the System Risk Indication (SyRI), a welfare fraud detection system in The Netherlands, which was introduced in 2010. SyRI used data from multiple governmental levels and agencies to conduct an artificial intelligence-based risk assessment, which indicated whether a person or a household was likely to engage in welfare fraud. Personal data of citizens was an inherent part of this process since multiple personal details (such as nationality and race) were determinants of whether a person was more likely to commit fraud (Giest & Klievink, 2024). Initially, the project was deemed to save millions of euros by potentially protecting the public budget against fraud through an automatic system that required little-to-no human intervention. However, the system gained public attention after around 270 thousand people (most of them individuals with immigrant backgrounds) were wrongly accused of fraud following the government's demand that they return the benefits received. An audit of the system revealed that nationality and appearance were taken into consideration when listing people as fraudsters, a clear violation of human rights in what was later called the "child benefit scandal" (Newman & Mintrom, 2023).

In a similar case, Norway's "Norwegian Labour and Welfare Administration" (Nye arbeids—og velferdsetaten, "NAV") is an agency responsible for processing several services and benefits in Norway, such as unemployment and sickness. In this context, NAV automated a great amount of its work, which meant translating national and European regulatory frameworks into code. The wrong implementation of social security regulations led to the denial of benefits and the request for repayments. One thousand and hundred people were forced to repay benefits to which they were entitled, 2,400 recipients were cut off from receiving benefits, and 86 persons were convicted of social benefit fraud, including jail time and expulsion from Norway. It took 26 years for the Norwegian government to admit the NAV scandal, and in 2019, a committee was appointed to investigate the situation. Unfortunately, few political and administrative changes were made, and a conviction by the European Court of Justice demanded the compensation of those affected (Rouwhorst, 2022).

In conclusion, smart governments are mechanisms of governance that are grounded in a perception that information-based decision-making, often automated through different mechanisms, may lead to a more effective, seamless, and less costly public administration. Nevertheless, in the three cases presented as examples of smart governments, it is possible to demonstrate how the use of "cold data"—which is taken out of context—creates a non-forgiving government that uses personal data as a form of public persecution disguised as efficiency. In this context, the next section will explore the harmful effects of smart governments.

Examining the harmful effects of smart governments

This section will focus on examining the harmful effects of smart governments following the analysis of their development and conceptualization. The backdrop to all of these harmful effects is the one-dimensional assumption that places technology as a beneficial, value-free driving force of change and progress (Foley & Alfonso, 2009). This naive belief prevents a balanced evaluation of the potentially harmful effects of these digital technologies that might be subject to individuals (McLoughlin & Wilson, 2013).

Internally, the digitalization of public administration has replaced traditional paper-based processes and face-to-face service channels with digital channels, such as websites, chatbots, smartphone apps, and SMS. Additionally, the internal structure of public administration has been modified by this digitalization process. Traditionally, governments have been organized in a conventional Weberian bureaucratic structure of silos consisting of separate public counters and agencies with separate files and records (Lips, 2019). Yet, with digitalization and the implementation of smart governments, public administration has replaced it with a large integrated dataset, which allows fluid data processing across different public sector divisions and single-citizen communication channels (Dunleavy et al., 2006). The decision to replace the traditional public administrative structure with a centralized dataset has multifaceted implications that transcend the mere reorganization of public administration. This transition reinforces a centralized, hierarchical power dynamic, effectively diminishing the influence of street-level bureaucrats while empowering automated computer decision-making systems.

Consequently, this paradigm shift has significantly altered the dynamics of citizen-government relations, as it changed the way in which decisions are made and implemented within the public sphere (Dunleavy, 2006; Lips, 2019). In traditional administrative settings, decision-making processes are strictly according to the law, respecting principles such as the rule of law, transparency, and accountability (OECD, 2023; Wieringa, 2023). Yet, with the automation of public tasks, these principles might be at risk since many of these smart government mechanisms are often opaque due to the variety, velocity, and volume of data constantly processed out of their initial processing context. As highlighted by Danielle Citron, opacity shields these automated systems from internal scrutiny under the disguise of cost savings, consistency, and responsiveness of the public sector. Other guarantees, such as human-in-the-loop, are also problematic since literature has shown that humans tend to perceive automated systems as error-free and are less likely to search for information by themselves, a phenomenon that is known as automation bias (Citron, 2007). In addition, the increasing reliance on automated processes elevates the potential for false positives caused by faulty algorithms or biased datasets, which may result in unnecessary public spending and tragic outcomes at the detriment of vulnerable individuals such as immigrants and socially excluded groups (Kordzadeh & Ghasemaghaei, 2022; Perez Vallejos et al., 2017; Citron, 2007).

In the previously highlighted examples, these internal consequences are visible. In the case of Norway's "Norwegian Labour and Welfare Administration" (Nye arbeids- og velferdsetaten, "NAV"), the system mishandled the processing of several services and benefits by incorrectly interpreting both national and European regulatory frameworks. This misinterpretation was not apparent to any public servant due to the opaqueness of the system. Automation bias could have played a large role since it took 26 years for the error to be identified. The same can be said about the SyRI scandal. The SyRI system was deemed to be "intentionally opaque," lacking the transparency required by any administrative practice—besides removing any type of internal and external oversight process—with no *ex-ante* or *ex-post* human intervention.

Externally, citizens are also greatly affected by smart government practices (Lyon, 2007). As previously mentioned, smart governments heavily rely on data to work a practice that, besides transforming individuals into "data points," violates their right to private life. This was the conclusion reached by the District Court of The Hague in its ruling on *NCJM* et al. *and FNV v The State of the Netherlands* related to the SyRi case. The Court mentioned practices that demand continuous widespread collection of citizen data, and that the processing of this data through artificial intelligence systems violates citizens' human rights and the right to private life. The Court emphasized that these governmental practices demand an intrusive system that proceeds with a large-scale, unstructured, automated linking of data from different sources, a practice that lacks proportionality in its violation of human rights (Rachovitsa & Johann, 2022).

The profiling and predictions that follow the widespread collection of data and back public policies with "data evidence" also create a non-empathetic and non-forgiving government since any mishap will reflect into the citizen's digital file, causing a butterfly effect within the whole administrative system due to its interconnection (Ranchordas & Scarcella, 2021). This impact is visible in the Chinese social scoring example, in which an individual who did not pay taxes is prevented from taking his children to a specific school or riding a high-speed train. Therefore, the smart government indeed becomes a seamless mechanism that weighs in citizens' lives, collecting information about all actions of individuals and registering every little misstep, similar to the novel *1984*s "Big Brother."

It is important to emphasize that vulnerable individuals are heavily impacted by smart government practices. This reality was visible in the SyRI, as families that were already on the fringe of society, such as single mothers and immigrants, were the ones that relied on social welfare benefits and were also more heavily targeted by algorithms as potential fraudsters (van Bekkum & Borgesius, 2021). The same can be observed in the Chinese social score system since this system depends on the digital interaction of citizens through digital apps, a practice that excludes digitally illiterate individuals, who will undoubtedly be overlooked by the government.

Concluding remarks and the path forward

The purpose of this study was to investigate the widespread use of technology by governments, known as "smart governments," and their negative effects, both internally within public administration and externally on citizens' rights and lives. Through this exploration, it became clear that the consequences of digitalizing public administration stem from the social impact of technology and the interaction between technology and individuals. It is crucial to focus on this interconnected relationship in order to fully acknowledge and address the harmful consequences of smart governments, as technology is often used as an opaque shield to avoid the accountability of public servants who implement it.

In this context, this chapter has shown the importance of abandoning the assumption that technology alone can solve all of the legal, technical, organizational, administrative, human, strategic, and political challenges faced by the public sector. It is crucial to assess which tasks can or should be automated, as well as the appropriate level of technology to be implemented by each ministry, office, and administrative employee (von Lucke & Grosse, 2017). This approach will help minimize automation risks and reduce the disruptive impact of haphazard technology adoption and deployment. Furthermore, the transformation of public sector values requires a reevaluation of the professional and ethical principles of public service, which should involve a democratic process engaging various stakeholders, including civil society (Lips, 2019).

It is important to establish limits and boundaries that restrict the use of automated decision-making in the public sector. This action will ensure that human decision-makers, who are properly trained to understand the full impact of their decisions, are more involved. Additionally, stronger protections should be put in place to uphold citizens' rights to due process in the context of digital administrative procedures based on due process and the right to informational self-determination (von Lucke & Grosse, 2017). This measure includes the implementation of internal mechanisms to ensure public administration principles and rules, such as transparency and due process, in the digital sphere.

To fully grasp the implications of these changes, it is essential to conduct comprehensive evaluations of both the technological solutions and the administrative processes that they seek to enhance. By involving a broad range of stakeholders—including public officials, technologists, ethicists, and the general public—we can ensure that the deployment of technology in public administration is both effective and ethically sound. This collaborative approach can help identify potential pitfalls and develop strategies to mitigate them, fostering a more transparent and accountable public administration. Moreover, public sector employees must be equipped with the necessary skills and knowledge to manage and operate these technologies effectively. Continuous training and education programs are vital to ensure that staff can navigate the complexities of digital tools while maintaining a focus on public service values. This measure not only enhances the efficiency of public administration, but also safeguards the rights and interests of citizens.

In conclusion, the integration of technology into public administration presents significant opportunities for improving efficiency and service delivery. However, it also poses substantial risks if not managed carefully.

Acknowledgment

The author has received funding from the European Union's Horizon 2020 research and innovation program under the GA n. 956562.

References

Abdoullaev, A. (2011). Keynote: A smart world: A development model for intelligent cities. In *11th IEEE International Conference on Computer and Information Technology (CIT)* (pp. 1–28). IEEE.

Andreassen, R., Kaun, A., & Nikunen, K. (2021). Fostering the data welfare state: A Nordic perspective on datafication. *Nordicom Review, 42*(2), 207–223.

Anthopoulos, L. G., & Reddick, C. G. (2016). Smart city and smart government: Synonymous or complementary? In *Proceedings of the 25th International Conference Companion on World Wide Web* (pp. 351–355). ACM.

Bellamy, C., & Taylor, J. A. (1998). *Governing in the information age*. Open University Press.

Bensaude Vincent, B. (2014). The politics of buzzwords at the interface of technoscience, market, and society: The case of 'public engagement in science'. *Public Understanding of Science, 23*(3), 238–253.

Budi, N. F. A., Fitriani, W. R., Hidayanto, A. N., Kurnia, S., & Inan, D. I. (2020). A study of government 2.0 implementation in Indonesia. *Socio-Economic Planning Sciences, 72*, 100920.

Cappers, R. T. J. (2006). The reconstruction of agricultural practices in ancient Egypt: An ethnoarchaeobotanical approach. *Palaeohistoria, 47*(48), 429–446.

Cellary, W. (2013). Smart governance for smart industries. In *Proceedings of the 7th International Conference on Theory and Practice of Electronic Governance* (pp. 91–93). ACM.

Chun, S. A., Shulman, S., Sandoval, R., & Hovy, E. (2010). Government 2.0: Making connections between citizens, data, and government. *Information Polity, 15*(1), 1.

Citron, D. K. (2007). Technological due process. *Washington University Law Review, 85*, 1249.

Curthoys, N., & Crabtree, J. (2003). *Smartgov: Renewing electronic government for improved service delivery*. Work Foundation.

Dunleavy, P., Margetts, H., Bastow, S., & Tinkler, J. (2006). New public management is dead—long live digital-era governance. *Journal of Public Administration Research and Theory, 16*(3), 467–494.

Elkin-Koren, N., & Gal, M. S. (2019). The chilling of governance-by-data on data markets. *The University of Chicago Law Review, 86*, 403.

Ellis, C. (2005). *Exploring the enigma*. University of Cambridge.

European Council of Lisbon. (2000). Europe – An information society for all. *Communication on a Commission initiative for the special European Council of Lisbon*, 23 and 24 March.

Foley, P., & Alfonso, X. (2009). eGovernment and the transformation agenda. *Public Administration, 87*(2), 371–396.

Fountain, J. E. (2004). *Building the virtual state: Information technology and institutional change*. Rowman & Littlefield.

Frank, T. (1924). Roman census statistics from 225 to 28 BC. *Classical Philology, 19*(4), 329–341.

Gauld, R., & Goldfinch, S. (2006). *Dangerous enthusiasms: E-government, computer failure and information system development*. University of Otago Press.

Giest, S. N., & Klievink, B. (2024). More than a digital system: how AI is changing the role of bureaucrats in different organizational contexts. *Public Management Review, 26*(2), 379–398.

Gil-Garcia, J. R., & Aldama-Nalda, A. (2013). Smart city initiatives and the policy context: The case of the rapid business opening office in Mexico City. In *Proceedings of the 7th International Conference on Theory and Practice of Electronic Governance* (pp. 234–237). ACM.

Gore, A. (1996). National partnership for re-inventing government. *National Press Club*. Retrieved December, 8, 2024. www.federalregister.gov/agencies/national-partnership-for-reinventing-government

Haggerty, K. D., Wilson, D., & Smith, G. J. D. (2011). Theorizing surveillance in crime control. *Theoretical Criminology, 15*(3), 231–237.

Halpern, O., Mitchell, R., & Geoghegan, B. D. (2017). The smartness mandate: Notes toward a critique. *Grey Room, 68*, 106–129.

Harlow, C. (1997). Back to basics: Reinventing administrative law. *Public Law, 2*, 245–261.

Harsh, A., & Ichalkaranje, N. (2015). Transforming e-government to smart government: A South Australian perspective. In *Intelligent Computing, Communication and Devices: Proceedings of ICCD 2014, Volume 1* (pp. 9–16). Springer India.

Hood, C. (1995). The "new public management" in the 1980s: Variations on a theme. *Accounting, Organizations, and Society, 20*(2–3), 93–109.

Janssen, D., Rotthier, S., & Snijkers, K. (2004). If you measure it they will score: An assessment of international eGovernment benchmarking. *Information Polity: The International Journal of Government and Democracy in the Information Age, 9*, 124–125.

Kaczorowski, W. (2014). *Die smarte Stadt-Den digitalen Wandel intelligent gestalten: Handlungsfelder Herausforderungen Strategien.* Richard Boorberg Verlag.

Kalogirou, V., & Charalabidis, Y. (2019). The European Union landscape on interoperability standardization: Status of European and national interoperability frameworks. In Keith Popplewell, Klaus-Dieter Thoben, Thomas Knothe, Raúl Poler (Eds.), *Enterprise Interoperability VIII: Smart Services and Business Impact of Enterprise Interoperability* (pp. 359–368). Springer International Publishing.

Kling, R., Crawford, H., Rosenbaum, H., Sawyer, S., & Weisband, S. (2000). *Learning from social informatics: Information and communication technologies in human contexts.* Center for Social Informatics, Indiana University.

Kordzadeh, N., & Ghasemaghaei, M. (2022). Algorithmic bias: Review, synthesis, and future research directions. *European Journal of Information Systems, 31*(3), 388–409.

Lee-Archer, B. (2023). *Effects of digitalization on the human centricity of social security administration and services.* International Labour Organization.

Lemke, F., Taveter, K., Erlenheim, R., Pappel, I., Draheim, D., & Janssen, M. (2020). Stage models for moving from e-government to smart government. In *Electronic Governance and Open Society: Challenges in Eurasia: 6th International Conference, EGOSE 2019, St. Petersburg, Russia, November 13–14, 2019, Proceedings 6* (pp. 152–164). Springer International Publishing.

Lips, M. (2019). *Digital government: Managing public sector reform in the digital era.* Routledge.

Lyon, D. (2007). *Surveillance studies: An overview.* Polity.

MacIntyre, A. (2007). *After virtue: A study in moral theory.* University of Notre Dame Press.

Matheus, R., Janssen, M., & Maheshwari, D. (2020). Data science empowering the public: Data-driven dashboards for transparent and accountable decision-making in smart cities. *Government Information Quarterly, 37*(3), 101284.

McLoughlin, I., & Wilson, R. (2013). *Digital government at work: A social informatics perspective.* OUP Oxford.

Melgaço, L., & van Brakel, R. (2021). Smart cities as surveillance theatre. *Surveillance & Society, 19*(2), 244–249.

Mellouli, S., Luna-Reyes, L. F., & Zhang, J. (2014). Smart government, citizen participation, and open data. *Information Polity, 19*(1–2), 1–4.

Montag, C., Becker, B., & Gan, C. (2018). The multipurpose application WeChat: A review on recent research. *Frontiers in Psychology, 9*, 408296.

Nam, T., & Pardo, T. A. (2011). Conceptualizing smart city with dimensions of technology, people, and institutions. In *Proceedings of the 12th Annual International Digital Government Research Conference: Digital Government Innovation in Challenging Times* (pp. 282–291). ACM.

Newman, J., & Mintrom, M. (2023). Mapping the discourse on evidence-based policy, artificial intelligence, and the ethical practice of policy analysis. *Journal of European Public Policy, 30*(9), 1839–1859.

OECD. (2023). The principles of public administration. *OECD.* www.sigmaweb.org/publications/Principles-of-Public-Administration-2023.pdf

Pentland, A. (2014). *Social physics: How good ideas spread-the lessons from a new science.* Penguin.

Perez Vallejos, E., Dowthwaite, L., Creswich, H., Gilbert, P., Koene, A., & Pereira, A. (2017). A critical reflection on the role of stakeholders in a public engagement process. *Social Science Computer Review, 35*(4), 602–619.

Pflücke, F. (2023). Interoperability in the EU: Paving the Way for Digital Public Services. *University of Luxembourg Law Research Paper*, 2023-14.

Prins, J. E. J., Broeders, D., & Griffioen, H. M. (2012). iGovernment: A new perspective on the future of government digitization. *Computer Law & Security Review, 28*(3), 273–282.

Rabinbach, A. (1992). *The human motor: Energy, fatigue, and the origins of modernity.* University of California Press.

Rachovitsa, A., & Johann, N. (2022). The human rights implications of the use of AI in the digital welfare state: Lessons learned from the Dutch SyRI case. *Human Rights Law Review, 22*(2), ngac010.

Ranchordas, S., & Scarcella, L. (2021). Automated government for vulnerable citizens: Intermediating rights. *William & Mary Bill of Rights Journal, 30,* 373.

Reitz, J. C. (2006). E-government. *The American Journal of Comparative Law, 54*(suppl_1), 733–754.

Roth, J., Greenburg, D., & Wille, S. (2004). *Monograph on terrorist financing* (p. 67). National Commission on Terrorist Attacks Upon the United States.

Rouwhorst, Z. (2022). *Internationale casusvergelijking socialezekerheidsschandaal.* Staat van de Uitvoering. Retrieved from https://staatvandeuitvoering.nl/onderzoek/internation ale-casusvergelijking-sociale-zekerheid-schandaal/

Schelin, S. H. (2007). E-government: An overview. In S. H. Schelin (Ed.), *Modern public information technology systems: Issues and challenges* (pp. 110–126). IGI Global Scientific Publishing.

Szreter, S., & Breckenridge, K. (2012, January). Recognition and registration: The infrastructure of personhood in world history. *Proceedings of the British Academy, 182,* 1–36.

Tapscott, D., Williams, A. D., & Herman, D. (2008). Government 2.0: Transforming government and governance for the twenty-first century. *New Paradigm, 1*(15), 1–21.

van Bekkum, M., & Borgesius, F. J. Z. (2021). Digital welfare fraud detection and the Dutch SyRI judgment. *European Journal of Social Security, 23*(4), 323–340.

Van Dijck, J. (2014). Datafication, dataism and dataveillance: Big Data between scientific paradigm and ideology. *Surveillance & Society, 12*(2), 197–208.

Van Zoonen, L. (2016). Privacy concerns in smart cities. *Government Information Quarterly, 33*(3), 472–480.

Von Lucke, J., & Grosse, K. (2017). Open approaches for smart government: Impulses from Germany. *Revue Internationale de droit des données et du numérique, 3,* 1–18.

Wieringa, M. (2023). "Hey SyRI, tell me about algorithmic accountability": Lessons from a landmark case. *Data & Policy, 5,* e2.

Wong, K. L. X., & Dobson, A. S. (2019). We're just data: Exploring China's social credit system in relation to digital platform ratings cultures in Westernised democracies. *Global Media and China, 4*(2), 220–232.

Yeung, K. (2023). The new public analytics as an emerging paradigm in public sector administration. *Tilburg Law Review, 27*(2), 1–32.

Yu, K. (2020). Towards graduated citizenship: A study of social credit systems in China. *Critique: A Worldwide Student Journal of Politics*, Spring 2020, 28–55.

7

AUGMENTING INEQUALITY

Socio-technical transformation of medicine and challenges to digital health citizenship (DHC) in the age of artificial intelligence (AI)

Gül Seçkin

Introduction

As we navigate the AI landscape, it is important to understand the implications, challenges, and opportunities arising from the exponential growth of healthcare data and technological advancements in natural language processing algorithms. This chapter examines how AI technologies pose challenges for medicine, clinical practice, and healthcare—specifically the impact on patient-doctor interaction, patient participation in clinical decision-making, patient empowerment, bias, diversity, equity, and social justice—all of which are critical considerations for promoting DHC (Petrakaki et al., 2021). With algorithms used to sense and interpret every patient's expression, behavior, and movement, the clinician's view of the patient becomes a data matrix that encodes their digital self. This assimilation of diverse data sources is pushing the limits of medical expertise, which could transform how we think about healthcare and challenge the traditional boundaries of medical expertise (Longoni et al., 2019). Therefore, SI research must understand how AI and other ICT technologies can influence the definitions and interpretations of health and disease.

The President's Council of Advisors on Science and Technology released a comprehensive report on June 30, 2020, which highlighted the need for significant investment in the field of artificial intelligence (U.S. DOE Office of Science, 2020). The report recommended that the federal government increase its funding for AI research and development by a factor of 10 over the next decade. The report noted that such investment would not only bolster research, but also support the development of AI applications in various fields, including healthcare, transportation, and national security. The report emphasized that the benefits of such investment would be substantial and far-reaching, both in terms of economic

DOI: 10.4324/9781032678542-11

growth and societal development. In recent years, programmers have focused on developing ML as a form of AI. ML teaches computer systems to recognize, sort, and predict outcomes by analyzing existing data sets. Computer scientists, engineers, and data scientists input existing data to train ML systems to make autonomous decisions. This decision-making then affects the social world, supporting or making determinations about various aspects of life, including medicine and health.

ML is emerging as a transformative force in the healthcare industry, leveraging vast datasets to enhance medical decision-making (Bhagat & Kanyal, 2024). This technology has the potential to revolutionize healthcare by enabling predictive analytics, personalized treatment recommendations, and the development of innovative diagnostic tools. However, it is imperative to understand how ML models are trained and the ethical considerations surrounding the usage of sensitive health data (Mestari et al., 2024). The European Union is governed by the General Data Protection Regulation (GDPR) for data privacy and protection, while the USA adheres to the Health Insurance Portability and Accountability Act (HIPAA) for health data. Various techniques are employed to ensure patient privacy while utilizing health data for training ML models. Data anonymization is a crucial step involving the removal of personally identifiable information before the data is used for training purposes (Zuo et al., 2021). This measure safeguards individual privacy while allowing the data to contribute to advancements in healthcare. Additionally, pseudonymization is employed, replacing personally identifiable information with unique identifiers to protect patient confidentiality further (Yadav et al., 2023). Understanding these safeguards is essential for the responsible and ethical use of healthcare data in training ML models, ultimately contributing to advancing patient care and healthcare innovation.

The interface between the health domain and other societal domains is creating new "health data protection grey zones" (Lievevrouw & Van Hoyweghen, 2019), where distinctions between different types of data (e.g., health versus lifestyle, sensitive versus non-sensitive, and personal vs. non-personal) and data uses (e.g., medical versus commercial) are becoming increasingly unclear (Marelli et al., 2020). With the increasing potential for integration and connection between different datasets, seemingly innocuous information such as shopping records and lifestyle habits could potentially reveal sensitive details, such as health status, or lead to assumptions about intimate aspects of an individual (Soumia et al., 2024). This reality is particularly relevant for "quasi-health data" encompassing personal information not explicitly related to health status—such as dietary, sleep, or exercise habits—yet capable of indicating a person's current or future physiological or pathological state (Ostherr, 2022). The boundary between non-sensitive and sensitive personal data is becoming less clear. The categorization of such data as sensitive, along with the potential eligibility for special protections under regulations like the GDPR, remains uncertain and is a subject of debate.

ML systems also draw on real-time data generated through the everyday use of computer technologies and sensor devices like smartphones and security cameras (Bi et al., 2019). These technologies disrupt the traditional boundaries between healthcare and other societal domains, making them increasingly unstable and porous (Marelli et al., 2020). As a result, any processing of regular data categories can quickly escalate into the processing of special categories of personal data. This complication undermines the original rationale for establishing this distinction, along with the regulatory framework built around it, while also diluting the significance and message conveyed by this framework regarding the heightened level of protection for sensitive data. This factor also challenges prevailing legal classifications of various types of data (such as sensitive, health-related, and anonymous data), which are currently placed in separate regulatory categories (Ostherr, 2022). Researchers have taken advantage of this data to further ML research and applications. The privacy of medical data is primarily governed by federal and state laws, with HIPAA being the main regulator. HIPAA oversees patient data collected by healthcare providers and their associates for treatment, payment, or healthcare operations. Privacy discussions often revolve around concerns regarding HIPAA, particularly the potential re-identification of de-identified data. Medical and health information outside of HIPAA may be shared voluntarily by consumers, recorded by companies tracking consumer behavior, or inferred through predictive models (Bi et al., 2019; Marelli et al., 2020).

It is important to recognize the different regulatory practices governing the collection, storage, and analysis of data within and outside of clinical settings. Traditional medical spaces like hospitals and physician offices are subject to laws such as HIPAA. As mentioned before, HIPAA is intended to safeguard personally identifiable health information and applies to "covered entities" such as doctors, hospitals, pharmacists, health insurers, and health maintenance organizations. However, the HIPAA Security Rule has a restricted scope and does not encompass numerous entities handling personal health information, including websites where consumers input health-related search terms, purchase non-prescription medications, or share personal health narratives (Ostherr, 2022). In essence, HIPAA solely pertains to personal health information in narrowly defined medical contexts, neglecting broadly interpreted health contexts.

As AI technologies evolve, it is crucial to understand how AI algorithms and digital data transform medical institutions, medical culture, and healthcare practices. Computer scientists and engineers must develop a deeper understanding of the implications, challenges, and opportunities arising from the exponential growth of natural language processing algorithms. Digital health technologies raise theoretical and political questions about how health, illness, and body concepts are generated or transformed for laypeople and professionals. These technologies have significant implications for medical power, knowledge, the doctor-patient relationship, and digital health citizenship. Due to ongoing technological advancements and the ability to link datasets, there is a heightened risk that supposedly anonymous data can be traced back to individuals. Even de-identified data carries a residual risk of re-identification in many cases, making current regulations around anonymous and identifiable data inadequate for protecting individuals' data. Scholars argue that these classifications are outdated and ineffective, especially in the post-digital era. With the challenges posed by AI, big data analytics, machine learning, and algorithms, data protection can no longer be static. Instead, regulations may need to be tailored to specific data processing activities, eliminating predefined distinctions based solely on the nature of the data.

SI researchers must therefore focus on these topics to understand the various dimensions of human data and how they intersect with systems of data regulation (Lazer et al., 2020; Cottom, 2020). The advancement of AI applications in healthcare is part of a broader shift toward digital health practices integrating data from both clinical and non-clinical settings (Ostherr, 2022). There are various applications of ML, including de-identifying personal health information, research subject recruitment, coding, and surveillance. Popular ML algorithms include artificial neural networks and decision trees to discern patterns in the data and make informed predictions or decisions based on these patterns. ML has been used to de-identify personal health information from clinical records, making them suitable for public research use without individual informed consent. Text mining and ML algorithms have also been used to identify patients who may benefit from participation in clinical studies. This process involves using algorithms that allows the computer to identify patterns in the data and make predictions or decisions based on those patterns (El Naqa & Murphy, 2015).

This chapter proposes that the DHC rely on the agency and rights of individuals and communities to control as well as benefit from data and information generated by AI health technologies and services, despite the belief held by AI practitioners that data generated about humans represents a single, objective reality. This assumption can exacerbate concerns about the potential for AI technology in healthcare to amplify existing inequalities (Wu et al., 2022). Data is not neutral, but rather value-laden, often contributing to social stratification. Differences reflect social relations not fully explained by the raw data points themselves. Computer scientists need to realize that data about one thing, such as ZIP codes or health records, may also be data about other things, such as class and race inequalities or socioeconomic status (Joyce et al., 2021). SI understands that what counts as data is socialized, politicized, and multi-layered, as data about humans often reflects structural inequalities related to gender, race, or class (Cirillo et al., 2020). It is therefore crucial to have a SI approach, as the uncritical use of human data in AI socio-technical systems will likely reproduce and even exacerbate pre-existing social inequalities.

SI in the context of AI

SI is a dynamic interdisciplinary field that explores information technologies' implications and outcomes in institutional and cultural contexts (Dourish, 2016; Kling, 2007). The research in this field focuses on the social aspects of computerization, examining the role of information technology in driving social and organizational changes, exploring the use of information technologies in social contexts, and analyzing how social forces and practices shape the social organization of information technologies. SI emphasizes empirical research to uncover the complex relationships among people, ICTs, and the social structures that shape their development and use (Pedersen & Sudzina, 2023; Longoni & Bonezzi, 2019).

The emergence of AI has sparked widespread discussion, but its impact on medicine and public health has yet to receive the attention that it deserves from researchers in SI. As AI becomes increasingly integrated into data organization, outcome prediction, and social information management systems, it becomes deeply embedded in our society as a socio-technical system. This term emphasizes recognizing the values, institutional practices, and inequalities built into AI's code, design, and usage. Designing AI is not merely about technological design, but also raises fundamental questions regarding power, social order, and digital health inequalities. Data are not inherently fair, objective, or impartial. Data often reflect societal biases and inequality, which can extend to predictive care models. During the early 2000s, scholars from various fields—such as social informatics, sociology, communication, and science and technology studies—began investigating algorithms, code, and platforms. They examined how algorithmic decision-making, social categories, and cultural contexts are interconnected. However, less attention has been paid to how complex social realities are transformed into algorithmic systems and the normative assumptions that drive these processes (Sikstrom et al., 2022). This topic is particularly important given that biases in AI models can have far-reaching consequences, such as perpetuating inequality and discrimination in areas like healthcare (Sasseville et al., 2023).

Algorithms cannot exist in isolation from the conditions under which they are created and used (Geiger et al., 2023; Kitchin, 2017). This is to say that algorithms have to be seen as interconnected, contingent, and influenced by the broader context in which they operate. From this perspective, an algorithm is just one part of a larger system and cannot be considered a purely technical, objective, or impartial form of knowledge or operation (Kitchin & Lauriault, 2018). In addition to critically examining the nature of algorithms, it is also important to consider their impact, effects, and power. Just as algorithms are not neutral or impartial expressions of knowledge, their actions are not without bias or political influence (Kitchin & Lauriault, 2018).

Algorithms search, organize, categorize, group, analyze, model, simulate, visualize, and regulate people, processes, and places. They shape our understanding of the world and actively contribute to altering the world through their use as software, with significant consequences (Kitchin & Dodge, 2011). In this sense, they actively influence outcomes and events (Mackenzie & Vurdubakis, 2011). The use of algorithms carries significant implications, as they are not neutral; rather, they construct and implement systems of power and knowledge. Algorithms have the potential to influence behavior and control interactions within various systems, whether they are designed for empowerment, entertainment, or enlightenment. They can also serve as pathways for capitalist power and may have unintended consequences if left unsupervised (Lash, 2007; Steiner, 2012). Additionally, algorithms can be biased or make errors due to bugs or miscoding (Diakopoulos, 2020; Drucker, 2013). It is important to recognize that algorithms are not solely the products of programmers but are part of a larger technological system that includes infrastructure, hardware, code platforms, data, and interfaces. Similarly, databases and repositories are not just technical means of assembling and sharing data but are complex socio-technical systems embedded within a larger institutional landscape (Kitchin, 2023; Ruppert, 2012). They are influenced by engineering and industrial practices, political agendas, and institutional ideologies—shaping what questions can be asked, how they are asked, and who can ask them (Hecht, 2001; Lauriault, 2012; Ruppert, 2012). Algorithms are not neutral; they create and enforce systems of power and knowledge (Kushner, 2013). Their use has normative implications and is used to influence, control, regulate, and guide interactions within different systems. This concept applies to systems designed for empowerment, entertainment, and enlightenment, all based on defined rule sets that determine system behavior in any given situation.

The role of algorithms in shaping behaviors is not only fascinating, but also significant.

Algorithms, often hidden, serve as channels through which capitalist power operates (Lash, 2007, p. 71). Additionally, algorithms can have unintended consequences and unforeseen side effects when unsupervised; they may carry out unanticipated actions (Steiner, 2012). Furthermore, algorithms can be biased or make errors due to bugs or coding mistakes (Diakopoulos, 2020; Drucker, 2013). In this sense, algorithms are not only defined by what programmers create or the effects that they have, but are integral parts of a technological stack that encompasses infrastructure, hardware, code platforms, data, and interfaces, and are influenced by various forms of knowledge, legalities, governmental processes, institutions, marketplaces, and finance, among other factors. A comprehensive understanding of algorithms, therefore, is not just a goal, but a necessity for anyone working in these fields, requiring a holistic examination of their entire socio-technical assemblage—including an analysis of the reasons behind subjecting the system to computational logic in the first place. Similarly, databases and repositories are not simply neutral technical means of assembling and sharing data but are bundles of contingent and relational processes that have real-world implications (Kitchin, 2023). They are complex socio-technical systems embedded within a larger institutional landscape of researchers, institutions, and corporations (Ruppert, 2012) and are subject to socio-technical regimes "grounded in ... engineering and industrial practices, technological artifacts, political programs, and institutional ideologies which act together to govern technological development" (Hetch, 2001, p. 257). Databases and repositories are expressions of knowledge and power, shaping what questions can be asked, how they are asked, how they are answered, how the answers are used, and who can ask them (Lauriault, 2012; Ruppert, 2012; Kitchin & Lauriault, 2018).

Machine learning

ML is a powerful subset of AI that enables computers to learn without explicit programming (Alpaydin, 2021). Instead of being explicitly programmed, ML systems learn from data to make predictions or classifications. ML can be broadly categorized into "supervised" and "unsupervised" learning. In supervised learning, the computer learns by fitting models to the data, usually with a known outcome. This process includes techniques like linear and logistic regression, as well as popular ML algorithms such as decision trees and support vector machines (Sidey-Gibbons & Sidey-Gibbons, 2019). On the other hand, unsupervised learning involves the algorithm identifying natural relationships and groupings within the data without any reference to a specific outcome. Unsupervised learning is similar to statistical approaches that aim to identify unspecified subgroups with similar characteristics, using clustering algorithms to group observations based on similar data characteristics.

The quality and quantity of data significantly impact the model's performance, highlighting the crucial role of data in the learning process. ML models learn by processing data through algorithms that iteratively adjust model parameters to minimize prediction errors. This data might include patient records, medical images, and genetic information in healthcare (Sidey-Gibbons & Sidey-Gibbons, 2019). Refining ML model parameters is a collaborative process involving ML engineers, data scientists, domain experts, and automated tools. The complexity of these processes can vary and may involve several stages of sophisticated human-machine interactions and decision-making. Combining human expertise and algorithmic optimization ensures that the model learns effectively from the data, achieving high performance in making predictions or decisions. This learning process underscores the importance of the data, as it allows the models to identify patterns and relationships in the data, enabling them to make predictions and decisions (Bi et al., 2019).

As the inner workings of most algorithmic systems are only understood by experts, it can be challenging for clinicians, patients, and families to understand their results. This difficulty is known as the black box problem of algorithmic systems (Sikstrom et al., 2022; Longoni et al., 2019). Machine learning models are designed to learn from data; as a result, they can potentially inherit any biases present in the data. This possibility is especially concerning in healthcare, where biased models could lead to unfair or inaccurate diagnoses (Kitchin & Lauriault, 2018). Such a plausible outcome suggests that AI could undermine patient autonomy and increase worries about the potential disempowerment of individuals in managing their health (Gupta & Mircheva, 2023). It is important to note that AI algorithmic bias extends beyond the technical definition and encompasses broader societal implications (Chen et al., 2023). There is also a risk of automation bias, as it could lead to an overreliance on AI systems. This possibility may result in patients placing more trust in machines than in doctors, which could have implications for the doctor-patient relationship—potentially impacting trust dynamics in healthcare settings (Jeyakumar et al., 2023).

There is a growing concern about the potential for these models to propagate or introduce biases toward susceptible groups based on characteristics such as: age, gender identity, sexual orientation, race, ethnicity, or socioeconomic status (Chu et al., 2022). Furthermore, there are theoretical and political questions about how health, illness, and body concepts are generated or transformed for laypeople and professionals by AI technologies, which—in turn—have significant implications for medical power, knowledge, doctor-patient relationships, professional work practices, and identities (Noble, 2018). It is imperative to critically evaluate and address these biases to ensure that machine learning models provide equitable and reliable insights into healthcare decision-making.

Artificial bias, real consequences

Large Language Models (LLMs), which are AI systems, can analyze text-based data such as electronic health records (EHR) and clinical notes to group patients into risk categories based on their likelihood of developing complications or experiencing disease progression. This functionality can help to identify individuals at high risk of developing specific diseases. LLMs equipped with natural language processing (NLP) capabilities can analyze vast amounts of patient data including symptoms, treatments, and outcomes. NLP is used to extract insights from the textual information in patient records, including structured and unstructured data. LLMs are particularly adept at understanding contextual nuances and relationships within natural language, enabling them to identify subtle factors in clinical narratives. They can identify patterns indicating disease progression or complications over time by analyzing the temporal sequence of events in patient records. Furthermore, LLMs can detect potential risk factors by recognizing correlations between different aspects of a patient's health history. They extract features from the text that may indicate risk factors, including mentions of symptoms, changes in medication, lifestyle factors, and other contextual information. LLMs can calculate a risk score—a probability indicating the likelihood of complications or disease progression based on the identified features. Based on the calculated risk scores, LLMs categorize patients into risk strata, such as low, medium, or high-risk categories. This ability allows for creating individualized risk profiles that can guide healthcare providers in tailoring treatment decisions and interventions to specific risk levels.

Algorithms are rules that guide how an AI system processes data and makes decisions. One concern with AI systems is that they may rely on biased algorithms. While algorithms can help to identify complex health needs and improve care management, they can exhibit significant racial bias (National Institute for Health Care Management, 2021). If an AI system considers race when assessing the likelihood of a disease or the need for treatment, it may not provide appropriate care to different racial groups (Noble, 2018). AI systems can produce social bias and discrimination based on data, algorithms, or models that do not consider the diversity of different social groups, such as those based on race, gender, age, or disability (Abnousi et al., 2019). These groups may not be adequately represented, accurately represented, or included in the design or evaluation of AI systems and the data used to train or test AI systems. If an algorithm is biased or unfair, it may use irrelevant or discriminatory factors, such as race or gender, to predict outcomes or allocate resources (Agency for Healthcare Research and Quality, 2023). Race and ethnicity are often associated with different health outcomes for minority patients compared to white patients. For example, an algorithm was found to recommend less healthcare for black patients than for white patients with the same conditions (Obermeyer et al., 2019). This discrimination could lead to unequal or inadequate treatment and biased or misleading outputs. AI systems may not even align with these social groups' values, needs, or preferences (Heinrichs, 2022).

Ensuring algorithmic fairness in medical practice is crucial to prevent ML from worsening healthcare inequalities (Grote & Keeling, 2022). However, it is surprising that there has been little discussion about this issue. The use of AI tools could intensify the structural inequalities that already exist (Wu et al., 2022). For example, if the data used to train an AI system are from a predominantly white and male population, the AI system may favor those characteristics over others. Similarly, if the data used are influenced by historical or structural inequalities—such as racism, sexism, ageism, or ableism—the AI system may reproduce or reinforce those inequalities (Joyce et al., 2021). This result is often due to the data sources or social contexts that shape the development and deployment of the AI system (Orwat, 2020). Additionally, if developers or users of the AI system have biases or stereotypes about certain groups of people, they may introduce or perpetuate those biases or stereotypes into the AI system (Stypińska & Franke, 2023; Sasseville et al., 2023). Significantly, social bias and discrimination in AI systems can threaten the accuracy, fairness, and impact of these systems on the health and well-being of different groups. Obermeyer et al. (2019) uncovered that AI systems utilized in US hospitals can generate discriminatory outcomes when decisions are solely based on insurance claims data. On the other hand, these biases are almost eliminated when the algorithm is trained on biological data from patients. Meanwhile, Murray et al. (2020) found that pre-installed AI tools for EHRs may classify personal traits such as ethnicity or religion as risk factors, thus perpetuating health disparities (Ostherr, 2022).

Different factors can influence AI bias, including data bias, which happens when the data used to train or test AI systems is not representative, accurate, or complete for the population or the problem (Wang et al., 2023). Collecting data for AI systems in healthcare involves gathering, organizing, labeling, and validating vast amounts of information from various sources like EHRs, medical images, genomic sequences, clinical trials, patient surveys, wearable devices, and social media. Different actors like healthcare providers, researchers, technology companies, governments, or patients can collect data for AI systems. For instance, if the data mostly comes from a particular group of people and excludes or underrepresents others, the AI system may perform poorly for those included (Fichman & Rosenbaum, 2014). Data bias can also result from errors or inaccuracies in the data collection or sampling. For example, if the data is labeled or categorized based on subjective and incorrect criteria like race or gender, the AI system may learn to associate these factors with the outcomes or decisions (NIH, 2024). When AI systems contain social bias and discrimination, it can lead to errors, inconsistencies, inaccuracies, or disparities that negatively affect certain groups' physical, mental, social, or economic health and well-being more than others (Leslie et al., 2021). An example of miscalibration in healthcare algorithms is using individual patients' health costs as the primary predictor. Black populations have limited access to healthcare due to various socioeconomic factors (Grote & Keeling, 2022). As a result, they may visit hospitals less frequently than their white counterparts, leading to disparities in health costs. When an algorithm utilizes previous healthcare spending to determine risk scores, this method can produce biased outcomes since black patients often have lower healthcare spending than white patients, even with the same health condition. This disparity results from the existing racial inequalities in the healthcare system. Improving the accuracy of health risk predictions for minority patients through algorithms involves addressing the lack of diversity in the training set, particularly regarding skin color. SI research must explore how these technologies might exacerbate or help to reduce social inequalities (Wu et al., 2022).

Bias in AI systems can occur for various reasons, like implicit bias and sampling bias. Implicit bias occurs when developers or users of AI systems have unconscious or hidden prejudices that affect their decisions and actions (Cirillo et al., 2020). Biases can also emerge when specific demographics are underrepresented during ML training (Grote & Keeling, 2022). Sampling bias occurs when the data used to train or test AI systems do not represent the population or domain that the systems are intended to serve. An AI system trained with data from one group may not generalize well to other groups, resulting in incorrect or inappropriate diagnoses and decisions (Murray et al., 2020). For instance, an AI system trained to detect skin cancer with data from mostly light-skinned individuals may exclude or underdiagnose individuals with different skin colors and/or skin features, creating a bias in the AI system that may fail to diagnose them correctly. Alternatively, an AI system trained with data from mostly male patients may fail to diagnose heart attacks in female patients. An AI system trained with data from mostly young adults may not recognize cognitive decline in older adults (Chu et al., 2022).

Algorithm bias can also result from errors or flaws in the algorithm design or implementation process, or when the algorithms used to process the data and make decisions are not fair, ethical, or accountable for the objectives and impacts (Karimian et al., 2022). For example, if the algorithms are not tested or validated for their performance and quality in diverse and realistic scenarios, the AI system may fail to generalize or adapt to new or changing situations. Output bias happens when the outputs produced by AI systems are not transparent, explainable, or understandable for users (Kawamleh, 2023). If the outputs are not clear or transparent about how or why the AI system makes decisions, users may unquestioningly trust or reject the outputs without knowing their validity or reliability. Output bias can also result from errors or misinterpretations in the output communication or presentation process. For example, if the outputs are tailored or customized for different audiences or purposes, users may need clarification. Therefore, data collection for AI systems in healthcare must ensure inclusiveness, diversity, transparency, and accountability of data sources, methods, and algorithms (Karimian et al., 2022; Green et al., 2024).

Privacy

As AI and related technologies become more integrated into the internet of health and medical things, there are increasing concerns that AI assessments of patients' digital footprints could map or even influence their healthcare experiences without their knowledge, consent, or ability to dispute the results (Winter & Davidson, 2020). A lawsuit known as Dinerstein v. Google has brought attention to privacy concerns regarding situations in which tech companies partner with clinical organizations to access health data for their AI systems. The case alleges that identifiable data from EHRs of thousands of patients treated at the University of Chicago Medical Center between 2009 and 2016 were shared with Google (Schencker, 2019). Despite being de-identified, the records contained time stamps that could easily re-identify a patient when combined with Google's access to geolocation and other types of data. This potential supports the plaintiff's claim that privacy rules were violated when Google obtained these records (Cohen & Mello, 2019). Recent reporting on another Google AI/EHR endeavor with Ascension health system shows that these efforts are part of a strategy to develop comprehensive digital health profiles of Google's enormous user base. Google filed a provisional patent in 2017 for a proprietary EHR system that would build on the company's mining of patient records to develop and sell AI-driven predictive EHRs for commercial gain. These privacy issues are similar to those of Google's DeepMind in 2017, when the company used patient records from the UK's National Health Service to build risk analytics tools without patient consent. Google still retains the capability to merge non-health-related consumer data and medical data without informing consumers or giving them the option to decline. These ethical and legal challenges like ensuring privacy, security, consent, and ownership of health data may affect data quality and reliability (Schneble et al., 2020; Yadav et al., 2023).

Socio-medical implications of AI from a SI perspective

The AI revolution is considered a new industrial revolution impacting all industries, including healthcare. The ability of AI to constantly capture and optimize vast amounts of data will significantly impact the accumulation and updating of medical knowledge, the discovery and acceleration of diagnostic methods, and the selection and implementation of treatment methods. In clinical medicine, advancements in AI technology and ML will significantly impact medical knowledge, diagnostic methods, and treatment selection. These technologies will change all aspects of medical practice and may influence the patient-doctor relationship. Even though AI has positive impacts, such as more accurate treatment selection and reduced workload for medical professionals, there are concerns about its limitations. It is therefore essential to understand the impact of AI on medical institutions and the implications for socio-medical interactions in the healthcare system (Tanaka et al., 2023).

The medical process of shared decision-making involves recognizing patients' unique life circumstances, preferences, and cultural backgrounds, which influence their healthcare choices. Collaborative decision-making involves patients and doctors working together to make treatment decisions considering medical expertise and patient preferences. This communication fosters empathy, humanizes medical care, and engenders a sense of agency for patients in their healthcare journeys. This approach encourages patient autonomy, empowering patients to take an active role in their medical care rather than being passive recipients of medical advice. AI may generate a different diagnosis than a human physician, and it may not be able to consider patients' values and preferences comprehensively (Tanaka et al., 2023). Human physicians are better equipped to consider patients' values, wishes, and contexts because such understanding involves multiple factors and elements (Tanaka et al., 2023).

The deployment of AI in medicine can be challenging to comprehend, mainly when it involves complicated algorithms or deep learning techniques (Oxholm et al., 2022). This shift is particularly relevant, as the patient-centered healthcare model emphasizes collaboration and shared decision-making within the healthcare ecosystem. Lack of transparency in data access and use could potentially erode patients' trust in using AI for care delivery (Jeyakumar et al., 2023). The involvement of AI in the decision-making process can create power imbalances. This possible outcome can affect the trust and confidence of both patients and healthcare professionals, making it difficult for them to question or challenge the decisions made by AI. For instance, if a patient is diagnosed with cancer, they would want to understand how AI technology arrived at that decision. Patients may not be satisfied with AI diagnosis or treatment without understanding its reasoning. They may perceive that AI, backed by advanced algorithms and data, has greater authority in decision-making, which could compromise the collaborative nature of the decision-making process.

To avoid creating a gap between AI algorithms and human understanding, we must focus on AI transparency. Moreover, patients value human judgment when making care decisions, even with the high accuracy and advancements in AI technologies. In addition, patients may find it challenging to form the same level of rapport and trust with AI systems as they do with human physicians (Dalton-Brown, 2020). Empathy, compassion, and trust play a significant role in the sustainability of AI innovations. Research has shown that patients value interaction with clinicians over AI technology alone (Jeyakumar et al., 2023). These socio-medical implications require careful consideration and proactive measures to ensure that the technology is used to enhance, rather than undermine, the human connection between patients and healthcare providers.

AI introduces new challenges, including low transparency and a high degree of autonomy for "black box" AI algorithms (Denecke et al., 2019). This lack of transparency raises concerns about accountability and trust in healthcare decision-making (Ostherr, 2022). The involvement of an algorithm as a third party in the therapeutic relationship can give rise to conflicts when the practitioner cannot justify the algorithm's suggestions or decisions. The inner workings of AI algorithms can be opaque to protect intellectual property, making it difficult to understand how they reach their conclusions (Lazer et al., 2020). Such opacity may impede the development of a shared understanding between the practitioner and the patient, ultimately leading to harm in the therapeutic alliance (Dalton-Brown, 2020). While AI offers efficiency and accuracy, it therefore raises concerns about shifting away from shared decision-making (Fossa et al., 2018). By ensuring transparency, AI systems can help healthcare professionals understand how it formulates its recommendations and explain its reasoning process to patients (Wang et al., 2023). This capability is particularly important for healthcare professionals and patients, who must trust that AI recommendations are well-founded and appropriate.

Patients prefer interacting with healthcare professionals who have clinical expertise and provide empathetic and compassionate care. However, establishing patient trust becomes increasingly difficult in a rapidly evolving digital space with complex and less transparent AI technologies. Patients expressed that physicians should verify the accuracy of the AI algorithm output and use it as a second opinion to inform clinical decisions. In a disagreement between the physician and the AI technology, patients prefer the physician's judgment as the final decision. Despite the use of AI to accelerate innovations in patient care and the need for patient voices, there is limited literature on patient engagement and their perceptions of how AI will affect care delivery (Jeyakumar et al., 2023). Patients who interacted solely with AI technologies reported a lack of compassion and empathy as well as limited opportunities to ask follow-up questions, discuss treatment options, and receive emotional support. It is therefore crucial to understand the challenges and opportunities arising from these fields' convergence.

The communication dynamics could change, with AI-generated data taking precedence over the patient's narrative, potentially disrupting the collaborative aspect of shared decision-making. AI may reduce the significance of the patient's subjective experience of illness, such as their symptoms, feelings, values, and preferences. This potential could make patients feel disempowered, with reduced agency and control over their health and treatment choices. In some cases, patients may feel ignored or dismissed by healthcare professionals who rely more on AI data than on the patient's account. The communication structure may change, as AI-driven information is presented technically, potentially reducing the interpersonal aspects of the relationship (Dalton-Brown, 2020). When or if patients feel that AI-generated decisions are prioritized over their input, they may feel powerless. The integration of AI into medical decision-making has the potential to strain the doctor-patient relationship. Patients' trust in doctors may be diminished as they question the role of AI in treatment decisions. Patients may question the reliability of AI-powered decisions that they do not fully understand. They may feel disconnected from shared experiences and empathetic interactions due to the perceived absence of human judgment. This information asymmetry could lead to a power struggle in which patients feel sidelined by an algorithmic approach that lacks human empathy (Kasapoglu, 2020).

The complexity of AI-generated explanations may make it difficult for patients to participate in decision-making actively. Such an outcome can hinder the natural flow of communication that builds the doctor-patient relationship. Patients may perceive themselves as passive receivers of predetermined algorithms, which can also limit their sense of control and agency. This shift disrupts the participative, human-centered decision-making process and can alienate patients (Longoni et al., 2019). As AI's role in medicine evolves, it lacks humans' empathetic touch and capabilities (NIH, 2024). AI-powered medical platforms should be seen as tools to enhance decision-making, not to replace human expertise and judgment (Green et al., 2024). Healthcare professionals must ultimately be responsible for decisions made using language-model-powered tools. It is vital to maintain a human-centered approach to healthcare (Kasapoglu, 2020; Johnson, 2022).

Promising potentials, implications, recommendations

Integrating human creativity and AI can revolutionize the healthcare industry as well as create a more equitable and efficient healthcare system (Bhagat & Kanyal, 2024). However, to maximize AI's benefits for all stakeholders, SI research must develop and implement fairness metrics and methods. Algorithmic bias is often a result of the human bias that individual programmers have coded into AI, and they require better training (NIH, 2024). Therefore, practical and actionable guidelines can help AI developers to design, test, and evaluate AI systems for fairness as well as reduce the risk of biased outcomes (Vorisek et al., 2023). Some detailed recommendations include:

1 *Inclusive Data Collection and Utilization*: To ensure that AI algorithms are fair, accurate, and representative of all communities, SI research must advocate

for the development and use of more comprehensive, diverse, and inclusive datasets. This aim can be achieved through collaborations among healthcare institutions, community organizations, and AI developers.

2 *Ethical Algorithm Design and Transparency*: To avoid biases and discrimination in AI, algorithms used within healthcare, ethical guidelines, and frameworks for designing AI algorithms should be designed. Transparency, fairness, and accountability should be prioritized throughout the AI development and implementation.

3 *Diverse Representation in AI Development:* One of the main challenges with AI in healthcare is the quality of data that it is trained on. To overcome this challenge, there is a need for more inclusive datasets that accurately reflect the health experiences of various marginalized social, racial, and ethnic groups. It is crucial to involve communities in developing and using AI to prevent biased outcomes and build trust among the most vulnerable stakeholders (Sasseville et al., 2023). By doing so, we can ensure that AI is used responsibly to improve healthcare and advance health equity (Hendricks-Sturrup et al., 2023; Berdahl et al., 2023). It is also essential to increase diversity and representation within the teams developing and deploying AI algorithms (Green et al., 2024). This aim can be achieved by providing opportunities for underrepresented groups and promoting diverse hiring practices.

4 *Establishment of Ethical Standards*: There is a need to formulate and implement clear ethical standards specific to AI applications in healthcare. These standards should focus on reducing biases in AI-driven models, ensuring transparency, and overseeing AI algorithms' responsible development and deployment to avoid exacerbating disparities. It is essential to involve all stakeholders in the development of these standards.

5 *Citizen Engagement:* Some communities may hesitate to use AI and ML technology due to concerns about privacy, data protection, and the potential for biased algorithms. A great deal of AI and ML today is developed without the meaningful engagement of individuals and communities, even when those individuals and communities have unknowingly generated data used by AI and ML models (Hendricks-Sturrup et al., 2023). This absence often leads to biased outcomes regarding who benefits from the technology's development and application. The under-engagement of communities in research, development, and use of AI and ML often needs to reflect more knowledge and crucial understandings about AI and ML, including how it is used in healthcare settings to advance health-related innovations and solutions (Hendricks-Sturrup et al., 2023).

6 *Fundamental Rights Impact Assessment*: Robust data anonymization techniques and strict access controls are essential to protect patients' privacy (Zuo et al., 2021). It is also vital to ensure that AI systems do not perpetuate biases. Rigorous testing for biases across different demographic groups is necessary. Additionally, transparency about data sources and model training can help to

identify and address any unintended biases. AI should augment human decision-making, not replace it entirely. Healthcare providers must retain the ability to override AI recommendations when necessary. Informed consent should cover AI involvement in diagnosis, treatment, and data sharing.

7 *Feminist Impact Assessment*: AI systems should be developed and trained using data that effectively represents women and other gender minorities, encompassing diversity in age, race, socioeconomic status, and health conditions. It is crucial to identify and mitigate biases in AI algorithms that could result in discriminatory practices (Kumar & Choudhury, 2022). For example, historical underrepresentation of women may lead to AI models performing less effectively when using women's data. It is imperative that AI systems do not perpetuate existing healthcare disparities. Intersectional factors that influence health outcomes—such as race, socioeconomic status, and disability—should be considered and reflected in the training data. Additionally, the development of AI systems supporting personalized medicine should consider gender differences in symptoms, disease progression, and treatment responses (Epker, 2023). AI systems should effectively address conditions that predominantly affect women, such as reproductive health issues, breast cancer, and autoimmune diseases. Importantly, training should be provided for developers and healthcare providers to recognize and address gender biases in AI.

Implementing these principles requires collaborative efforts from developers, healthcare providers, policymakers, and communities to create a more equitable healthcare system.

Conclusions

While AI has essential potential in healthcare, factors such as varying socioeconomic conditions, healthcare infrastructures, regulatory frameworks, and cultural factors can significantly impact the adoption and effectiveness of AI technologies (Upadhyay et al., 2023). Improving the trustworthiness of AI-based applications is particularly crucial in the medical field, and explainability plays a vital role in achieving this goal (Wang et al., 2023). Ensuring that AI algorithms are technically sound as well as culturally and linguistically appropriate is critically essential. It is worth noting that these challenges may vary within specific regions and may evolve over time (Upadhyay et al., 2023). This complexity requires a multifaceted approach integrating technical advancements, policy standardization, capacity building, and global collaboration. Another important consideration is that cultural and ethical nuances may differ, influencing the acceptance and adoption of AI-based healthcare solutions. Overcoming these disparities in AI healthcare implementation requires careful consideration and a flexible approach that complies with local laws, respects cultural norms, and develops customized solutions. To maximize the potential of AI in healthcare across diverse regions worldwide, it is essential to take a comprehensive approach that considers all of these factors. By doing so, we can ensure that the deployment of AI in healthcare is not only technically sound, but also culturally appropriate and equitable (Green et al., 2024).

Despite the above discussed concerns, there is a rapid push to accelerate AI development in the United States. On February 11, 2019, then-President Trump signed Executive Order 13859, announcing the American AI Initiative: the U.S. national strategy on AI. SI researchers acknowledge that the design and use of information systems are not solely technical, but also involve social factors (Sawyer & Tyworth, 2006). By exploring the complex interplay between technology and society, SI offers a comprehensive framework for understanding how information technologies shape and are shaped by social norms, power relations, and cultural values. SI is, therefore, a crucial field of study that offers valuable insights into the complex interactions between technology and society. By understanding how ICTs are designed, used, and experienced in different social contexts, we can develop more effective policies and technologies that benefit everyone in society (Sawyer & Tyworth, 2006). Introducing new technologies can lead to unforeseen consequences. As we continue to develop more advanced ICT technologies and use them in various aspects of social life, we encounter new theoretical challenges for SI (Kling, 2007; Dourish, 2016). In this respect, the SI approach provides an invaluable theoretical framework and analytical foundation (Wu et al., 2022).

References

Abnousi, F., Rumsfeld, J. S., & Krumholz, H. M. (2019). Social determinants of health in the digital age: Determining the source code for nurture. *Journal of American Medical Association, 321, 3*, 247–248.

Agency for Healthcare Research and Quality. (2023). *Impact of healthcare algorithms on racial and ethnic disparities in health and healthcare*. Agency for Healthcare Research and Quality.

Alpaydin, E. (2021). *Machine learning*. MIT Press.

Berdahl, C. T., Baker, L., Mann, S., Osoba, O., & Girosi, F. (2023). Strategies to improve the impact of artificial intelligence on health equity: Scoping review. *JMIR AI, 2*, e42936.

Bhagat, S. V., & Kanyal, D. (2024). Navigating the future: The transformative impact of artificial intelligence on hospital management-a comprehensive review. *Cureus, 16*(2), e54518. https://doi.org/10.7759/cureus.54518

Bi, Q., Goodman, K. E., Kaminsky, J., & Lessler, J. (2019). What is machine learning? A primer for the epidemiologist. *American Journal of Epidemiology, 188*(12), 2222–2239.

Chen, Y., Clayton, E. W., Novak, L. L., Anders, S., & Malin, B. (2023). Human-centered design to address biases in artificial intelligence. *Journal of Medical Internet Research, 25*, e43251.

Chu, C. H., Leslie, K., Shi, J., Nyrup, R., Bianchi, A., Khan, S. S., Rahimi, S. A., Lyn, A., & Grenier, A. (2022). Ageism and artificial intelligence: Protocol for a scoping review. *JMIR Research Protocol, 11*(6), e33211.

Cirillo, D., Catuara-Solarz, S., & Morey, C., Guney, E., Subirats, L., Mellino, S., Gigante, A., Valencia, A., Rementeria, M. J., Santuccione Chadha, A., & Mavridis, N. (2020).

Sex and gender differences and biases in artificial intelligence for biomedicine and healthcare. *npj Digital Medicine, 3*(81), 111.

Cohen, G., & Mello, M. (2019). Big data, big tech, and protecting patient privacy. *Journal of American Medical Association, 322*(12), 1141–1142.

Cottom, M. T. (2020). Where platform capitalism and racial capitalism meet: The sociology of race and racism in the digital society. *Sociology of Race and Ethnicity, 6*(4), 441–449.

Dalton-Brown, S. (2020). The ethics of medical AI and the physician-patient relationship. *Cambridge Quarterly of Healthcare Ethics, 29*, 115–121.

Denecke, K., Gabarron, E., Grainger, R., Stathis, T. K., Lau, A., Rivera-Romero, O., Miron-Shatz, T., & Merolli, M. (2019). Artificial intelligence for participatory health: Applications, impact, and future implications. *Yearbook of Medical Informatics, 28*(1), 165–173.

Diakopoulos, N. (2020). Accountability, transparency, and algorithms. In M. D. Dubber, F. Pasquale, & S. Das (Eds.), *The Oxford handbook of ethics of AI* (Vol. 17, No. 4, p. 197). Oxford University Press.

Dourish, P. (2016). Algorithmic culture in context. *Big Data & Society, 3*(2), 1–11.

Drucker, A. (2013). High-confidence predictions under adversarial uncertainty. *ACM Transactions on Computation Theory (TOCT), 5*(3), 1–18.

El Naqa, I., & Murphy, M. J. (2015). *What is machine learning?* (pp. 3–11). Springer International Publishing.

Epker, E. (2023). Artificial intelligence in women's health: The pros, the cons, and the guardrails needed to improve care. *Forbes*. www.forbes.com/sites/evaepker/2023/08/01/artificialintelligence-in-womens-health-the-pros-the-cons-and-the-guardrails-needed-to-improve-care/

Fichman, P., & Rosenbaum, H. (2014). *Social informatics: Past, present and future.* Cambridge Scholars Publishing.

Fossa, A. J., Sigall, K. B., & DesRoches, C. (2018). Open notes and shared decision making: A growing practice in clinical transparency and how it can support patient-centered care. *Journal of American Medical Informatics Association, 25*(9), 1153–1159.

Geiger, R., Tandon, U., Gakhokidze, A., Song, L., & Irani, L. (2023). Rethinking Artificial Intelligence: Algorithmic bias and ethical issues| making algorithms public: Reimagining auditing from matters of fact to matters of concern. *International Journal of Communication, 18*, 22. R

Green, B. L., Murphy, A., & Robinson, E. (2024). Accelerating health disparities research with artificial intelligence. *Frontiers in Digital Health, 6*, 1330160.

Grote, T., & Keeling, G. (2022). On algorithmic fairness in medical practice. *Cambridge Quarterly of Healthcare Ethics, 31*, 1, 83–94.

Gupta, K., & Mircheva, I. (2023). Ethical implications of artificial intelligence in population health and the public's role in its governance: Perspectives from a citizen and expert panel. *Journal of Medical Internet Research, 25*, e44357.

Hecht, J. G. (2001). Technology, politics, and national identity in France. In M. T. Allen & G. Hecht (Eds.), *Technologies of power: Essays in honor of Thomas Parke Hughes and Agatha Chipley Hughes* (pp. 253–293). MIT Press.

Heinrichs, B. (2022). Discrimination in the age of artificial intelligence. *AI & Society, 37*, 143–154. https://doi.org/10.1007/s00146-021-01192-2

Hendricks-Sturrup, R., Simmons, M., Anders, S., Aneni, K., Wright, C. E., Coco, J., Collins, B., Heitman, E., Hussain, S., Joshi, K., Lemieux, J., Novak, L. L., Rubin, D. J., Shanker, A., Washington, T., Waters, G., Webb, Harris, J., Yin, R., Wagner, T., Yin, Z., & Malin, B.

(2023). Developing ethics and equity principles, terms, and engagement tools to advance health equity and researcher diversity in AI and machine learning: Modified Delphi approach. *JMIR AI, 2*, e52888.

Jeyakumar, T., Younus, S., Zhang, M., Clare, M., Charow, R., Karsan, I., Dhalla, A., AlMouaswas, D., Scandiffio, J., Aling, J., Salhia, M., Lalani, N., Overholt, S., & Wiljer, D. (2023). Preparing for an artificial intelligence-enabled future: Patient perspectives on engagement and health care professional training for adopting artificial intelligence technologies in health care settings. *JMIR AI, 2*, e40973.

Johnson, S. (2022). Racing into the fourth industrial revolution: Exploring the ethical dimensions of medical AI and rights-based regulatory framework. *AI Ethics, 2*, 227–232.

Joyce, K., Smith-Doerr, L., Alegria, S., Bell, S., Cruz, T., Hoffman, T. G., Noble, S. U., & Shestakofsky, B. (2021). Toward a sociology of artificial intelligence: A call for research on inequalities and structural change. *Socius: Sociological Research for a Dynamic World, 7*, 1–11.

Karimian, G., Petelos, E., & Evers, S. M. A. (2022). The ethical issues of the application of artificial intelligence in healthcare: A systematic scoping review. *AI Ethics, 2*, 539–551.

Kasapoglu, A. (2020). Sociology of artificial intelligence: A relational sociological investigation in the field of health. *Reports on Global Health Research, 3*(112), 1–13.

Kawamleh, S. (2023). Against explainability requirements for ethical artificial intelligence in health care. *AI Ethics, 3*, 901–916.

Kitchin, R. (2017). Thinking critically about and researching algorithms. *Information, Communication & Society, 20*(1), 14–29.

Kitchin, R. (2023). *Digital timescapes: Technology, temporality and society*. John Wiley & Sons.

Kitchin, R., & Dodge, M. (2011). *Code/space: Software and everyday life*. MIT Press.

Kitchin, R., & Lauriault, T. (2018). Towards critical data studies: Charting and unpacking data assemblages and their work. In J. Thatcher, J. Eckert, & A. Shears (Eds.), *Thinking big data in geography: New regimes, new research* (pp. 3–20). University of Nebraska Press.

Kling, R. (2007). What is social informatics and why does it matter? *The Information Society, 23*(4), 205–220.

Kumar, S., & Choudhury, S. (2022). Gender and feminist considerations in artificial intelligence from a developing-world perspective, with India as a case study. *Humanities and Social Science Communications, 9*, 31.

Kushner, S. (2013). The freelance translation machine: Algorithmic culture and the invisible industry. *New Media & Society, 15*(8), 1241–1258.

Lash, S. (2007a). Power after Hegemony: Cultural studies in mutation. *Theory, Culture & Society, 24*(3), 55–78.

Lauriault, T. P. (2012). Data, infrastructures and geographical imaginations (Doctoral dissertation, Carleton University).

Lazer, D. M. J., Pentland, A., Watts, D. J., Aral, S., Athey, S., Contractor, N., Freelon, D., GonzalezBailon, S., King, G., Margetts, H., Nelson, A., Salganik, M. J., Strohmaier, M., Vespignani, A., & Wagner, C. (2020). Computational social science: Obstacles and opportunities. *Science, 369*(6507), 1060–1062.

Leslie, D., Mazumder, A., Peppin, A., Wolters, M. K., & Hagerty, A. (2021). Does "AI" stand for augmenting inequality in the era of Covid-19 healthcare? *British Medical Journal, 372*, n304.

Lievevrouw, E., & Van Hoyweghen, I. (2019). The social implications of digital health technology. In S. Claes, D. Berckmans, L. Geris, I. Myin-Germeys, C. Van Audenhove,

I. Van Diest, C. Van Hoof, I. Van Hoyweghen, S. Van Huffel, & E. Vrieze (Eds.), *Mobile health revolution in healthcare: Are we ready?*. Metaforum position paper (Vol. 17, pp. 1–67). Working Group Metaforum.

Longoni, C., Bonezzi, A., & Morewedge, C. K. (2019). Resistance to medical artificial intelligence. *Journal of Consumer Research, 46*(4), 629–650.

Mackenzie, A., & Vurdubakis, T. (2011). Codes and codings in crisis: Signification, performativity and excess. *Theory, Culture & Society, 28*(6), 3–23.

Marelli, L., Lievevrouw, E., & Van Hoyweghen, I. (2020). Fit for purpose? The GDPR and the governance of European digital health. *Policy Studies, 41*(5), 447–467.

Mestari, S. Z. E., Lenzini, G., & Demirci, H. (2024). Preserving data privacy in machine learning systems. *Computers & Security, 137*, 103605.

Murray, S. G., Wachter, R. M., & Cucina, R. J. (2020). Discrimination by artificial intelligence in a commercial electronic health record. A case study. *Health Affairs Blog*, January 31.

National Institute of Health (NIH). (2024). *Artificial intelligence and your health. How computers are helping medicine*. Available at Artificial Intelligence and Your Health | NIH News in Health. https://newsinhealth.nih.gov/2024/01/artificial-intelligence-your-health

National Institute for Health Care Management. (2021). *Racial bias in health care artificial intelligence*. National Institute for Health Care Management. Available at https://nihcm.org/publications/artificial-intelligences-racial-bias-inhealth-care?ssp=1&setlang=tr-TR&safesearch=moderate

Noble, S. U. (2018). *Algorithms of oppression: How search engines reinforce racism*. University Press.

Obermeyer, Z., Powers, B., Vogeli, C., & Mullainathan, S. (2019). Dissecting racial bias in an algorithm used to manage the health of populations. *Science, 366*(6464), 447–453.

Orwat, C. (2020). *Risks of discrimination through the use of algorithms*. Federal AntiDiscrimination Agency.

Ostherr, K. (2022). Artificial intelligence and medical humanities. *Journal of Medical Humanities, 43*, 211–232.

Oxholm, C., Christensen, A. M., & Nielsen, A. S. (2022). The ethics of algorithms in healthcare. *Cambridge Quarterly of Healthcare Ethics, 31*(1), 119–130.

Pedersen, E. R., & Sudzina, F. (2023). Relationship between citizens' perspective on digital health and underlying health risks. *Digital Health, 9*, 20552076231191045.

Petrakaki, D., Hilberg, E., & Waring, J. (2021). The cultivation of digital health citizenship. *Social Science & Medicine, 270*, 113675.

Ruppert, E. (2012). The governmental topologies of database devices. *Theory, Culture & Society, 29*(4–5), 116–136.

Sasseville, M., Ouellet, S., Rhéaume, C., Couture, V., Després, P., Paquette, J. S., Gentelet, K., Darmon, D., Bergeron, F., & Gagnon, M. P. (2023). Risk of bias mitigation for vulnerable and diverse groups in community-based primary health care artificial intelligence models: Protocol for a rapid review. *JMIR Research Protocol, 12*, e46684.

Sawyer, S., & Tyworth, M. (2006). Social informatics: Principles, theory, and practice. In *Social Informatics: An Information Society for All? In Remembrance of Rob Kling: Proceedings of the Seventh International Conference on Human Choice and Computers (HCC7), IFIP TC 9, Maribor, Slovenia, September 21–23, 2006* (pp. 49–62). Springer US.

Schencker, L. (2019). How much is too much to tell Google? Privacy lawsuit alleges U. of C. Medical Center went too far when sharing patient data. *Chicago Tribune*. Available at www.chicagotribune.com/2019/06/27/how-much-is-too-much-to-tell-google-privacy-lawsuit-alleges-u-of-c-medical-center-went-too-far-when-sharing-patient-data/

Schneble, C. O., Elger, B. S., & Shaw, D. M. (2020). Google's Project Nightingale highlights the necessity of data science ethics review. *EMBO Molecular Medicine, 12*(3), e12053.

Seckin, G., Hughes, S., Campbell, P., & Lawson, M. (2021). In internet we trust: Intersectionality of distrust and patient non-adherence. *Information, Communication & Society, 24*(5), 751–771.

Sidey-Gibbons, J., & Sidey-Gibbons, C. (2019). Machine learning in medicine: A practical introduction. *BMC Medical Research Methodology, 19*, 64.

Sikstrom, L., Maslej, M. M., Hui, K., Findlay, Z., Buchman, D. Z., & Hill, S. L. (2022). Conceptualising fairness: Three pillars for medical algorithms and health equity. *BMJ Health & Care Informatics, 29*(1), e100459.

Soumia, Z. E. M., Lenzini, G., & Demirci, H. (2024). Preserving data privacy in machine learning systems. *Computers & Security, 137*, 103605.

Steiner, C. (2012). *Automate this: How algorithms took over our markets, our jobs, and the world.* Penguin.

Stypińska, J., & Franke, A. (2023). AI revolution in healthcare and medicine and the (re-) emergence of inequalities and disadvantages for ageing population. *Frontiers in Sociology, 7*, 1038854.

Tanaka, M., Matsumura, S., & Bito, S. (2023). Roles and competencies of doctors in artificial intelligence implementation: Qualitative analysis through physician interviews. *JMIR Formative Research, 7*, e46020.

Upadhyay, U., Gradisek, A., & Iqbal, U. (2023). Call for the responsible artificial intelligence in the healthcare. *BMJ Health Care Informatics, 30*, e100920.

U.S. DOE Office of Science. (June, 2020). *Recommendations for strengthening American leadership in industries of the future. A report to the President of the United States of America.* The President's Council of Advisors on Science and Technology. Available at PCAST Report to the President of the United States of America June2020 (osti.gov)

Vorisek, C. N., Stellmach, C., Mayer, P. J., Klopfenstein, S. A. I., Bures, D. M., Diehl, A., Henningsen, M., Ritter, K., & Thun, S. (2023). Artificial intelligence bias in health care: Web-based survey. *Journal of Medical Internet Research, 25*, e41089.

Wang, C., Liu, S., Yang, H., Guo, J., Wu, Y., & Liu, J. (2023). Ethical considerations of using ChatGPT in health care. *Journal of Medical Internet Research, 25*, e48009.

Winter, J., & Davidson, E. J. (2020). Harmonizing regulatory spheres to overcome challenges for governance of patient-generated health data in the age of artificial intelligence and big data. In *TPRC48: The 48th Research Conference on Communication, Information and Internet Policy.* Available at https://ssrn.com/abstract=3749529h

Wu, H., Wang, M., Sylolypavan, A., & Wild, S. (2022). Quantifying health inequalities induced by data and AI models. In *31st International Joint Conference on Artificial Intelligence, Vienna* (pp. 5192–5198). IJCA.

Yadav, N., Pandey, S., Gupta, A., Dudani, P., Gupta, S., & Rangarajan, K. (2023). Data privacy in healthcare: In the era of artificial intelligence. *Indian Dermatology Online Journal, 14*(6), 788–792.

Zuo, Z., Watson, M., Budgen, D., Hall, R., Kennelly, C., & Al Moubayed, N. (2021). Data anonymization for pervasive health care: Systematic literature mapping study. *JMIR Medical Informatics, 9*(10), e29871.

8

A SOCIO-TECHNICAL INTERACTION NETWORK (STIN) PERSPECTIVE ON TIKTOK FAKE NEWS

The case of the Russia-Ukraine War

Bevis Hsin-Yu Chen and Pnina Fichman

Introduction

In the era of social media, the phenomena of coordinated adversarial behaviors (e.g., cyberbullying, disinformation, doxing, and trolling) have raised major concerns (Stringhini, 2019). One prominent aspect of these phenomena is the proliferation of fake news on social media; scholars found that fake news had an impact on the 2016 United States presidential election outcomes (Allcott & Gentzkow, 2017), tapered public trust in news media (Wasserman & Madrid-Morales, 2019), and negatively affected people's perceptions of health information during the COVID-19 pandemic—the infodemic (World Health Organization, 2022).

Fake news, which refers to the intentional and unintentional spread of false or inaccurate information (i.e., disinformation and misinformation) (Hassan et al., 2020), has become a major concern following the Russian interference in the 2016 United States presidential election. Not a new phenomenon, fake news has existed for centuries (Khan et al., 2021), but with the rapid growth of social media platforms in recent years, fake news has spread more widely and quickly (Langin, 2018). For example, falsehood on Twitter diffused significantly faster, broader, and deeper than the truth, reaching far more people than the truth (Vosoughi et al., 2018). Social media platforms enable fake news dissemination due to low cost and high reach (Daud & Zulhuda, 2020; Muhammed & Mathew, 2022). The cost of creating and spreading falsehood on social media is relatively low (Daud & Zulhuda, 2020), and it achieves significant communication outreach due to the sizable number of users who are active on social media (Murero, 2023). In short, social media has significantly shaped the ways that people share and consume information and disinformation, making the fake news problem worse than it ever was before.

DOI: 10.4324/9781032678542-12

We claim that one way to gain a better understanding of fake news on social media is through a socio-technical framework that accounts for the interactions among people and technologies in context. Braccini (2020), for example, argues that the fake news phenomenon can be understood as a socio-technical problem because it involves complex relationships between many actors. On the social side, heterogeneous actors—such as activists, social media users, and platform administrators—are participating in the process of creating, spreading, and receiving disinformation (Braccini, 2020). On the technical side, the functions and affordances of social media platforms allow people to connect with others in different ways (Braccini, 2020). Other scholars also suggest that a socio-technical framework can help researchers in their efforts to map out key actors and the interrelationship between people and technology (Marwick, 2018; Westlund et al., 2022). Further, social informatics scholars contend that the socio-technical interaction between people and technology always occurs in context that affects it (Fichman et al., 2015). Creech (2020) pointed out that context should not be ignored, as the fake news problem is embedded in political, economic, legal, and cultural conditions that shape the creation, dissemination, and use of fake news. Kim et al. (2021) suggested that research that applies socio-technical frameworks is needed to better understand the complex characteristics of fake news.

Addressing these calls, this chapter analyzes the phenomenon of the spread of fake news on social media using a specific social informatics perspective, and utilizes the socio-technical interaction network (STIN) framework. The STIN framework is a useful approach because it provides a systematic, socio-technically-oriented framework to study the networks of technology and people in context (Fichman et al., 2015; Kling et al., 2003; Shachaf & Rosenbaum, 2009). It can help scholars map the complex interrelationships between people, social media, and society. To illustrate the utility of this approach, this chapter focuses on the spread of fake news during the early days of the Russia-Ukraine War on TikTok as a case study. We chose disinformation about the Russia-Ukraine War on TikTok for two reasons. First, TikTok is one of the fastest-growing social media platforms, where fake news is rife (Hsu, 2022). Second, during the Russia-Ukraine War, social actors have used TikTok as a propaganda machine for spreading disinformation (Klepper, 2022). Using this case study, we demonstrate how the STIN framework can contribute to and inform research on fake news on social media.

This chapter is structured as follows. The first section introduces the fake news phenomenon on TikTok as a socio-technical problem. Section two presents the STIN framework and illustrates how it can be applied to understand fake news on social media. In section three, this chapter begins to apply the STIN approach to analyze fake news on social media, using the spread of fake news about the Russia-Ukraine War on TikTok as a case study. This chapter then concludes by highlighting its contributions and limitations, and it suggests future research directions.

Fake news on TikTok

The section first describes TikTok's popularity and the socio-technical affordances of the platform. Then, it discusses the fake news phenomenon and its manifestation on TikTok as a socio-technical problem.

TikTok's popularity and affordances

TikTok is a popular social media platform used primarily for sharing short-form mobile videos. Launched in 2016 by the Chinese technology company ByteDance, TikTok has rapidly grown in popularity in recent years (Iqbal, 2023). According to statistics, TikTok reached 1.6 billion users in the fourth quarter of 2022 and is used by 18% of global internet users aged 16–64 (Iqbal, 2023). The majority of TikTok users are young, and most users (52.8%) are aged between 18 and 24 (Aslam, 2023). While TikTok is available in more than 150 countries, it is banned in several countries, including India, Iran, Pakistan, and Syria ("TikTok," 2023). Besides China, the United States has the most TikTok users worldwide; the latest statistic shows over 150 million active TikTok users in the United States (Lee, 2023). In short, TikTok has become one of the most popular social media platforms that impact society (Brandon, 2022).

TikTok's enormous success can be attributed to three powerful affordances of the platform (Guinaudeau et al., 2022): the televisual medium, algorithmic recommendation, and mobile-only interface design. To elaborate, televisual medium means that users are easily attracted by visual and audio content; algorithmic recommendations help users navigate the content; mobile-first design targets smartphone users. Rach and Peter (2021) argue that TikTok's user-focused algorithm outperforms that of other social media platforms. Specifically, TikTok feeds do not only focus on users' friendship networks, but also provide users with personalized content through their user-centric recommendation algorithms. TikTok is also easy to use, allowing users to make and share short-form and highly engaging videos, which blurs the line between content creators and consumers (Hern, 2022a). More importantly, TikTok encourages its users to engage with each other by offering various interactive functions (e.g., likes, comments, shares, follows, and hashtags). From users' perspectives, TikTok is a virtual space for self-expression, emotional expression, and the exchange of social support (Barta & Andalibi, 2021; Omar & Dequan, 2020).

TikTok can be understood as a socio-technical system with complex relationships between the platform, various social actors (e.g., individual users, organizations, and governments), and the contexts in which these dynamic relationships exist and evolve. These socio-technical relationships are evident at the societal, national, organizational, and individual levels of analysis. The complex interrelationships between governments and the parent company of TikTok—ByteDance—for example, have led to at least twelve countries banning or limiting the use of the platform (Chan, 2023). TikTok has also cooperated with many fact-checking organizations and non-governmental organizations (NGOs) to combat disinformation (Bettadapur, 2020), demonstrating interorganizational relationships. At the individual level, the socio-technical interactions involve, for example, TikTok's unique personalized recommendation algorithms, drawing them to continue and extend their use of the platform. Evidently, as many actors are involved in this socio-technical system, interacting with one another in contexts, we contend that researchers should be aware of the intertwined relationships between technology and people in context when conducting research on the spread of fake news on TikTok.

Fake news on TikTok as a socio-technical problem

With more than 1.6 billion users, TikTok has become a major digital platform for the dissemination of information, including fake news. In this chapter, "fake news" refers to the intentional and unintentional spread of false or inaccurate information (Hassan et al., 2020), including both disinformation (intentional) and misinformation (unintentional). Several recent studies pointed out that TikTok has become a hotbed of mis- and disinformation (Alonso-López et al., 2021; Harrison, 2022; Meyers, 2022). According to a research report, nearly 20% of TikTok research results contain misleading or false information (Klepper, 2022). Research also showed that TikTok algorithms usually directed users to fake news about war (Hern, 2022b). Take the Russia-Ukraine War as an example. Since Russia invaded Ukraine in early 2022, the Russian government and state-controlled media have continuously used TikTok to spread disinformation that describes Ukraine as the aggressor (O'Connor, 2022). At that time, the Russian government also passed a new law criminalizing the spread of fake news, which led TikTok to suspend some services in Russia (Tiku, 2022). Taken together, the fake news phenomenon in this context is a socio-technical interaction network that includes interrelationships between the platform, people, organizations, and governments.

Marwick (2018) used a socio-technical framework to explore why people share fake news on social media, suggesting that researchers consider three crucial aspects of the fake news phenomenon: actors, messages, and affordances. First, from a socio-technical perspective, identifying who participates in creating, disseminating, and consuming media messages is essential. Different groups of actors (e.g., users, politicians, and governments) play unique roles in the process. The more we know about the actors involved, the more we can understand their roles. Second, analyzing and understanding media messages are important. Understanding the meanings of messages helps us understand the relationship between media, power, and social control. Third, affordances matter. Affordances refer to the features and functionality of the communication medium. Consider TikTok as an example; its powerful algorithms spread fake news that TikTok users create and share on the platform more quickly and broadly (Hern, 2022b).

In response to the fake news problem, social media users, governments, NGOs, and TikTok's parent company have all developed solutions. For instance, TikTok has adopted measures to combat fake news by updating misinformation policies, improving algorithms, broadening partnerships with fact-check organizations, and collaborating with experts (TikTok, n.d.). In addition, governments play an important role in fighting against fake news, and many countries, including the United States, have passed new laws to regulate fake news on social media. Zhu and Yang (2023), focusing on how the U.S. and Chinese governments regulate fake news, for example, used a socio-technical framework to examine how different national contexts affect policy design and identified the stakeholders of fake news. To conclude, fake news is a socio-technical problem embedded in complex contexts. We introduce a specific socio-technical framework—the STIN—that we will utilize in this chapter beginning in the next section.

Theoretical framework

Socio-technical interaction network (STIN)

The socio-technical interaction network (STIN) is a conceptual framework developed by social informatics scholar Rob Kling and his colleagues (Kling et al., 2003). Kling et al. (2003) defined the STIN as "a network that includes people (including organizations), equipment, data, diverse resources (money, skill, status), documents and messages, legal arrangements and enforcement mechanisms, and resource flows." Specifically, the STIN approach examines interactive relationships among people, institutions, technologies, and social contexts (Fichman et al., 2015; Kling et al., 2003). Kling and other social informatics researchers claim that technologies and their users do not exist or interact in isolation; instead, they are highly embedded in a complex socio-technical network (Fichman et al., 2015; Kling et al., 2003). Social informatics scholars consider the socio-technical systems and the reciprocal relationships among various social actors while analyzing the roles and impacts of technologies on society, organizations, and people.

According to Kling et al. (2003), the STIN approach has four fundamental assumptions. First, the social and the technological are not meaningfully separable. Because technology and society co-constitute each other and are highly intertwined, they are not meaningfully divisible in understanding how technology works. Second, theories of social behavior should influence technical design choices. The design and implementation of technologies are socio-technical activities (Fichman et al., 2015). Previous research emphasized that the use of technology can influence the design, use, and implementation of technologies in an iterative and reciprocal process (Fichman et al., 2015). Third, participants are embedded in multiple, overlapping, and non-technologically mediated social relationships. Meyer (2006) echoed the idea that the STIN framework not only includes various social actors, but also examines their complex relationships. Fourth, the sustainability of the technology and its routine operations are critical. To some extent, the sustainability of a technological system depends on participants' interactions with it and with each other. The system will become unsustainable if participants no longer want to participate (Kling et al., 2003). The core concept that unites the four STIN assumptions is that technologies are embedded in and intertwined with the environment, as social actors, technologies, and the environment are mutually shaping each other. One of the reasons that this specific socio-technical framework is of interest to us is its unique emphasis on excluded actors in STIN, whereas other socio-technical frameworks largely ignore them.

The STIN framework can help us understand the complex relationships between people and technology in various contexts. Over time, the STIN framework has been applied to examine scholarly communication forums (Kling et al., 2003), digital libraries (Rosenbaum & Joung, 2004), free and open-source software development (Scacchi, 2005), digital photography (Meyer, 2007), e-learning (Walker & Creanor, 2009), question answer sites (Shachaf & Rosenbaum, 2009), and data dashboard in higher education (McCoy, 2020). Shachaf and Rosenbaum (2009) suggest that the STIN framework has the potential for wider applicability because it includes heterogeneous human and non-human participants. In addition, the STIN looks beyond the socio-technical system itself and examines how other actors' social worlds are connected to the understanding of technology use (Shachaf & Rosenbaum, 2009).

However, the use of the STIN framework has some limitations (Meyer, 2006). First, the STIN has mainly been adopted by Kling's colleagues and students. This gap can be bridged only when more scholars start applying the STIN framework to their research areas and further develop it to adapt to the changing socio-technical environment. This chapter does that; it demonstrates the applicability of the STIN framework beyond this limited group of scholars, and expands its utility to social media research. Second, the STIN has an organizational bias that constrains its ability to incorporate social implications of technology beyond organizational boundaries (Meyer, 2006). Indeed, most STIN studies involved digital organizations (Kling et al., 2003; Meyer, 2007; McCoy, 2020; Rosenbaum & Joung, 2004; Scacchi, 2005; Walker & Creanor, 2009), and only one limited effort was made to extend its reach beyond those boundaries (Shachaf & Rosenbaum, 2009). Because the framework was proposed before the era of social media and its prior applications were confined to organizational contexts, its potential utility for social media studies has not been explored. Clearly, human-technology interaction is more complicated outside the organization because it involves complex contexts with more actors and interactions. Thus, we aim to extend the STIN's applicability beyond organizational boundaries and demonstrate how it might be relevant to today's digital society. Furthermore, compared with most previous STIN studies that focused on neutral or positive examples of social-technical systems, our research employs the STIN to analyze disinformation, an example of a problematic socio-technical system. We adopt the STIN framework to explore the fake news phenomenon on TikTok and gain a better understanding of the complex relationships among relevant actors, technology, and contexts.

TikTok as a STIN

We claim that the STIN approach can be applied to TikTok research and that TikTok can be described and analyzed as a STIN. According to Kling et al. (2003)'s definition, "the elements of a STIN are heterogeneous," and "the network relationships between these elements include social, economic, and political interactions." We begin by describing TikTok as a STIN, where various individuals (e.g., TikTok users), organizations (e.g., fact-checking organizations and tech companies), and governments get involved in the process of creating, spreading, and curbing information, including fake news. These actors and technologies are engaged in relations of dependency and mutual shaping. For instance, social media users rely on TikTok to acquire information, and TikTok offers personalized content by collecting users' data and tracking their online activities (Brandon, 2022; Mozur et al., 2022). The TikTok algorithms depend on user activities to feed into it, and users extend their engagement with the platform due to its algorithms as they are consuming, creating, and disseminating content. To gain a better understanding of the fake news phenomenon on TikTok, we next utilize the STIN framework and describe the complex relationships among different interactors, focusing on the case of fake news on TikTok about the Russia-Ukraine War.

A case study: Fake news on TikTok about the Russia-Ukraine War

The Russia-Ukraine War has been called "the world's first TikTok war," as increasing fake news spreads across the platform (Chayka, 2022). During the war, TikTok was weaponized by governments to spread disinformation, and its users were frequently exposed to fake news about the war (Brown, 2022; Sardarizadeh, 2022). Moreover, the TikTok algorithm worsened the problem by continuously recommending false videos to its users (Hern, 2022b). While the socio-technical affordances of specific social media platforms enable different degrees of disinformation and trolling (Fichman & Rathi, 2023), TikTok's recommendation algorithms and its asymmetric network enable the fast spread of short video content and the widespread distribution of disinformation more than on any other platform.

To explore the fake news phenomenon on TikTok using the STIN framework, we began by following Kling et al. (2003)'s steps. We focus here on identifying the critical social actors and their interrelationships to demonstrate the utility of the STIN framework.

STIN steps:

1 Identify a relevant population of system interactors
2 Identify core interactor groups

3 Identify incentives
4 Identify excluded actors and undesired interactions
5 Identify existing communication systems
6 Identify resource flows
7 Identify system architectural choice points
8 Map architectural choice points to socio-technical characteristics

Following Kling et al. (2003)'s first two steps, we initially identify core interactor groups and the population of system interactors. This process mainly aims to understand the scope of the interactors and their different social roles in the fake news phenomenon. Recognizing that the socio-technical system is large and complex, we only account for the most relevant and significant actors that participate in creating, sharing, and curbing fake news during the Russia-Ukraine War (Table 8.1). We illustrate how the various interactors participate in this system

TABLE 8.1 Key actors and their activities on TikTok during the Russia-Ukraine War

Interactors	Activities
TikTok's parent company (ByteDance)	• Develop and use algorithms to facilitate content creation, use, and dissemination • Develop and use algorithms to collect users' data and feed content • Set up mis- and disinformation policies • Develop and use algorithms to detect and avoid falsehoods • Interact with governments, policymakers, and other organizations (e.g., fact-checking NGOs) • Disclosure (e.g., transparency reports)
Users/individuals	• Create, watch, and share content • Create, watch, share, and report false content • Interact with content and with other users (e.g., likes, comments, tags, and follows)
Governments	• Regulate tech industry • Regulate fake news through legislation or policies • Create and spread fake news • Cooperate with tech companies to address problems • Promote information literacy education
International organizations (e.g., E.U., U.N.)	• Set up standards for regulating tech companies and their platforms • Set up and monitor human rights frameworks
Fact-check NGOs	• Detect and verify false videos • Promote information literacy education
Competitors (e.g., Meta, Twitter)	• Develop and use algorithms to facilitate content creation, use, and dissemination • Compete with TikTok concerning users' engagement

and provide examples of their relevant activities. Each interactor has unique roles and interrelationships with other actors.

Besides identifying key interactors, recognizing the incentive structure of TikTok's socio-technical system is a critical step because it helps us understand what motivates interactors to participate in the system (Kling et al., 2003). In the Russia-Ukraine War, each interactor has a distinct motive for engaging in information warfare on the TikTok platform. For instance, the Russian and Ukrainian governments used the TikTok platform as a propaganda tool. The Russian government has been using TikTok as a platform to spread disinformation and undermine Western support for Ukraine (Seldin, 2023). Meanwhile, the Ukrainian government has been using the TikTok platform to debunk Russian propaganda by launching an official TikTok account (York, 2023). In doing so, both the Russian and Ukrainian governments used the platform to create and spread false information, demonstrating both the governments' motivations for using the platform and one angle of TikTok-government relationships.

The fourth step for modeling the STIN framework is identifying excluded interactors and undesired social interactions, such as monitoring and surveillance (Kling et al., 2003). This step highlights one of the unique features of the STIN, and one of the main reasons that we chose it as the specific socio-technical framework in this chapter. Take the TikTok-government relationship as an example. In 2022, the Russian government passed a new law criminalizing the spread of fake news. If anyone describes Russia's attack against Ukraine as an "invasion," the person was to face a threat of a 15-year prison sentence (Tiku, 2022). In response to the law, TikTok suspended both live-streaming and new content services in Russia, thus affecting its users (Tiku, 2022). The suspense of TikTok services can be regarded as an example of a critical system choice point, following step seven in modeling STIN. An architectural choice point means a social arrangement in which the technology designer can select alternatives, and some choice points can be restrictions on the ability to use the technological instrument (Kling et al., 2003). In the case of the Russia-Ukraine War, TikTok's design choice was to suspend its services and restrict users' ability to use TikTok. TikTok users in Russia were then excluded from using the socio-technical system, because the new law passed by the Russian government posed a threat to the safety of TikTok users and employees (Tiku, 2022).

Next, we describe the existing communication system through the technological features and affordances of TikTok, and we explore their influence on the proliferation of fake news during the Russia-Ukraine War. TikTok's recommendation algorithms are primarily based on user's preferences, interests, and video-watching behaviors (Kang & Lou, 2022), which is an exemplary demonstration of human-machine interaction (Kang & Lou, 2022). During the Russia-Ukraine War, TikTok's algorithms frequently directed users to fake news about the war (Hern, 2022b). Specifically, if users often consume posts containing false information, TikTok's algorithms will recommend more of those types of posts (Milmo & Farah, 2022).

TikTok's powerful algorithms have raised many concerns, and some people urge that algorithmic technologies need stricter regulation (Rothkopf, 2023). For instance, the U.S. Congress asked TikTok to disclose more information about its algorithms (Agustin, 2021), and several members of the U.S. Congress have expressed concerns that TikTok's algorithms are "dangerous" and deliberately showcase controversial content (Agustin, 2021; Lasarte, 2023). Clearly, the mutual relationships between users and the social media platform occur in a more complex context that involves governments. For example, following the Russian invasion of Ukraine, Russia introduced strict new media censorship (Ljunggren & Porter, 2022), resulting in TikTok's ban on all international content for users in Russia, which contributed to Russia's disinformation monopoly over its citizens (Groenewald, 2023). This example of TikTok-government relationships alludes not only to the Russian citizens as excluded interactors (step four), but also to the system's architectural choice points (step seven). Specifically, the TikTok company's decision to suspend its services in Russia reflects the designers' intention to prevent users from utilizing the technological instrument due to the threat posed by Russian law. In short, the above examples demonstrate how TikTok and various social actors interact in context.

The strength of the STIN framework is that it can map multiple and critical relationships between technology, social actors, and society (Kling et al., 2003; Sawyer & Tyworth, 2006) as well as account for excluded actors and undesired interactions. To better understand the complex interactions between key interactors in context, we created a relational graph (Figure 8.1).

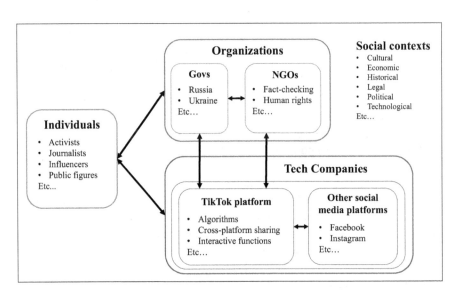

FIGURE 8.1 Socio-technical interaction network diagram of the fake news phenomenon on TikTok.

Figure 8.1 shows that many stakeholders, individuals, and organizations are involved in disseminating, sharing, and curbing fake news during the Russia-Ukraine War. As the above discussion of TikTok-government relationships highlights, mutual shaping and interactions among actors are complex and multidimensional. Each of the actors depicted in Figure 8.1 has multiple social positions and relationships with one another; in this chapter, we chose to illustrate the utility of the map by describing some aspects of the relationships. Because the spread of fake news is a socio-technical problem, it calls for socio-technical understandings and solutions, which entails accounting for the technology (the TikTok platform and its algorithms) and the organizations behind it (the TikTok company). That means that we refer to TikTok here as both the company behind the technology and the platform's algorithms, as we clearly distinguish between the two.

The TikTok company's interrelationships with users, governments, NGOs, and other tech companies are complex. For example, TikTok built cooperation with about a dozen fact-checking NGOs to identify the accuracy of content in 30 languages. According to TikTok, once content is verified as fake news, the company removes it and notifies the creator (TikTok, n.d.).

TikTok-government relationships in the context of fake news are complex. On the one hand, some governments and politicians use the platform to create and spread fake news; on the other hand, governments regulate misinformation and social media use. In the case of the Russia-Ukraine War, both the Russian and Ukrainian governments use TikTok as a propaganda tool to spread fake news (Klepper, 2022; Majumder, 2022). Contexts, however, differ greatly from country to country; governments design, adopt, and implement information policies that take into account their unique and complex contexts (Zhu & Yang, 2023). These policies are also important for understanding the spread of fake news on TikTok. Many countries have passed laws to address the fake news problem (Santuraki, 2019; Zhu & Yang, 2023). For example, during the COVID pandemic, the U.S. and Chinese governments' misinformation policies resulted from their unique political and cultural contexts (Zhu & Yang, 2023).

Individual TikTok users also play an essential role in this socio-technical interaction system of fake news. Lamb and Kling (2003) pointed out that people who use digital technologies have multiple complex roles; the roles and identities of individuals affect how they use technologies. Furthermore, technologies, individuals, and social contexts are not isolated entities; rather, they coexist and interact with each other (Fichman et al., 2015). In the context of TikTok's fake news, those that participate in creating, spreading, and combating fake news are diverse in their motives, values, and methods. For example, it is believed that certain TikTok influencers were paid by the Russian government to promote pro-Kremlin narratives about the conflict in Ukraine through their videos (Gilbert, 2022). At the same time, journalists and fact-checkers work together to verify the content of Russia-Ukraine War-related videos on TikTok (Thomson, 2022). TikTok also partners with experts to shape content moderation policies and enables users to report misleading or harmful information that they encounter (Pappas, 2020).

Furthermore, the TikTok platform competes and coexists alongside other social media platforms and algorithms. The cross-platform connectivity of TikTok is a good example of this context. TikTok is designed to connect with other international platforms, such as Facebook, Instagram, Twitter, and YouTube, which allows users to share videos more easily and quickly (Kaye et al., 2021). However, because some social media platforms—such as Facebook and Instagram—are currently banned in Russia (Sauer, 2022), TikTok users in Russia cannot share videos from the banned social media sites with TikTok. This fact demonstrates not only how platforms coexist, but also how social context affects the affordances of TikTok and its users' behaviors.

The previous examples show that the fake news phenomenon is multifaceted, involving a diverse range of actors and complex interrelationships between technology and various social actors in complex and dynamic contexts. The social contexts can significantly influence social actors' behaviors and interrelationships (Sawyer & Tyworth, 2006). In the context of fake news, actors are embedded within an enabling and constraining social setting as much as by technological affordances. We claim that while analyzing how TikTok is used in the context of fake news, researchers should consider different contextual aspects—including the local, institutional, international, political, economic, cultural, historical, and legal conditions.

Limitations

As an exploratory paper, this chapter has some limitations. First, as a conceptual chapter, it mainly relies on the theoretical assumptions of the STIN and lacks empirical data. Future studies may further revise and apply this conceptual framework to conduct empirical research. Second, this chapter primarily focuses on the fake news phenomenon on TikTok, which is relatively narrow, and the scope and scale of this STIN network are therefore limited. On other platforms or concerning other phenomena, the socio-technical system's structure and contexts vary and may be more complex. Future socio-technical research on social media platforms' ecologies is still much needed. Third, while we demonstrated the STIN's applicability to social media research, we hope that future research may propose new heuristics for the STIN model to further develop the STIN framework.

Conclusions

As a multifaceted socio-technical problem, the fake news phenomenon involves complex relationships between people, technology, and social context, causing a tremendous impact on individuals and society. To investigate the fake news phenomenon, we adopted the STIN framework and identified the intertwined relationships between interactors and their positions within the socio-technical system. This chapter suggests that a comprehensive understanding of the socio-technical system's structure is required for addressing the fake news problem, in which active involvement and cooperation of various social actors are evident. Utilizing the STIN framework to identify the relationships between technology, social actors, and social contexts, we first identified key social actors and their relationships with technology and society, and then we mapped the socio-technical networks of the fake news phenomenon on TikTok concerning the Russia-Ukraine War.

This chapter makes three major contributions with implications for theory and practice. First, compared with previous STIN studies in organizations, this chapter extends the STIN's applicability to a non-organizational context. In doing so, we began to address one of the research gaps in STIN research: that the STIN framework's inherent organizational bias limits its ability to analyze the broader non-organizational social implications of technology.

Second, unlike most previous STIN studies—which mainly explored neutral or positive examples of social-technical systems—this conceptual chapter extends the STIN's applicability to an undesirable case of disinformation.

Third, aiming to gain a better understanding of the socio-technical networks in contemporary social media platforms, this chapter applies the STIN framework in TikTok research. Specifically, we demonstrate how the spread of fake news about the Russia-Ukraine War on TikTok can be defined and analyzed as a socio-technical interaction network. We showed how this problem has emerged and expanded from both social and technical causes. On the social side, diverse actors—such as governments, NGOs, social media users, and the TikTok company—are participating in creating, spreading, receiving, and combating fake news. On the technical side, the affordances of TikTok enable social actors to disseminate and curb fake news. TikTok's algorithms can both trigger and solve some fake news problems. Besides the social and technical factors, the broader context shapes the fake news phenomenon and actors' participation in the network.

References

Agustin, F. (2021, November 10). Congress demands TikTok share information about its 'dangerous' algorithm after oversight committee finds the platform is serving harmful content to underage users. *Insider*. www.businessinsider.com/congress-demands-tiktok-share-information-about-dangerous-algorithm-2021-11

Allcott, H., & Gentzkow, M. (2017). Social media and fake news in the 2016 election. *Journal of Economic Perspectives, 31*(2), 211–236.

Alonso-López, N., Sidorenko-Bautista, P., & Giacomelli, F. (2021). Beyond challenges and viral dance moves: TikTok as a vehicle for disinformation and fact-checking in Spain, Portugal, Brazil, and the USA. *Anàlisi: Quaderns de comunicació i cultura, 64*, 65–84.

Aslam, S. (2023, February 27). TikTok by the numbers: Stats, demographics & fun facts. *Omnicore*. www.omnicoreagency.com/tiktok-statistics/

Barta, K., & Andalibi, N. (2021). Constructing authenticity on TikTok: Social norms and social support on the "fun" platform. *Proceedings of the ACM on Human-Computer Interaction, 5*(CSCW2), 1–29.

Bettadapur, A. N. (2020, October 1). TikTok partners with fact-checking experts to combat misinformation. *TikTok.* https://newsroom.tiktok.com/en-au/tiktok-partners-with-fact-checking-experts-to-combat-misinformation

Braccini, A. M. (2020, June 8–9). The (un) invited in collective action on social media: A socio-technical perspective of fake news. *The 6th International Workshop on Socio-Technical Perspective in I.S. Development (STPIS'20), Virtual Conference.* https://ceur-ws.org/Vol-2789/paper24.pdf

Brandon, J. (2022, April 28). One reason TikTok is the most popular social media App of the year so far. *Forbes.* www.forbes.com/sites/johnbbrandon/2022/04/28/one-reason-tiktok-is-the-most-popular-social-media-app-of-the-year-so-far/?sh=5d114 4e241ed

Brown, S. (2022, April 6). In Russia-Ukraine war, social media stokes ingenuity, disinformation. *MIT Sloan.* https://mitsloan.mit.edu/ideas-made-to-matter/russia-ukraine-war-social-media-stokes-ingenuity-disinformation

Chan, K. (2023, April 4). Here are the countries that have bans on TikTok. *A.P. News.* https://apnews.com/article/tiktok-ban-privacy-cybersecurity-bytedance-china-2dce297f0aed0 56efe53309bbcd44a04

Chayka, K. (2022, March 3). Watching the world's first "TikTok war." *The New Yorker.* www.newyorker.com/culture/infinite-scroll/watching-the-worlds-first-tiktok-war

Creech, B. (2020). Fake news and the discursive construction of technology companies' social power. *Media, Culture & Society, 42*(6), 952–968.

Daud, M., & Zulhuda, S. (2020). Regulating the spread of false content online in Malaysia: Issues, challenges and the way forward. *International Journal of Business & Society, 21*(S1), 32–48.

Fichman, P., & Rathi, M. (2023). Trolling CNN and Fox News on Facebook, Instagram, and Twitter. *Journal of the Association for Information Science and Technology, 74*(5), 493–505.

Fichman, P., Sanfilippo, M. R., & Rosenbaum, H. (2015). *Social informatics evolving.* Morgan & Claypool Publishers.

Gilbert, D. (2022, March 11). Russian TikTok influencers are being paid to spread Kremlin propaganda. *VICE News.* www.vice.com/en/article/epxken/russian-tiktok-influencers-paid-propaganda

Groenewald, A. (2023, February 5). TikTok bans foreign content in Russia while claiming to curb misinformation. *Privacy Hub.* www.cyberghostvpn.com/en_US/privacyhub/tik tok-bans-foreign-content-russia/

Guinaudeau, B., Munger, K., & Votta, F. (2022). Fifteen seconds of fame: TikTok and the supply side of social video. *Computational Communication Research, 4*(2), 463–485.

Harrison, M. (2022, October 26). Research confirms TikTok is a cesspool of misinformation. *Futurism.* https://futurism.com/tiktok-political-misinformation

Hassan, I., Azmi, M. N. L., & Abdullahi, A. M. (2020). Evaluating the spread of fake news and its detection. Techniques on social networking sites. *Romanian Journal of Communication and Public Relations, 22*(1), 111–125.

Hern, A. (2022a, October 24). How TikTok's algorithm made it a success: 'It pushes the boundaries.' *The Guardian.* www.theguardian.com/technology/2022/oct/23/tiktok-rise-algorithm-popularity

Hern, A. (2022b, March 21). TikTok algorithm directs users to fake news about Ukraine war, study says. *The Guardian.* www.theguardian.com/technology/2022/mar/21/tiktok-algori thm-directs-users-to-fake-news-about-ukraine-war-study-says

Hsu, T. (2022, November 4). Worries grow that TikTok is new home for manipulated video and photos. *The New York Times.* www.nytimes.com/2022/11/04/technology/tiktok-deepfakes-disinformation.html

Iqbal, M. (2023, January 9). TikTok revenue and usage statistics. *Business of Apps.* www.bus inessofapps.com/data/tik-tok-statistics/

Kang, H., & Lou, C. (2022). A.I. agency vs. human agency: Understanding human–A.I. interactions on TikTok and their implications for user engagement. *Journal of Computer-Mediated Communication, 27*(5), 1–13.

Kaye, D. B. V., Chen, X., & Zeng, J. (2021). The co-evolution of two Chinese mobile short video apps: Parallel platformization of Douyin and TikTok. *Mobile Media & Communication, 9*(2), 229–253.

Khan, T., Michalas, A., & Akhunzada, A. (2021). Fake news outbreak 2021: Can we stop the viral spread? *Journal of Network and Computer Applications, 190*, 103112.

Kim, B., Xiong, A., Lee, D., & Han, K. (2021). A systematic review on fake news research through the lens of news creation and consumption: Research efforts, challenges, and future directions. *PloS One, 16*(12), e0260080. https://doi.org/10.1371/journal.pone.0260080

Klepper, D. (2022, February 26). War via TikTok: Russia's new tool for propaganda machine. *A.P. News.* https://apnews.com/article/russia-ukraine-technology-europe-media-national ism-2186dbc533560cb666f59655ecf1ee8e

Kling, R., McKim, G., & King, A. (2003). A bit more to it: Scholarly communication forums as socio-technical interaction networks. *Journal of the American Society for Information Science and Technology, 54*(1), 47–67.

Lamb, R., & Kling, R. (2003). Reconceptualizing users as social actors in information systems research. *MIS Quarterly, 27*(2), 197–235.

Langin, K. (2018, March 8). Fake news spreads faster than true news on Twitter—thanks to people, not bots. *Science.* www.science.org/content/article/fake-news-spreads-faster-true-news-twitter-thanks-people-not-bots

Lasarte, D. (2023, March 30). A US senator is slowing down the process to ban TikTok, citing free speech concerns. *Quartz.* https://qz.com/a-us-senator-is-slowing-down-the-process-to-ban-tiktok-1850284854

Lee, C. E. (2023, March 19). TikTok now has 150 million active users in the U.S., CEO to tell Congress. *NBC News.* www.nbcnews.com/politics/congress/tiktok-now-150-mill ion-active-users-us-ceo-tell-congress-rcna75607

Ljunggren, D., & Porter, M. (2022, December 16). TikTok says it will cut staff in Russia-company statement. *Reuters.* www.reuters.com/technology/tiktok-cut-staff-rus sia-ria-2022-12-16/

Majumder, B. G. (2022, March 24). Information war: TikTok is giving fake news on Russia-Ukraine conflict to new users, says report. *News18.* www.news18.com/news/tech/info rmation-war-tiktok-is-giving-fake-news-on-russia-ukraine-conflict-to-new-users-says-report-4901945.html

Marwick, A. E. (2018). Why do people share fake news? A socio-technical model of media effects. *Georgetown Law Technology Review, 2*(2), 474–512.

McCoy, C. (2020). *Socio-material interaction networks, data dashboards, and decision makers' practices: A study of data dashboards in higher education institutions* (Publication No. 28025017) [Doctoral dissertation Indiana University-Bloomington]. *ProQuest Dissertation and Theses Global.*

Meyer, E. T. (2006). Socio-technical interaction networks: A discussion of the strengths, weaknesses and future of Kling's STIN model. In J. Berleur, M. I. Nurminen, & J. Impagliazzo (Eds.), *Social informatics: An information society for all? In remembrance of Rob Kling* (pp. 37–48). Springer.

Meyer, E. T. (2007). *Socio-technical perspectives on digital photography: Scientific digital photography use by marine mammal researchers* (Publication No. 3278467) [Doctoral dissertation Indiana University-Bloomington]. ProQuest Dissertation and Theses Global.

Meyers, D. (2022, September 15). TikTok has become a hotbed of misinformation. *Fulcrum.* https://thefulcrum.us/big-picture/Media/tiktok-misinformation

Milmo, D., & Farah, H. (2022, March 5). War as seen on TikTok: Ukraine clips get views whether true or not. *The Guardian.* www.theguardian.com/technology/2022/mar/05/tik tok-ukraine-russia-invasion-clips-get-views-whether-true-or-not

Mozur, P., Mac, R., & Che, C. (2022, August 19). TikTok browser can track users' keystrokes, according to new research. *The New York Times.* www.nytimes.com/2022/08/19/technol ogy/tiktok-browser-tracking.html

Muhammed, T. S., & Mathew, S. K. (2022). The disaster of misinformation: A review of research in social media. *International Journal of Data Science and Analytics, 13*(4), 271–285.

Murero, M. (2023). Coordinated inauthentic behavior: An innovative manipulation tactic to amplify COVID-19 anti-vaccine communication outreach via social media. *Frontiers in Sociology, 8,* 1141416. https://doi.org/10.3389/fsoc.2023.1141416

O'Connor, C. (2022, March 2). #Propaganda: Russia state-controlled media flood TikTok with Ukraine disinformation. *Institute for Strategic Dialogue.* www.isdglobal.org/dig ital_dispatches/propaganda-russia-state-controlled-media-flood-tiktok-with-ukraine-dis information/

Omar, B., & Dequan, W. (2020). Watch, share or create: The influence of personality traits and user motivation on TikTok mobile video usage. *International Journal of Interactive Mobile Technologies, 14*(4), 121–137.

Pappas, V. (2020, March 18). Introducing the TikTok content advisory council. *TikTok.* https://newsroom.tiktok.com/en-us/introducing-the-tiktok-content-advisory-council

Rach, M., & Peter, M. K. (2021). How TikTok's algorithm beats Facebook & Co. for attention under the theory of escapism: A network sample analysis of Austrian, German and Swiss users. In F. J. Martínez-López & D. López López (Eds.), *Advances in digital marketing and ecommerce* (pp. 137–143). Springer.

Rosenbaum, H., & Joung, K. (2004). Socio-technical interaction networks as a tool for understanding digital libraries. *Proceedings of the American Society for Information Science and Technology, 41*(1), 206–212.

Rothkopf, D. (2023, March 24). TikTok isn't the sole problem. Tech needs tougher regulation. *Daily Beast.* www.thedailybeast.com/tiktok-isnt-the-solo-problem-tech-needs-tougher-regulation

Santuraki, S. U. (2019). Trends in the regulation of hate speech and fake news: A threat to free speech? *Hasanuddin Law Review, 5*(2), 140–158.

Sardarizadeh, S. (2022, April 25). Ukraine war: False TikTok videos draw millions of views. *BBC News.* www.bbc.com/news/60867414

Sauer, P. (2022, March 21). Russia bans Facebook and Instagram under 'extremism' law. *The Guardian.* www.theguardian.com/world/2022/mar/21/russia-bans-facebook-and-instagram-under-extremism-law

Sawyer, S., & Tyworth, M. (2006). Social informatics: Principles, theory, and practice. In J. Berleur, M. I. Numinen, & J. Impagliazzo (Eds.), *Social informatics: An information society for all? In remembrance of Rob Kling* (pp. 49–62). Springer.

Scacchi, W. (2005). Socio-technical interaction networks in free/open source software development processes. In S. T. Acuña & N. Juristo (Eds.), *Software process modeling* (pp. 1–27). Springer.

Seldin, J. (2023, March 30). Russia using TikTok to push pro-Moscow narrative on Ukraine. *Voice of America*. www.voanews.com/a/russia-using-tiktok-to-push-pro-moscow-narrat ive-on-ukraine-/7029637.html

Shachaf, P., & Rosenbaum, H. (2009, February 8–11). Online social reference: A research agenda through a STIN framework. *Proceedings of the iConference 2009*. Chapel Hill, NC. https://scholarworks.iu.edu/dspace/bitstream/handle/2022/25095/online_social_re ference_proceedings.pdf?sequence=1&isAllowed=y

Stringhini, G. (2019). Adversarial behaviours knowledge area. In A. Rashid, H. Chivers, G. Danezis, E. Lupu, & A. Martin (Eds.), *The cyber security body of knowledge* (pp. 223–250). The National Cyber Security Centre.

Thomson, T. J. (2022, February 28). How to spot fake or misleading footage on social media claiming to be from the Ukraine war. *PBS*. www.pbs.org/newshour/world/how-to-spot-fake-or-misleading-footage-on-social-media-claiming-to-be-from-the-ukraine-war

TikTok. (n.d.). Safety partners. *TikTok*. www.tiktok.com/safety/en/safety-partners/

"TikTok." (2023, March 20). *Wikipedia*. https://en.wikipedia.org/wiki/TikTok

Tiku, N. (2022, March 6). TikTok suspends posting new video from Russia over the country's recent 'fake news' law. *The Washington Post*. www.washingtonpost.com/tec hnology/2022/03/06/tiktok-russia-putin-fake-news-law/

Vosoughi, S., Roy, D., & Aral, S. (2018). The spread of true and false news online. *Science, 359*, 1146–1151.

Walker, S., & Creanor, L. (2009). The STIN in the tale: A socio-technical interaction perspective on networked learning. *Educational Technology & Society, 12*(4), 305–316.

Wasserman, H., & Madrid-Morales, D. (2019). An exploratory study of "fake news" and media trust in Kenya, Nigeria and South Africa. *African Journalism Studies, 40*(1), 107–123.

Westlund, O., Larsen, R., Graves, L., Kavtaradze, L., & Steensen, S. (2022). Technologies and fact-checking: A socio-technical mapping. In J. C. Correia, P. Jerónimo, & I. Amaral (Eds.), *Disinformation studies: Perspectives from an emerging field* (pp. 193–236). LabCom.

World Health Organization. (2022, September 1). Infodemics and misinformation negatively affect people's health behaviors: New WHO review finds. *WHO*. www.who.int/europe/ news/item/01-09-2022-infodemics-and-misinformation-negatively-affect-people-s-hea lth-behaviours--new-who-review-finds

York, J. (2023, February 24). 'World's first TikTok war': Ukraine's social media campaign 'a question of survival.' *France 24*. www.france24.com/en/europe/20230224-world-s-first-tiktok-war-ukraine-s-social-media-campaign-a-question-of-survival

Zhu, X., & Yang, S. (2023). Toward a socio-technical framework for misinformation policy analysis. In S. Yang, X. Zhu, & P. Fichman (Eds.), *The usage and impact of ICTs during the Covid-19 pandemic* (pp. 11–45). Routledge.

SECTION IV

Opportunities and challenges with digital technology domestication

9

SOCIO-ECOLOGICAL MODEL OF INTERNET CHALLENGES

Pnina Fichman and Patrick Sullivan

Introduction

TikTok, Instagram, Facebook, and other social media platforms enable the rise in popularity of internet challenges (ICs), some of which become viral. Over time, some ICs lose public interest and disappear while others continue to change as they spread. The impact of some popular ICs spills over into offline activities, bearing implications for individuals, groups, and organizations beyond their original online popularity. While research concerning ICs increased as the phenomenon became popular, most studies focused on individuals' motivations for participation in ICs (e.g., Burgess et al., 2018; Deslandes et al., 2020; Falgoust et al., 2022; Feijoo et al., 2023; Roth et al., 2022; Shroff et al., 2021) or their spread in networks that resembles the spread of viral information typically following a power law distribution (e.g., Burgess et al., 2018; Ortega-Barón et al., 2023; Pressgrove et al., 2018). Yet, while these ICs spread within a complex contextual setting, which includes the specific sociotechnical affordances of platforms, researchers have generally ignored other political, economic, social, and technological factors influencing the evolutionary pattern of ICs in their sociotechnical contexts. To address this gap, we propose a socio-ecological model of IC evolution, which is illustrated by two ICs that were popular during the early days of the COVID-19 lockdown. This chapter uses the metaphor of an organism to analyze and examine the evolution of ICs, relying on Bronfenbrenner's socio-ecological theory (Bronfenbrenner, 1977, 1986, 1989). This metaphor is useful here since the evolution of ICs resembles that of other organisms—with their complex structure of interdependent elements—as their existences evolve over time. Frequently, the evolutionary patterns of ICs follow the patterns of spread of other online information. Take the spread of viral information as an example. Nahon

DOI: 10.4324/9781032678542-14

and Hemsley (2013) argue that the process of social information flow follows an S-shape curve, with a slow beginning and a fast increase after reaching a critical mass that later slows down, much like the diffusion of technological innovation and other epidemic models. However, that viral information spread also follows a power law distribution with a sharp acceleration that is followed by a quick decay (Nahon & Hemsley, 2013). Ecological models like Bronfenbrenner's theory, which helps us to understand how an organism develops over time as a complex system of relationships affected by multiple levels of the surrounding environment, have been widely used in the study of individuals, groups, and organizations; these models have inspired better understandings of social media phenomena as diverse as collective trolling events or crowdfunding (Inbar & Barzilay, 2014; Lin & Lin 2006; Sun & Fichman, 2020).

Bronfenbrenner's (1977) socio-ecological theory deals with the ecology of human development and posits that the individual develops within an environment (also referred to as a context or system) that includes four levels. These levels are: microsystems (e.g., family, peers, school, and health system), mesosystem (interactions between microsystems), exosystem (e.g., mass media, local politics, neighbors, and industry), and macrosystem (attitudes and ideologies of the culture) (Bronfenbrenner, 1977). The theory "was illustrated by nesting circles that place the individual in the center surrounded by various systems" (Kilanowski, 2017, p. 295). Bronfenbrenner (1986) later revised his theory to focus on the interaction between processes, persons, context, and time, known as the PPCT model, which was followed by his ecological system theory (Bronfenbrenner, 1989). Bronfenbrenner's PPCT model, importantly, adds the process of interaction with certain parts of the environment (proximal) over time, in which the form, power, and content of the interaction instrumentally shape the organism. While various socio-ecological models have been widely adopted in research beyond child development, Bronfenbrenner's theory was particularly appealing in two other specific subject domains: (1) public health (e.g., Kilanowski, 2017); and (2) crowdfunding (e.g., Inbar & Barzilay, 2014; Lin & Lin, 2006). The latter is of particular interest to us because these studies utilize Bronfenbrenner's socio-ecological theory in the context of online platforms.

Inspired by Lin and Lin's (2006) ecological model of communities of practice (CoP), based partially on Bronfenbrenner's work, Inbar and Barzilay (2014) proposed that online platforms (e.g., the crowdfunding platform Kickstarter) are "a hierarchy of multiple, partially competing communities ... that evolve and change over time" (p. 1) with shifting member interest and participation. Their theory was validated by studying participation patterns of users in crowdfunding campaigns over five years. They found that while the growth of some communities impacted their crowdfunding performance, "some communities, despite high participation rates, had negative impacts on crowdfunding campaign success" (Inbar & Barzilay, 2014, p.1). This decrease varied across the 13 Kickstarter categories; it was most noticeable in campaigns in the Games category and least noticeable in campaigns in the Art and Photography categories. It is unclear why the Art and Photography categories demonstrate a different pattern of CoP members' behaviors over time than members in the Games CoP. Herding behaviors, according to Inbar and Barzilay (2014), explained some of the changes that they observed in crowdfunding campaigns over time, with two peaks in funding level. It is unclear if other instances of herding behaviors, such as those manifested by ICs, will follow a similar pattern in these communities. Interestingly, a participation pattern with two peaks also characterized the evolution of an online case of mass Chinese collective trolling (Sun & Fichman, 2020), which resembles the fast spread of ICs. Researchers have not yet explored what causes some ICs and some CoPs to demonstrate this kind of evolutionary pattern.

We propose a socio-ecological model of ICs that is informed by Bronfenbrenner's theory, and we demonstrate the potential utility of the model for explaining the evolution in participation patterns over time. We demonstrate the utility of this model with two ICs, each of which formed their own CoPs: one surrounding a painting recreation challenge (Between Art and Quarantine) and the other surrounding a photography challenge (View from My Window).

We pose a few assumptions:

1 An IC evolves within the context of other ICs that have different types (e.g., dance, art, music, and cooking).
2 As ICs are shared on different platforms (e.g., TikTok, Instagram, and Facebook), they utilize a range of sociotechnical affordances that enable and constrain their spread.
3 ICs are nested in their general environment that includes political, economic, social, and technological forces, along with international, legal, health, and cultural settings.
4 Over time, ICs evolve and spread within this context.

An examination of an IC's various environmental factors is critical to understanding its nature and spread.

Internet challenges

Research concerning the spread of ICs is relatively new. Academic literature regarding this subject dates back to around 2014 in response to the Ice-Bucket Challenge. Early examples of studies focused on IC participation (e.g., Ni et al., 2014; Phing & Yazdanifard, 2014) originate in 2014 and analyze the proliferation of this particularly popular challenge, which began in that year. However, it was not until 2020 that scholars took especial interest in the development of ICs. As explained by researchers such as Klug (2020), Falgoust et al. (2022), and Fichman and Dedema (2023), these ICs provided a form of socialization amidst the isolation of social distancing. As 2020 marked the beginning of COVID-19 lockdowns, which in turn encouraged public interest in ICs, so too did the year mark an increase in scholarly interest in IC proliferation.

Among the variety of theories that guide scholarly analyses of ICs, virality is perhaps the most broadly applicable. Although *viral* has a loose, colloquial meaning, researchers have provided the concept with a more concrete understanding as a defined process. For instance, Hemsley (2011) defines virality as an informational diffusion involving word-of-mouth discussions, connected personal networks, and exponential growth in exposure. As popular ICs spread in a manner generally understood as viral, researchers have repeatedly analyzed these challenges as viral processes (e.g., Burgess et al., 2018; Ortega-Barón et al., 2023; Pressgrove et al., 2018; Shroff et al., 2021). Wenger's (1998, 2001) communities of practice theory, which focuses on the social process of learning in communities of practice, informed Fichman and Dedema's (2023) analysis of ICs. Other theories utilized to analyze ICs include the Integrated Behavioral Model, a framework for human behavior centered upon intention and motivation (e.g., Khasawneh et al., 2021a; Roth et al., 2022), and the Behavioral Contagion Theory, which posits that individuals repeat behaviors that they witness others performing (e.g., Abraham et al., 2022; Park et al., 2023).

Scholars applied either a qualitative or quantitative approach. Those in the former group generally analyze common themes and trends among a relevant dataset, such as videos of ICs (e.g., Deslandes et al., 2020; Khasawneh et al., 2020; Khasawneh et al., 2021b; Klug, 2020), interviews with IC participants (e.g., Falgoust et al., 2022; Feijoo et al., 2023; Roth et al., 2022), and online posts discussing ICs (e.g., Park et al., 2023; Pressgrove et al., 2018). Researchers conducting quantitative IC studies predominantly analyze metadata related to videos of challenges, such as Bonifazi et al. (2022), who create models that track the lifespans of ICs based upon video characteristics and the social parameters of those spreading the challenges. Others analyzed demographics of participants to draw conclusions regarding which groups are most likely to partake in a challenge (e.g., Khasawneh et al., 2021a; Ng et al., 2021; Shroff et al., 2021).

Most of these studies focus on the motivations encouraging IC participation and the relationship between demographic groups and involvement in ICs. Findings show that participants in ICs act out of a desire to achieve perceived benefits such as positive socialization and enjoyment. Burgess et al. (2018), for example, find that ICs are best considered "as creative and inclusive challenges, rather than sheepish acts of conformity" (p. 1048), explaining that those involved typically take part in a challenge due to personal incentives including social prestige and amusement. Other researchers (e.g., Deslandes et al., 2020; Falgoust et al., 2022; Feijoo et al., 2023; Roth et al., 2022) likewise determine that individuals predominantly partake in ICs because they find these challenges enjoyable and socially rewarding, as opposed to acting out of a sense of pressure or expectation. Some studies focused on the role of gender in IC participation. Ortega-Barón et al. (2023), for instance, find that boys are more likely to perform dangerous

ICs than girls, and Ward et al. (2021) find that males are more likely to perform dangerous ICs than females in certain circumstances. Shroff et al. (2021) conclude that the more traits considered masculine an individual has, the more likely that individual is to participate in an IC, while the inverse is true for traits considered feminine. In the specific case of an individual dance challenge, however, Klug (2020) determined that teenage girls were the most represented demographic. Furthermore, Ward et al. (2021) conclude that individuals with high perceived popularity are more likely to partake in dangerous ICs, and Shroff et al. (2021) conclude that individuals belonging to a social group are more likely to participate in challenges overall. Together, these studies suggest that demographics correlate with participation in these challenges. Researchers have further directed particular attention to ICs that pose risks, such as challenges that might cause bodily harm, as they consider these examples especially important to address. Accordingly, many studies concerning ICs (e.g., Deslandes et al., 2020; Khasawneh et al., 2020; Khasawneh et al., 2021b; Park et al., 2023; Ward et al., 2021) center on dangerous challenges in order to provide potential manners through which to combat their spread and harmful effects. This emphasis has given particular focus to the topic of risky challenges and has directed some attention away from non-dangerous challenges as a result.

This chapter occupies a unique space in the present literature concerning ICs and proposes a socio-ecological model. Rather than centering its examination on individuals' motivations to participate in ICs or ICs' networks and virality, this chapter describes ICs as communities in relation to various social contexts including economic forces and cultural settings. In doing so, it provides a new lens through which one can view ICs and their spread within a socio-ecological theoretical framework. Importantly, rather than focusing on dangerous challenges, we focus on non-dangerous challenges.

Art internet challenges during COVID lockdown

In the early days of the COVID-19 pandemic, governments around the globe enacted "stay-at-home" orders, known as lockdowns. These lockdowns triggered an unprecedented reliance on information technology among large segments of the world population for most of their daily activities. The intended and unintended consequences of information technology use attracted much media and scholarly attention (Yang et al., 2023). During these early days of the pandemic, individuals from around the globe who were isolated in their homes bonded online, united by their creative participation in various internet challenges. While health, economy, and political considerations emphasized national boundaries, internet challenges on social media enabled secluded individuals to emerge from isolation and find common ground with others. Participation in these internet challenges supported the well-being of individuals around the globe, disregarding nationality, demography, or socio-economic status. Participating in each of these challenges, members shared their creations—which utilized common household items and tools—with like-minded peers. Users posted their creations, and others liked and commented on them on social media platforms. This study examines the evolution of two internet challenges from this period. One is an Instagram painting recreation challenge, and the other is a Facebook photography challenge. Both challenges attracted many posts and are still active at the time of writing; they received media attention and resulted in the publications of catalogs, books, and museum exhibitions. Scholars have previously studied an internet challenge as a CoP (Fichman & Dedema, 2023).

The two ICs were at the peak of their popularity during the COVID-19 lockdown. The Between Art and Quarantine (BAaQ) IC was created by museum employees, who used their Instagram accounts to call their followers to post a picture replicating an artwork using items that they had at home (Fichman & Dedema, 2023). Around the same time, Barbara Duriau created the public Facebook group "View from My Window" (VfMW) with the goal of "connect[ing] people from all around the World during these tough times" (Duriau, 2020, 2021; Sleith, 2020). The group, which asked members to photograph and share the view from one's window or balcony, rapidly grew and had at some point 42 moderators and a backlog of posts that at times were shared over a month after submission.

Clearly, each of the two ICs had a specific purpose and common rules to follow. All ICs are embedded in particular sociotechnical types and platforms that enable them through the platform's affordances (e.g., sharing, liking, tagging, using hashtags, creating closely moderated groups, texts, visuals, and networks) and the technical practices enforced by their types (e.g., dance, baking, and photography). Specifically, BAaQ utilizes Instagram's hashtags, tagging, liking, sharing, and commenting, taking advantage of the platform's visual and textual affordances. To participate in BAaQ, there are little to no barriers, as it only requires an Instagram account and a camera. However, there are more barriers to participate in the VfMW challenge, as one needs to be a member of the group, adhere to the group rules, and wait within the moderators' backlog. This IC utilizes Facebook's groups capabilities, including: sharing, liking, commenting, and moderating, and the platform's visual and textual affordances. Furthermore, these two ICs, like other ICs, are nested in the larger environment. Also as with other ICs, the sociotechnical affordances of platforms support other activities and process, which in turn impact the spread of ICs by utilizing the platform's networks on one hand, and users' skillsets on the other. Importantly, however, the spread of specific ICs on particular platforms is intertwined with the specific context of COVID-19, and the global, health, legal, and political environment. Specifically, both ICs were triggered by the health crisis of the COVID-19 pandemic and the resultant lockdown enacted by governments around the globe, which caused people all over the world to use technology to conduct their work and social needs (Yang et al., 2023).

Art internet challenges as communities of practice

We describe each of the challenges and argue that both ICs are CoPs, and that they have similarities and differences in their community features. Fichman and Dedema (2023) studied four communities of practice from around the globe that posted content on Instagram with variations on the community of Between Art and Quarantine—the first of the ICs. We describe the challenge and then explain it as a CoP. Next, we likewise describe the second challenge (View from My Window) and explain it as a CoP as well.

Internet challenge #1: Between Art and Quarantine

The Between Art and Quarantine internet challenge began in the early days of the COVID-19 pandemic lockdown (March 2020) on Instagram. It was created by museum employees (e.g., those of the Rijsmuseum in Amsterdam and the Getty Museum in the USA), who promoted it on their Instagram accounts, and they encouraged followers to post a picture of an art recreation using household items (Fichman & Dedema, 2023). They called on their followers to use hashtags such as #betweenartandquarantine or #tussenkunstenquarantaine (translated from Dutch to "Between Art and Quarantine") in their posts. Later in 2020, Getty Publications published a printed catalog of recreation posts, and an exhibition of the recreations from the challenge opened to visitors at the Palais des Beaux-Arts de Lille in France. For an example of the BAaQ challenge, one can view an Instagram post by Laura Belconde. In her post from May of 2020, Belconde recreates a sixteenth-century portrait of Ana de Mendoza, Princess of Eboli, painted by Alonso Sanchez Coello. Positioning a photograph of herself next to the original artwork for comparison, she utilizes everyday objects to imitate some of its aspects, including using a teabag as an eyepatch and rolls of toilet paper as a ruff collar. Her caption includes hashtags such as #betweenartandquarantine and #tussenkunstenquarantaine, which identify the post as participating in the challenge (Belconde, 2020).

As previously articulated by Fichman and Dedema (2023), BAaQ fits Murillo's (2008) five key characteristics of a virtual CoP: mutual engagement, joint enterprise, shared repertoire, community, and learning or identity acquisition. IC participants collaborated with each other through actions such as sharing posts, providing feedback, and discussing related topics, thereby conducting mutual engagement. The Instagram accounts of the Getty Museum and the Rijksmuseum contributed to BAaQ's joint enterprise—building a common understanding of the community's activities and creating a differentiated space for it—by announcing the challenge, encouraging followers to participate, and displaying examples of art recreations. Those involved in the IC used a shared repertoire, such as specific hashtags, to identify their posts and communicate information. Moreover, participants connected with each other and developed an online community of peers with a shared interest in fine art, and they acquired identities as members of this community. Accordingly, BAaQ, as a challenge that displays the five fundamental aspects described by Murillo (2008), is an example of a CoP.

Internet challenge #2: View from My Window

On March 23, 2020, Barbara Duriau, a graphic designer living in Amsterdam, created the public Facebook group "View from my window" for the purpose of bringing people from around the globe together amidst the isolation of social distancing. Initially, "344 people accepted [Duriau's] invitation. The following day there were 2,675. One week later, 50,000. April 15th, 1 million" (Duriau, 2020, p.8). By June 2020, VfMW boasted 2.3 million members. VfMW became a supportive community that provided crisis relief to millions of users during the lockdown, when the view from one's window was, for most, the only bridge to the outside world. The internet challenge called users to "take a photo of the view from your own home, either from your window or your balcony and then share it with the group … [no] close-ups of pets or flowers, multiple or panoramic photos, videos, people you could clearly identify" (Duriau, 2020, p.10). Users were then informed that, "by contributing to this group, and posting [their] photo[s], [participants] agree to give out [their] photo... free of rights" ("View From my Window" – Life after Facebook, 2020). Group members' willingness to donate money to the cause of creating an exhibition, website, and book were noticeable. On May 14, 2020, Duriau launched a Kickstarter campaign with a goal of reaching €70,000 (~$79,399). Her goal was exceeded, with over 3,000 people backing the project, raising €138,580 (~$155,912) ("View From my Window" – Life after Facebook, 2020). In November 2020, Duriau (2020) self-published the first volume, made up of many of the photos from the VfMW group, and exactly a year later, she released her second volume. As the community grew, Duriau gathered a team of volunteers to assist her with moderating VfMW and processing photographs. By June 2020, 42 people were listed as either administrators or moderators. On June 14, Duriau posted to the Facebook group that she and her team had made the decision to stop accepting any more members or photos because "the concept of the group [was] linked to lockdown" ("View From my Window" – Life after Facebook, 2020), and lockdown was coming to an end in many countries. This decision was short-lived, however, as the group was experiencing an "exponential curve that didn't show any signs of falling" (Duriau, 2020, p.13). The group's popularity, as well as the positive response that Duriau received when asking users for their reasons for wanting the group to continue, motivated her to keep the group open for an indefinite time with the intent of helping members to "keep the connections [that they had] made and to nurture them" ("View From my Window" – Life after Facebook, 2020). One example of the VfMW challenge is a Facebook post in the VfMW group by Marie Tirrell dated April 7, 2020. The post includes a photo of the New York City skyline during the daytime. In her caption, Tirrell explains that the image is the view from a twenty-sixth-floor balcony, and she writes that New Yorkers regularly stand on their balconies to cheer medical personnel for their efforts combating the pandemic. She also offers well wishes to viewers, notes that she cannot wait to visit their cities and countries in person again, and she tells them to stay home and stay safe (Tirrell, 2020).

The VfMW challenge fits the five key characteristics that Murillo (2008) assigns to a virtual CoP, as we describe here, similar to the description of the BAaQ challenge. Firstly, participants mutually engage with each other by sharing their photos and interacting through likes or comments on posts. The IC's hashtag is additionally an example of shared repertoire, and Duriau's Facebook group—by acting as a differentiated space for the IC and listing its parameters, such as prohibiting close-ups of pets and flowers—provides joint enterprise. Lastly, participants created a community based upon their interconnections formed through the Facebook group, and they subsequently adopted identities as community members. In this challenge, a group of CoP members became more involved with the community through moderation and participation in enforcing and further developing community norms. Taking these elements into account, as in the case of BAaQ, we understand VfMW as a CoP because it exhibits all five core components of such a community listed by Murillo (2008).

Art internet challenges' development in context

Examining the development over time of these two ICs represents a challenging task. First, the BAaQ challenge involved multiple hashtags, forming communities around each of them, with some overlap among community members (Fichman & Dedema, 2023). As part of the same art recreation challenge, hashtags evolved and peaked sometimes independently of each other, reflecting the specific context of their unique community members. For example, the Dutch hashtag was the first to appear due to the earlier spread of COVID in European countries. The Russian hashtag, by contrast, appeared later and, perhaps due to the different script of Cyrillic, was employed by some users with less overlap concerning the other three hashtags and with different styles of social media usage. Examining only one hashtag would provide a limited account of the IC, and examining them all together would miss the nuanced contextual variations between the four hashtags. Hence, an accurate analysis of this IC's development requires considering its complex socio-cultural context; yet, existing approaches to the study of IC development largely ignore this context. They instead focus on other areas of research including gender and motivation to participate in dangerous challenges. Those that examine the context of ICs mainly focus on virality of information, tracking diffusion and exponential growth in exposure through the network. As they focus on the process of sharing, they place less emphasis on the ways that the content changes as it spreads—the evolutionary pattern's contents. The nuanced differences between posts are lost in this type of research that mostly confirms the power law distribution of information in the network. These lost nuances are critical because scholars found that these challenges are best considered "as creative and inclusive challenges, rather than sheepish acts of conformity ... Participating in a VCM [viral challenge meme] involves adding to a social practice that diffuses in a wave-like fashion, and it requires contributors to have an intuitive social sense of the challenge's permutations, life-cycle and currency" (Burgess et al., 2018, p. 1048). Thus, analyses of the IC lifecycle should not ignore the uniqueness of each post in the challenge and should go beyond the diffusion patterns of challenges.

Additionally, the VfMW challenge poses distinct problems when considering its evolution over time. First, because different parts of the world went into stay-at-home orders with different types of restrictions and timelines, an analysis of the IC's diffusion and growth that does not account for these factors' implications concerning the challenge's development is problematic. The sociotechnical context of the challenge complicates an accurate analysis. Second, because the challenge was triggered with the intention to create an exhibition or publish a book, and due to its clear rules for participation (e.g., only one post per users that strictly adhere to the IC's criteria), it required manual moderation. The enforcement of the challenge's rules through group moderation on Facebook resulted in significant delay in posting new images. This postponement became evident not only from moderators' posts, but also from the content of the posts themselves. Many of the posts adhere to the challenge's requirement to include a date, and the gap between the post date and the date on which it was shared on the platform was significant, limiting the ability to accurately examine the evolution of the challenge over time. Here again, it is critical to consider sociotechnical contextual factors in examining the development of the challenge over time. Simply relying on the date of the post would provide an inaccurate storyline.

Thus, both examples raise the need to incorporate contextual factors into the study of IC evolution, and we deem ecological theories of development to be an appropriate path of exploration to address this necessity. Specifically, we propose the socio-ecological model.

A socio-ecological model of internet challenges

We describe the socio-ecological model and demonstrate its utility for understanding the two ICs. Figure 9.1 illustrates the socio-ecological model of ICs, showing that an IC evolves within the context of an ecosystem that includes other ICs. ICs vary in their contents (e.g., dance, art, music, and cooking). They are shared on different platforms (e.g., TikTok, Instagram, and Facebook), and at times they spill over from one platform to another. ICs utilize a range of platform-specific sociotechnical affordances that impact the spread of each challenge. Various ICs present different risk levels, and these ICs evoke a range of motives for participation. ICs involve content created and shared on the internet, and as such they are part of internet content more broadly. Like other content on the internet, ICs are nested in the general environment that includes political, economic, social, and technological

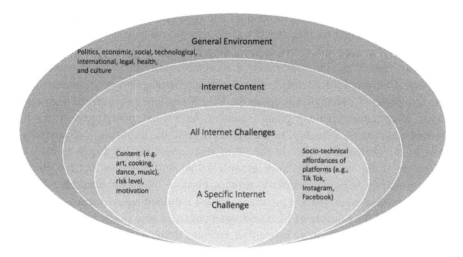

FIGURE 9.1   Socio-ecological model of internet challenges.

forces, along with international, legal, health, and cultural settings. To form a good understanding of the nature and spread of an IC, an examination of its environment's various factors is critical. Each IC evolves and spreads over time within this context and is marked at the center of our nested circles; specific ICs are at the center-most position.

We explain the utility of the model and its various components, demonstrating its value by using the two ICs: BAaQ and VfMW. Each of the two challenges has a purpose and common rules to follow. BAaQ challenges individuals to recreate fine art masterpieces with common household items, take a picture, and share on Instagram. Likewise, VfMW challenges individuals to take a photo of the view from their windows (without people in it) and share on Facebook with a description, date, and location. Participants join these challenges for the aesthetics, creativity, and to be part of the art enthusiasts' communities.

ICs are enabled by the sociotechnical affordances of social media platforms (e.g., sharing, liking, tagging, using hashtags, creating closely moderated groups, textual-visual, and networks) and the technical practices enforced by their particular content (e.g., dance, baking, and photography). Specifically, the BAaQ challenge utilizes Instagram's hashtags, tagging, liking, sharing, and commenting; the challenge takes advantage of the platform's visual and textual affordances. There are little barriers to participation in this challenge, as it only requires an Instagram account and a camera to participate. This challenge used several other hashtags, creating communities of practice with permeable boundaries between them and many overlapping posts (Fichman & Dedema, 2023). At the same time, the VfMW challenge utilizes the capabilities of Facebook's groups, including sharing, liking, commenting, and moderating, and it also takes advantage of the platform's visual and textual affordances. However, this challenge involves more barriers to participation than the BAaQ challenge, including: the need to be a member of the group and accept its rules; the barrier of moderators and the backlog that was created; and the strict rules for acceptable posts, allowing only one post per user. Compared with BAaQ's use of Instagram hashtags to create communities, the utilization of Facebook Groups in the VfMW challenge encouraged a stronger sense of community among group members. As a result, participants in this IC shared additional information in their posts beyond the information requested as part of the challenge's rules. In the posts' texts, users quickly began to include messages to the community, such as well wishes and greetings, but the photos adhered to the rules more strictly, perhaps because the moderators focused on enforcing these rules. While a picture is worth a thousand words, the text attached to it affected the number of likes and comments on these posts, and posts with personal stories evoked more supportive reactions from the community. Clearly, in each challenge, participants made use of the platform's sociotechnical affordances to create and share their posts, and to interact with each other.

ICs are nested in the larger internet ecosystem, and the sociotechnical affordances of platforms allow for many other activities and processes beyond the platform or the ICs. Importantly, however, the initiation and development of ICs are triggered by, and intertwined with, the general environment. For example, the two ICs analyzed in this chapter were triggered by the context of the COVID-19 lockdown; they evolved as lockdown orders changed globally in timelines and rules. The two ICs originated during this lockdown, when people all over the world used technology to conduct their work and social needs (Yang et al., 2020, 2023). Both ICs were popular around the same time, yet some other ICs that were triggered by the COVID-19 lockdown varied significantly from one country to another or were limited to particular regions or countries. Factors in the general environment—such as those of global, health, legal, and political contexts—trigger ICs and impact their content and spread.

The socio-ecological model in Figure 9.1 does not include a time dimension to understand the development of ICs, but it provides a framework useful for understanding the nuanced development of ICs in context. Adding Bronfenbrenner's PPCT model strengthens the nested circles in the socio-ecological model that we illustrate above by suggesting that the various contextual forces impact the organism differently over time, as processes are crucial for the development of an organism. In particular, the lockdown mandates with country-specific stipulations and timelines affected the global spread of BAaQ, and the bottleneck and posting delay created by VfMW moderators affected the spread of the latter IC. Indeed, time plays a crucial role in the development of ICs. Other scholars found an ecological understanding of phenomena to be useful (Fichman & Dedema, 2023; Sun & Fichman, 2020), particularly because of its shared emphasis on the importance of context. The socio-ecological model we propose aligns well with this body of work.

Conclusions

This chapter argues that we can gain a better understanding of the spread of ICs when we examine them within their contexts, and it provides a socio-ecological model that is informed by Bronfenbrenner's theory for that purpose. The model suggests that an IC can be perceived as an organism that evolves over time within the context of its environment, taking into account that the environment allows for a nuanced understanding of its development over time that is otherwise missed. This chapter makes the argument that analyzing ICs as CoPs can be useful, providing two IC examples that demonstrate the utility of the socio-ecological model; the spread of both ICs could not be accurately described and explained without considering their environmental factors. Rather than focusing on individuals who participate in ICs, or on IC spread in networks, this chapter argues that this model can be helpful in analyses of other internet challenges as CoPs.

References

Abraham, J., Roth, R., Zinzow, H., Madathil, K. C., & Wisniewski, P. (2022). Applying behavioral contagion theory to examining young adults' participation in viral social media challenges. *Transactions on Social Computing, 5*(1–4), 1–34. https://dl-acm-org. proxyiub.uits.iu.edu/doi/full/10.1145/3538383

Belconde, L. [@laurabelconde]. (2020, May 9). *« Ana de Mendoza de la Cerda, la princesse d'Eboli », Alonso Sanchez Coello – Reproduction spéciale confinement: collerette de pq + sachet de thé*❀ [Photograph]. Instagram. www.instagram.com/p/B_-HB0IDitQ/

Bonifazi, G., Cecchini, S., Corradini, E., Giuliani, L., Ursino, D., & Virgili, L. (2022). Extracting time patterns from the lifespans of TikTok challenges to characterize non-dangerous and dangerous ones. *Social Network Analysis and Mining, 12,* 62. https:// doi-org.proxyiub.uits.iu.edu/10.1007/s13278-022-00893-w

Bronfenbrenner, U. (1977). Toward an experimental ecology of human development. *American Psychologist, 32,* 513–531. https://doi.org/10.1037/0003-066X.32.7.513

Bronfenbrenner, U. (1986). Ecology of the family as a context for human development: Research perspectives. *Developmental Psychology, 22*(6), 723–742. https://doi.org/10.1037/0012-1649.22.6.723

Bronfenbrenner, U. (1989). Ecological systems theory. In R. Vasta (Ed.), *Annals of child development* (Vol. 6, pp. 187–249). Jessica Kingsley Publishers.

Burgess, A., Miller, V., & Moore, S. (2018). Prestige, performance and social pressure in viral challenge memes: Neknomination, the Ice-Bucket Challenge and SmearForSmear as imitative encounters. *Sociology, 52*(5), 1035–1051. https://journals-sagepub-com. proxyiub.uits.iu.edu/doi/full/10.1177/0038038516680312

Deslandes, S. F., Coutinho, T., de Souza Costa Ferreira, T. R., & Flach, R. M. D. (2020). Online challenges among children and adolescents: Self-inflicted harm and social media strategies. *Salud Colectiva, 16,* e3264. https://doi-org.proxyiub.uits.iu.edu/10.18294/ sc.2020.3264

Duriau, B. (2020). *View from my window.* BXRBXRX.

Duriau, B. (2021). "The Backstory", View from My Window, https://viewfrommywindow. world/the-backstory/

Falgoust, G., Winterlind, E., Moon, P., Parker, A., Zinzow, H., & Chalil Madathil, K. (2022). Applying the uses and gratifications theory to identify motivational factors behind young adult's participation in viral social media challenges on TikTok. *Human Factors in Healthcare, 2*. https://doi-org.proxyiub.uits.iu.edu/10.1016/j.hfh.2022.100014

Feijoo, B., Sádaba, C., & Segarra-Saavedra, J. (2023). Viral challenges as a digital entertainment phenomenon among children. Perceptions, motivations and critical skills of minors. *Communications*. https://doi-org.proxyiub.uits.iu.edu/10.1515/com mun-2022-0044

Fichman, P., & Dedema, M. (2023). Boundary crossing through text and image on Instagram in an online community of practice. *Proceedings of the 56th Hawai'i International Conference on System Sciences* (HICSS-56), pp. 3507–3516. IEEE Press. https://hdl.han dle.net/10125/103062

Hemsley, J. (2011). Virality: Developing a rigorous and useful definition of an information diffusion process. *Social Science Research Network*. https://papers.ssrn.com/sol3/papers. cfm?abstract_id=3129424#

Inbar, Y., & Barzilay, O. (2014). Community impact on crowdfunding performance (November 15, 2014). Available at https://ssrn.com/abstract=2524910 or http://dx.doi. org/10.2139/ssrn.2524910

Khasawneh, A., Chalil, M. K., Dixon, E., Wiśniewski, P., Zinzow, H., & Roth, R. (2020). Examining the self-harm and suicide contagion effects related to the portrayal of the Blue Whale Challenge on YouTube and Twitter (Preprint). *JMIR Mental Health*. https://par. nsf.gov/biblio/10142273. https://doi.org/10.2196/15973

Khasawneh, A., Chalil, M. K., Zinzow, H., Rosopa, P., Natarajan, G., Achuthan, K., & Narasimhan, M. (2021a). Factors contributing to adolescents' and young adults' participation in web-based challenges: Survey study. *JMIR Pediatrics and Parenting, 4*(1). https://doi-org.proxyiub.uits.iu.edu/10.2196/24988

Khasawneh, A., Madathil, K. C., Zinzow, H., Wisniewski, P., Ponathil, A., Rogers, H., Agnisarman, S., Roth, R., & Narasimhan, M. (2021b). An investigation of the portrayal of social media challenges on YouTube and Twitter. *ACM Transactions on Social Computing, 4*(1), 1–23. https://doi-org.proxyiub.uits.iu.edu/10.1145/3444961

Kilanowski, J. (2017). Breadth of the socio-ecological model. *Journal of Agromedicine, 22*(4), 295–297. https://doi.org/10.1080/1059924X.2017.1358971

Klug, D. (2020). "It took me almost 30 minutes to practice this." Performance and production practices in dance challenge videos on TikTok. *arXiv preprint*. arXiv:2008.13040.

Lin, S., & Lin, F. (2006). Towards an ecological perspective on the evolution of online communities of practice. *Proceedings of the 39th Annual Hawaii International Conference on System Sciences* (pp. 134a–134a). IEEE. https://doi.org/10.1109/HICSS.2006.493

Murillo, E. (2008). Searching Usenet for virtual communities of practice: Using mixed methods to identify the constructs of Wenger's theory. *Information Research: An International Electronic Journal, 13*(4), 1–36.

Nahon, K., & Hemsley, J. (2013). *Going viral*. Polity Press.

Ng, L. H. X., Tan, J. Y. H., Tan, D. J. H., & Lee, R. K.-W. (2021). Will you dance to the challenge?: Predicting user participation of TikTok challenges. *Proceedings of the 2021 IEEE/ACM International Conference on Advances in Social Networks Analysis and Mining* (pp. 356–360). ACM. https://doi-org.proxyiub.uits.iu.edu/10.1145/3487 351.3488276

Ni, M. Y., Chan, B. H., Leung, G. M., Lau, E. H., & Pang, H. (2014). Transmissibility of the Ice Bucket Challenge among globally influential celebrities: Retrospective cohort study. *BMJ* (Clinical Research ed.). https://doi.org/10.1136/bmj.g7185

Ortega-Barón, J., Montiel, I., González-Cabrera, J., & Machimbarrena, J. M. (2023). Viral internet challenges scale in preadolescents: An exploratory study. *Current Psychology, 42*(15), 12530–12540. https://doi-org.proxyiub.uits.iu.edu/10.1007/s12 144-021-02692-6

Park, J., Wisniewski, P., Lediaeva, I., Lopez, M., Godfrey, A., Madathil, K. C., & Zinzow, H. (2023). How affordances and social norms shape the discussion of harmful social media challenges on reddit. *Human Factors in Healthcare, 3*. https://doi-org.proxyiub. uits.iu.edu/10.1016/j.hfh.2023.100042

Phing, A. N. M., & Yazdanifard, R. (2014). How does ALS Ice Bucket Challenge achieve its viral outcome through marketing via social media. *Global Journal of Management and Business Research, 14*(7), 56–63.

Pressgrove, G., McKeever, B. W., & Jang, S. M. (2018). What is contagious? Exploring why content goes viral on Twitter: A case study of the ALS Ice Bucket Challenge. *International Journal of Nonprofit & Voluntary Sector Marketing, 23*(1), 1. https://doi-org.proxyiub.uits.iu.edu/10.1002/nvsm.1586

Roth, R., Ajithkumar, P., Natarajan, G., Achuthan, K., Moon, P., Zinzow, H., & Madathil, K. C. (2022). A study of adolescents' and young adults' TikTok challenge participation in South India. *Human Factors in Healthcare*. https://doi-org.proxyiub.uits.iu.edu/10.1016/j.hfh.2022.100005

Shroff, N., Shreyass, G., & Gupta, D. (2021). Viral internet challenges: A study on the motivations behind social media user participation. In T. Senjyu, P. N. Mahalle, T. Perumal, & A. Joshi (Eds.), *Information and communication technology for intelligent systems*. ICTIS 2020. *Smart innovation, systems and technologies*, vol. 196. Springer. https://doi.org/10.1007/978-981-15-7062-9_30

Sleith, E. (2020). "View from My Window" Facebook page becomes a global phenomenon. *Sunday Times*. www.timeslive.co.za/sunday-times/lifestyle/travel/2020-06-21-in-pics-view-from-my-window-facebook-page-becomes-a-global-phenomenon/

Sun, H., & Fichman, P. (2020). The collective trolling lifecycle. *Journal of the American Society for Information Science and Technology, 71*(7), 770–783.

Tirrell, M. (2020, April 7). *Sunday, April 5, New York City from the 26th floor balcony* [Image attached] [Photograph]. Facebook. www.facebook.com/photo?fbid=1022335741 1749067&set=gm.573087386653567

"View From my Window" – Life after Facebook. (2020). In Kickstarter. www.kickstarter. com/projects/barbaraduriau/view-from-my-window-life-after-facebook/description

Ward, S., Dumas, T. M., Srivastava, A., Davis, J. P., & Ellis, W. (2021). Uploading risk: Examining the social profile of young adults most susceptible to engagement in risky social media challenges. *Cyberpsychology, Behavior, and Social Networking, 24*(12), 846–850. https://doi-org.proxyiub.uits.iu.edu/10.1089/cyber.2020.0846

Wenger, E. (1998). *Communities of practice: Learning, meaning, and identity*. Cambridge University Press.

Wenger, E. (2001). *Supporting communities of practice: A survey of community-oriented technologies*. Retrieved from www.ewenger.com/tech/index.html

Yang, S., Fichman, P., Zhu, A., Sanfilippo, M. R., Zhang, S., & Fleischmann, K. R. (2020). The use of ICT during COVID-19. *Proceedings of the 83rd Annual Conference of the American Society of Information Science and Technology, 57*, e297. https://doi.org/10.1002/pra2.297

Yang, S., Zhu, X., & Fichman, P. (Eds.). (2023). *The usage and impact of ICTs during the Covid-19 pandemic* (1st ed.). Routledge. https://doi.org/10.4324/9781003231769

10

ROLE EXPANSION OF SOCIAL MEDIA GROUPS

Example from the online activity for Roman Zadorov in Israel

Azi Lev-On

Introduction

This chapter delves into a captivating and unexplored social media phenomenon: the "role expansion" of social media groups. Namely, in certain circumstances, groups formed for a specific purpose redirect their activities toward related or analogous goals that surpass their original scope. This chapter sheds light on the character of this phenomenon and provides an initial explanation for its underlying mechanisms.

This research on the "role expansion" phenomenon within social media groups contributes to the literature in the field of social informatics. Social informatics is concerned with the study of how information and communication technologies (ICTs) impact and are influenced by social structures, human behaviors, and organizational practices (Kling, 2007; Smutny & Vehovar, 2020; Fichman et al., 2022). The "role expansion" phenomenon is an intriguing dimension of social informatics, as it explores how online groups, originally formed for specific purposes, adapt and evolve over time in response to changing circumstances and member needs.

This study resonates with existing social informatics research that examines the complex dynamics of online communities (Preece, 2000; Lev-On, 2013), highlighting their ability to serve as platforms for multifaceted discussions that transcend their initial objectives. The study serves as a significant addition to social informatics literature, providing insights into the ways in which online groups engage with a variety of social issues, ultimately broadening our understanding of the role of ICTs in shaping contemporary public discourse.

As a case study, I analyze social media activity advocating justice for Roman Zadorov in Israel. Zadorov was found guilty in 2010 of murdering a young girl and was sentenced to life in prison. After a retrial, Zadorov was acquitted in 2023.

DOI: 10.4324/9781032678542-15

Despite being convicted of the murder in 2010, a large majority of Israelis believed that he was innocent. Over the following decade, numerous Facebook groups promoting justice for Zadorov emerged, with the largest boasting over 300,000 members—one of the largest groups on Facebook in Israel.

The existing body of literature on social media activity within groups dedicated to rectifying wrongful convictions indicates that the discussions within these groups can generally be classified into two distinct categories. The first category encompasses conversations about evidence, narratives, and the underlying reasons that led to the miscarriage of justice. In contrast, the second category goes beyond the specifics of individual cases and engages in a critical and anti-establishment dialogue. This discourse sheds light on instances of unprofessionalism and corruption within the justice system, expressing skepticism about its capacity to conduct impartial investigations and accurately identify the true perpetrators (Gerbaudo, 2017; Savage et al., 2007).

The study reveals a similar intriguing phenomenon that exists within the groups advocating justice for Roman Zadorov. Using content analysis, I found that most of the content in the two large groups advocating justice for Zadorov centers on the Zadorov case itself. Still, a significant portion of it pertains to cases with a "family resemblance," such as institutional injustices, innocence of falsely convicted people, cases of violence and murder, and more. While these cases are not directly related to the Zadorov case, they are frequently presented to illustrate that the Zadorov affair is part of a larger set of phenomena. Arguably, by gaining familiarity with this broader context, a more comprehensive understanding of the Zadorov case can be achieved.

The phenomenon of "role expansion" within online groups advocating against miscarriages of justice can also be attributed to the imperative of maintaining the audience's sustained interest. Insights gleaned from interviews with group administrators underscore the fluctuating nature of public attention toward the Zadorov case. Periods of intense scrutiny alternate with phases of minimal coverage. During these periods of diminished attention, administrators are challenged to sustain engagement and provide relevant information. Consequently, the original "role" of the group broadens to encompass these gaps in attention and maintain ongoing reader engagement.

Role expansion of organizations

There is a scarcity of literature that specifically discusses the concept of "role expansion." However, existing literature in this area revolves around the notion that organizations and groups are established with a *clear purpose of fulfilling certain roles*. These roles can span across diverse domains such as social, economic, and leisure activities, among others. Sometimes, these roles are explicitly defined from the outset of the organization's formation, while in other instances, they might be more loosely outlined. Regardless, the members or participants of the organization generally have a shared understanding of the underlying purpose that drove its creation.

This concept is rooted in the notion that organizations initially adopt specific roles to fulfill within a particular context. However, organizations are far from being rigid entities; they often demonstrate adaptability by revising their plans and strategies to meet evolving member needs and changing external circumstances. For instance, trade unions have historically championed the cause of workers, tirelessly striving to enhance their working conditions. However, in certain instances, these unions broaden their scope to encompass areas such as recreation and housing. What may have initially been established to better the conditions of workers eventually evolves and takes on a "life of its own," becoming independent of the organization's original role. This phenomenon of role expansion has been documented in the literature (Ben-Ari, 2018; Lewis & Vandekerckhove, 2018; Lissak, 1976), highlighting the dynamic character of organizations as they adapt and develop to meet changing demands.

Role expansion of social media groups

Similar to trade unions and various other organizations, social media groups often come into existence with a defined purpose. Yet, it is not uncommon for them to undergo development and adopt a slightly altered trajectory over time. The initial intent of these groups can often be inferred from disclaimers, cover photos, pinned messages, posts, interviews with administrators or key figures, and other indicators.

Still, a social media group might originate with a distinct objective, such as advocating for a specific cause or creating a platform for discussions about a particular subject. However, with the passage of time, the group could organically evolve into a more inclusive support network, fostering a safe haven for members to share their stories and connect with others experiencing analogous challenges.

As far as our current understanding goes, there exists a dearth of literature that systematically investigates the concept of 'role expansion' within the realm of social media groups. This notion pertains to the phenomenon wherein social media groups, initially established for specific purposes, broaden their roles to encompass additional and interconnected functions. The present chapter seeks to bridge this gap by examining instances of role expansion within social media groups, thereby extending the application of this concept beyond its traditional organizational context and into the domain of online social media platforms.

Research environment: The activity for justice for Roman Zadorov in Israel

To explore the phenomenon of "role expansion" within social media groups, I will delve into a case study that focuses on social media activism related to the pursuit of justice concerning the Roman Zadorov case. The primary goal is to exemplify how the initial engagement, which revolved around a singular case, expanded its reach, gained momentum, and underwent transformations to encompass a multitude of comparable cases. This case study serves as an illustrative representation of the role expansion phenomenon previously elucidated.

On December 6, 2006, 13-year-old Tair Rada was discovered murdered at her school in Katzrin, Israel. Roman Zadorov, a flooring installer who worked at the school, was arrested six days later and confessed to the murder a week after his arrest. However, he immediately recanted and has since denied any involvement in the crime. Despite this development, Zadorov was convicted of murder in 2010 and received a life sentence. Zadorov's appeal to the Supreme Court was denied in 2015.

However, the court's verdict contradicts public opinion, as numerous opinion polls have shown that an overwhelming majority of the public believes that Zadorov is innocent. In 2021, a Supreme Court judge decided to grant Zadorov a retrial, and he was acquitted in 2023.

The murder of Tair Rada, a young girl killed in her school in broad daylight, immediately drew public attention. This attention was further fueled by Tair's mother, who expressed doubts about Roman Zadorov's involvement shortly after he confessed to the murder. As time went on, issues with Zadorov's confession and the reconstruction of the crime only added to the doubts surrounding his guilt. Additionally, alternative theories began to emerge about who the real culprit(s) might be, how the murder was carried out, and what the motives behind it were.

Another significant factor contributing to widespread public interest in the case is the extensive use of social media to promote Zadorov's innocence. Since 2009, numerous Facebook groups have been established to discuss and debate the case. In 2015, following the rejection of Zadorov's appeal to the Supreme Court, the membership of these groups skyrocketed. The largest of these groups, "All the Truth about the Murder of the Late Tair Rada," became one of the biggest Facebook groups in Israel (Ben-Israel, 2016). Additionally, the investigation materials were made available on the "Truth Today" website starting in 2016. Several YouTube channels also feature videos related to the case, including investigative footage, conversations with the police informant, and the reconstruction of the crime scene.

Apart from its scope, the activity for Zadorov on social media is unique in other aspects (Grossman & Lev-On, 2023; Lev-On, 2023c):

1 The context: The activity takes place in the context of a murder trial and a call for justice for a putative false conviction. In contrast, the findings and products of police investigations and legal proceedings are typically far from the public eye.
2 The identity of participants in the discourse: Typically, participants in the public discourse regarding law and justice are "insiders"—police officers, lawyers, judges, reporters, and legal commentators. In the Zadorov case, however, the involvement of "outsiders" is evident, including activists who are familiar with small and large issues.

3 The activity is also unique in its significant effects including, for example, effects on public opinion concerning the functioning of the relevant state institutions and Zadorov's guilt/innocence (Lev-On, 2023a, 2023b).

In addition, this activism is unique in how it has led to many discoveries by activists who pore through investigation materials, including those who led to the decision to hold a retrial for Zadorov (Lev-On, 2023c). For these reasons, activism on behalf of Zadorov represents a fascinating case for examining the characteristics and effects of social media activism.

Through a separate investigation, I uncovered notable disparities across various groups concerning factors such as size and characteristics. This subsequent study identified two of the most prominent and impactful groups, namely "All the Truth about the Murder of the Late Tair Rada" (referred to as "All the Truth") and "Demanding a Just Trial in the Late Tair Rada Murder Case" (referred to as "Demanding Justice"), upon which the research is primarily focused. Notably, "All the Truth" boasts a membership count in the hundreds of thousands, whereas "Demanding Justice" comprises several tens of thousands of members. These distinctions extend beyond mere size, encompassing the very character of the groups; the larger entity fosters heightened participation and discourse, albeit potentially at the expense of accuracy in the content shared. Conversely, the smaller group places a premium on maintaining precision, even if it entails a reduction in ongoing interactions and conversations (Lev-On, 2022).

Method

To delve into the perspectives presented within the advocacy groups promoting justice for Roman Zadorov, and to explore the potential for "role expansion" within this context, I documented and analyzed all of the posts that surfaced on the two prominent online forums dedicated to the Zadorov case: "All the Truth" and "Demanding Justice." This comprehensive scrutiny encompassed the time span of January 2017 to September 2018—a period characterized by limited legal and media developments related to the Zadorov case.

For the purpose of this analysis, I manually archived all posts that emerged within both groups during the specified timeframe—a total of 1,460 posts from the "All the Truth" group, alongside 1,052 posts from the "Demanding Justice" group. Owing to the constraints of the prevailing Facebook API during the study period, which lacked the functionality for automated post retrieval, the task necessitated a hands-on approach to preserve the posts. To accomplish this undertaking, the involvement of three research assistants was essential. They actively joined the groups and meticulously accessed and retrieved the content—including any associated images—in a reverse chronological sequence. Subsequently, these materials were painstakingly organized and systematically cataloged into a structured table format.

The posts were systematically categorized into two distinct groups: "Posts directly addressing the Zadorov affair" ("Yes") and "Posts unrelated to the Zadorov affair" ("No"). The "Yes" category encompassed posts that directly related to the Zadorov case, covering subjects such as the Tair Rada murder, various investigative processes, Zadorov's detention and interrogations, and more. Posts that did not possess direct relevance to the Zadorov affair were categorized as "No." Approximately 10% of the dataset underwent coding by the principal investigator and three research assistants. This process continued until a consensus of nearly 100% agreement was achieved. Once this consensus point was reached, the remaining portion of the dataset was categorized by the research assistants.

In addition to the content that was collected from both groups, a total of 25 interviews were conducted with administrators of different social media groups. These interviews covered various aspects, including the interviewees' background information (biographical details, knowledge, and opinions about the case), perceptions of the goals and impact of activism, issues regarding group management, the perceived effects of their activities, and (most relevant to this chapter), questions about handling off-topic and even irrelevant content uploaded by group members. Each interview lasted approximately one to one-and-a-half hours and took place in relaxed settings, such as cafes, to foster open and comfortable interactions.

The interviews were conducted by four interviewers under the supervision of the author. All interviews were recorded and transcribed verbatim to ensure accuracy. Following transcription, the interviews underwent a rigorous thematic analysis process, which was conducted by the author in collaboration with a team of research assistants.

To begin the thematic analysis, we employed Braun and Clarke's (2006) six-phase framework. First, all team members immersed themselves in the data by reading and re-reading the transcripts. This initial phase aimed to ensure a deep understanding of the content. Notes and initial observations were made during this process. Then, codes were assigned to segments of data that appeared relevant or interesting. This coding was done independently by the author and each research assistant to ensure a wide range of perspectives.

Thirdly, the codes were collated into potential themes. This step involved grouping codes that shared similar patterns or meanings. Fourth, the preliminary themes were reviewed and refined, and all of the data extracts were collated according to each theme to ensure coherence and consistency.

Fifth, once we were satisfied with the thematic map, we further refined each theme, ensuring each one captured the essence of the coded data. Clear definitions and names for each theme were developed. Sixth and last, we weaved together the analytic narrative and data extracts to illustrate the themes compellingly.

Throughout this process, we adhered to principles of reflexivity and transparency, regularly discussing and documenting our analytic decisions. This collaborative and iterative approach helped to enhance the reliability and validity of our thematic analysis, ensuring that the identified themes were robust and reflective of the interview data. By employing this comprehensive approach, we were able to extract nuanced and meaningful themes that provide a rich understanding of the research topic.

Findings

The findings reveal that approximately one-third of the posts within the studied timeframe were dedicated to subjects that are not directly intertwined with the Zadorov case. To provide a quantitative breakdown: among the 1,460 posts in the "All the Truth" group, 428 posts (29.3%) were classified as not pertinent to the Zadorov case. Likewise, out of the 1,052 posts within the "Demanding Justice" group, 404 posts (38.4%) were identified as posts that did not have direct relevance to the Zadorov case.

The coders systematically established six categories to comprehensively organize posts that were *not* directly related to the Zadorov case, with five of these categories containing a substantial number of posts. These categories encompassed subjects pertaining to institutional injustices, assertions of innocence, incidents involving violence and murder, accounts of victimization, and events in the northern region of Israel—including Katzrin. Note that certain posts were categorized under more than one of these categories.

Significant variations emerged in the distribution of topics between the two groups. The "Demanding Justice" group exhibited a marked emphasis on matters related to institutions and claims of innocence. Conversely, the "All the Truth" group displayed a higher proportion of posts delving into topics related to violence and the narratives of victimized experiences. In the forthcoming paragraphs, I outline the specific issues that surfaced within both groups.

Institutional injustices (and ways to correct them)

A total of 327 posts in the "All the Truth" group (76.4% of the sample) and 343 posts in the "Demanding Justice" group (84.9% of the sample) were dedicated to addressing institutional injustices.

A notable portion of the posts in this category centered on *police investigations and broader concerns within law enforcement*. These discussions encompassed a wide array of topics, including: investigative methods, the use of polygraph tests, the competency of interrogators in detecting deception, the utilization of unethical tactics during investigations, concerns regarding evidence contamination, the implications of using criminal informants, instances of compromised police informants, and the importance of establishing a digitized repository for cataloging evidence.

Furthermore, posts within this category delved into the *behavior of police officers*, covering issues such as: underreporting of crimes, cases of sexual harassment involving police personnel, traffic violations committed by police officers, instances of perjured testimony by police officers, mishandling of police records, and instances in which investigative files inexplicably went missing.

This category also encompassed discussions about *DNA and post-mortem procedures*. Such conversations spanned a spectrum of subjects, including: an examination of the operations of the Institute of Forensic Medicine, calls for the establishment of an independent secondary pathological institute in Israel, instances of questionable shifts in pathological report lacking adequate justification, and cases in which confidential material from the pathological institute was allegedly leaked to legal practitioners contrary to the law.

Moreover, posts within this category tackled matters concerning *evidence*, ranging from advancements in DNA testing—particularly the extraction of DNA from deceased individuals—to considerations surrounding scientific evidence's role in convictions. These discussions touched on: the potential implications of convictions hinging on DNA findings, advancements in DNA and genetic genealogy studies, legal quandaries related to mental health conditions, the prevalence of convictions in the judicial system, and more.

Additionally, posts scrutinized the *legal process* itself, including: critiques of the prosecution's audit system, instances of contentious plea bargains, cases in which murderers seemingly evaded due prosecution, allegations of preferential treatment for prosecution and defense witnesses, issues concerning the transfer of evidence from the prosecution to the defense, the dynamics between judges and prosecutors, and concerns surrounding the appointments of judges.

Finally, a handful of posts within this category touched upon matters related to the Israeli *Prison Service*, discussing topics such as the curbing of prisoners' furloughs and incidents of violence within prison facilities.

Innocence

A thorough analysis revealed a total of 143 posts within the "All the Truth" group (33.4% of the sample) and 146 posts within the "Demanding Justice" group (36.1% of the sample) that were dedicated to discussing issues relating to *innocence.*

This category encompasses a significant number of posts that revolve around the *indictment of innocent people.* Such topics include: instances in which efforts to indict suspects were unsuccessful, allegations of wrongful indictment of innocent individuals based on testimonies from state witnesses, cases of individuals being released after serving lengthy prison sentences for crimes that they did not commit, and references to the Innocence Project in the US—which focuses on re-evaluating forensic findings at crime scenes.

Moreover, posts in this category address matters related to *retrials*, discussing topics such as the criteria for submitting a request for a retrial and critiquing instances in which requests for retrials were denied.

Additionally, posts delved into the topic of *false confessions* and their implications. Such discussions encompass: an examination of the phenomenon of false confessions and its underlying causes, the intricacies of false memory formation and why individuals remember events that never transpired, calls for the establishment of a committee to prevent false confessions, cases within Israel in which false confessions led to wrongful convictions that were subsequently overturned, and conversations about compensating individuals who were wrongfully convicted based on false confessions.

Cases of violence and murder

A total of 126 posts within the "All the Truth" group (29.4% of the sample) and 46 posts within the "Demanding Justice" group (11.4% of the sample) were dedicated to discussing *cases of violence and murder*, particularly those involving teenagers.

Posts within this category encompassed a range of issues, such as unresolved murder mysteries and instances of missing persons.

Victims and victimhood

Within the "All the Truth" group, 88 posts (20.6% of the sample) focused on the experiences of victims, particularly those who had suffered from abuse—most notably teenagers. In contrast, the "Demanding Justice" group contained only seven posts (1.7% of the sample) that focused on similar themes. These posts delved into a variety of topics, including: calls for boycotting teenagers, discussions about instances of violent communication within WhatsApp groups, and conversations surrounding teen suicide.

Occurrences in the northern region of Israel (where the murder occurred)

The "All the Truth" group contained 79 posts (18.5% of the sample) and the "Demanding Justice" group featured 15 posts (3.7% of the sample) discussing events in the northern region of Israel, which were notably centered on Katzrin—the very town where the murder occurred. These posts covered a range of topics, including: the commemoration of Katzrin's 40th anniversary, efforts to locate a missing individual in the northern region, and conversations surrounding incidents of animal abuse within Katzrin.

Why does the phenomenon exist? Insights from interviews

The findings presented thus far demonstrate that the observed groups have undergone a phenomenon known as "role expansion." Originating with discussions closely related to the Zadorov case—emphasizing Tair Rada's life, advocating for justice in Zadorov's case, and critiquing establishment actions in this affair—these groups have now embarked on a trajectory that actively engages in critical and anti-establishment pursuits across various pertinent domains. These domains encompass instances such as: cases of violence and murder, wrongful confessions of innocent people, and institutional injustices extending beyond the Zadorov case. This role expansion signifies a broader commitment to addressing systemic issues and advocating for justice on a wider scale, illustrating the groups' evolutions from single-issue focuses to multifaceted activisms.

The question arises: why does this phenomenon occur? Insights gleaned from interviews with group administrators shed light on this phenomenon. Administrators allow posts not directly tied to the Zadorov case for two primary reasons. Firstly, there are practical considerations aimed at *maintaining an ongoing volume of discussions, even during periods of lower activity*. This concern ensures that the group remains active and engaging for its members, preventing stagnation and disinterest. Secondly, administrators aim to underscore that the Zadorov case is merely one example among many similar incidents. By highlighting other cases, they *draw attention to broader patterns of injustice and mobilize support for systemic change*. This strategic broadening of focus helps to sustain member engagement and fosters a sense of collective purpose.

For example, one of the interviewees stated that "There haven't been many recent developments to report. However, considering that the posts are likely being published by managers, it's understandable that they may want to demonstrate their own ongoing relevance and activity." This comment underscores the administrators' role in keeping the group dynamic and relevant, even when specific case updates are lacking. Another interviewee stated: "administrators seem to employ a strategic approach to uphold the groups' engagement levels. By delving into related issues, they effectively maintain their communities' vitality and relevance." This strategy not only keeps the discussions vibrant, but also broadens the scope of issues addressed, thereby attracting a wider audience. A third interviewee stated: "by embracing a variety of relevant subjects, administrators … provide a space for broader societal discussions … thus the administrators skillfully cater to members' interests while maintaining the groups' overall purpose." This approach allows the group to serve as a platform for critical discourse about various social issues, enhancing its impact and reach.

Furthermore, this role expansion can be seen as a response to the members' evolving interests and the need to address a range of injustices that resonate with the group's original mission. By expanding their focus, administrators can tap into a broader spectrum of concerns, thereby maintaining the group's relevance and engagement. This evolution reflects a strategic adaptation to the dynamic nature of social movements and online communities, for which continuous relevance is crucial for sustained activism and member retention. The shift toward a broader agenda also aligns with growing awareness and activism surrounding social justice issues, suggesting that the group's expansion is both a reflection of and a response to wider societal trends.

Thus, it seems that the phenomenon of role expansion among these groups highlights a deliberate and strategic effort by administrators to sustain engagement and broaden their impact. By incorporating a wider range of issues, they ensure that the groups remain active, relevant, and aligned with their overarching mission of advocating for justice and addressing systemic injustices. This approach not only benefits the groups by keeping members engaged, but also contributes to the larger discourse concerning social justice, amplifying their collective voice and influence.

Discussion and conclusions

This chapter delves into the captivating phenomenon of "role expansion" of social media groups. This phenomenon has predominantly been explored in contexts unrelated to media, such as trade unions. Significantly, this study represents a pioneering effort to investigate "role expansion" within the realm of social media.

Social groups typically come together with well-defined objectives that are often discernible through disclaimers, cover photos, pinned messages, posts, and even interviews with administrators or key figures. However, these groups are susceptible to evolving their original intents gradually—influenced by diverse factors such as shifting circumstances, changes in group administration, or waning interest in the initial subject matter.

Despite the prevalence of this phenomenon, comprehensive studies have been in short supply. Even the term "role expansion" lacks a robust and firmly established conceptual framework. In this chapter, I undertake a preliminary exploration of this phenomenon within the specific context of groups overseeing activity related to Roman Zadorov—whose distinctive case stands out due to its magnitude and influence. The analysis delves into the posts made during the 2017–2018 timeframe, a period marked by the absence of sensational events associated with the Zadorov case, which originally spurred the creation of these groups. Confronted with this void in content, group administrators addressed the issue by incorporating more than a third of the posts, which focused on different subjects altogether.

A significant proportion of these posts revolves around concerns related to institutional injustices, emerging as a prevailing theme among the members of these groups. Additionally, discussions encompassing themes of innocence, violence, and murder also hold prominent positions. While there are variations in the frequency of these themes between the two groups, a consistent pattern emerges: approximately one-third of the posts address similar subjects tangentially linked to the Zadorov case. These matters remain intricately connected to the Zadorov case; however, it is intriguing to observe that roughly one-third of the discussions concerning them branch out into distinct contexts.

Insights gleaned from interviews with group administrators indicate that this phenomenon can be primarily attributed to two key factors: firstly, maintaining engagement during periods of reduced interest in the Zadorov case; and secondly, emphasizing the notion that while the discourse is centered on Zadorov, analogous phenomena also warrant attention. This strategic approach becomes particularly relevant when alternative topics are limited, thereby prompting the exploration of related phenomena to invigorate discussions.

The implications of this research extend beyond its contribution to the existing body of knowledge in social informatics, and they have practical significance for both research and practice in this field. Firstly, the study highlights the need for a more nuanced understanding of the evolving character of online communities and their ability to adapt to the changing information landscape. It calls for further investigation into the mechanisms behind "role expansion" within social media groups, offering valuable insights for researchers interested in studying the dynamics of online platforms. Researchers in social informatics can use the findings of this research as a foundation for exploring similar phenomena in different online contexts, providing a more comprehensive understanding of how digital technologies shape and are shaped by evolving social structures and interactions.

From a practical perspective, this research has implications for the management of online communities and social media groups. Administrators and moderators of such groups can draw on the insights from this study to better understand how to engage and sustain the interest of their members, especially during periods of reduced activity. By recognizing the potential for "role expansion," administrators can strategically guide discussions back to the group's central topic when relevant events occur. Additionally, this research underscores the role of online groups as platforms for diverse societal discussions, which can be leveraged for raising awareness, advocacy, and information dissemination. Overall, this research has practical implications for enhancing the effectiveness and impact of online communities in social informatics research and practice.

This preliminary exploration serves as a foundation for future investigations. Subsequent studies could delve deeper into similar phenomena present within diverse contexts of social media groups, whether on platforms such as Facebook or others that facilitate conversation and discourse.

Another intriguing avenue for exploration lies in conducting a comprehensive analysis of group activity patterns during periods of reduced engagement in comparison to periods of heightened activity. Specifically, does the phenomenon of "role expansion" manifest exclusively during lulls in relevant events, or does it persist even when pertinent occurrences are prevalent? A more extensive scrutiny of this aspect could lead to more robust conclusions regarding the specific contexts and timeframes in which administrators of social media groups strategically guide discussions back to the central topic for which the group was initially formed, as opposed to instances in which such guidance might be less stringent.

Acknowledgments

I thank Shira Krisher, Inbal Laks-Freund, Hodaya Abekasis, and Inbar Malka for their assistance in preparing this manuscript for publication.

References

Ben-Ari, E. (2018). *Military, state, and society in Israel: Theoretical and comparative perspectives*. Routledge.

Ben-Israel, D. (2016, February 15). "The Tube" celebrates 900K and Ynet is in a hysterical pressure: Ranking of Facebook pages for January 2016. *Mizbala*. http://mizbala.com/digital/social-media/109150.

Braun, V., & Clarke, V. (2006). Using thematic analysis in psychology. *Qualitative Research in Psychology, 3*(2), 77–101.

Fichman, P., Sanfilippo, M. R., & Rosenbaum, H. (2022). *Social informatics evolving*. Springer Nature.

Gerbaudo, P. (2017). Cahiers de doleance 2.0: Crowd-sourced social justice blogs and the emergence of a rhetoric of collection in social media activism. In V. Pickard & G. Yang (Eds.), *Media activism in the digital age* (pp. 139–150). Routledge.

Grossman, N., & Lev-On, A. (2023). Social media jurors: Conceptualizing and analyzing online public engagement in reference to legal cases. *Crime Law and Social Change, 79*(3), 223–240.

Kling, R. (2007). What is social informatics and why does it matter? *The Information Society, 23*(4), 205–220.

Lev-On, A. (2013). Communities, crowds and focal sites: Fine-tuning the theoretical grounding of cooperation online. *Journal of Community Informatics, 9*(3).

Lev-On, A. (2022). Polarization of deliberative and participatory activists on social media. *Media and Communication, 10*(4), 56–65.

Lev-On, A. (2023a). Democratizing the discourse on criminal justice in social media: The activity for justice for Roman Zadorov as a case study. *Humanities and Social Sciences Communications, 10*, Article 770.

Lev-On, A. (2023b). Making sense of murder: Stories in social media groups dedicated to justice for wrongfully convicted. *Media Culture and Society, 45*(8), 1708–1719.

Lev-On, A. (2023c). *The murder of Tair Rada and the trial of Roman Zadorov: Establishment, justice, citizens and social media*. Yedioth Books.

Lewis, D., & Vandekerckhove, W. (2018). Trade unions and the whistleblowing process in the UK: An opportunity for strategic expansion? *Journal of Business Ethics, 148*(4), 835–845.

Lissak, M. (1976). *Military roles in modernism* (Vol. 8). Sage.

Preece, J. (2000). *Online communities: Designing usability and supporting socialbilty*. John Wiley & Sons.

Savage, S. P., Grieve, J., & Poyser, S. (2007). Putting wrongs to right: Campaigns against miscarriages of justice. *Criminology & Criminal Justice, 7*, 83–105.

Smutny, Z., & Vehovar, V. (2020). Social informatics research: Schools of thought, methodological basis, and thematic conceptualization. *Journal of the Association for Information Science and Technology, 71*(5), 529–539.

11

SOCIAL MEDIA AFFORDANCES FOR MEDIATED SCIENCE COMMUNICATION DURING THE COVID-19 PANDEMIC

Noriko Hara and Seung Woo Chae

Introduction

One of the key characteristics of social informatics research is paying attention to the attributes of artifacts, i.e., information communication technologies (ICTs). Kling et al. (2005) emphasize that computing has both communication and technology capacities. In fact, in a personal conversation with the late Rob Kling, he lamented that there are few social science theories that explicitly include technologies. However, there are a few exceptions, such as Actor Network Theory (Latour, 2007). Moreover, among social informatics scholars, Meyer (2014) argued that the hyphen is the most important part of the socio-technical interaction network framework. In other words, when we conceptualize ICT-related phenomena, we need to pay equal attention to the integrative nature of both their social and technical aspects. In addition, others focus their investigations on the nature of artifacts, including ICTs. Scott and Orlikowski (2012), for example, discuss the materiality of ICTs in organizations, while Gaver (1991) articulates affordances of technologies.

In this chapter, we pay attention to social media platforms' affordances by examining science communication mediated by social media as an example of online knowledge sharing. Scientific knowledge is shared not only by scientists, but also by the non-expert public (herein called the public), especially in interactive mediated environments such as social media (Hara & Sanfilippo, 2016; Hara et al., 2019; Chen et al., 2021). Knowledge sharing occurs with both the support and hindrances of affordances created between users and various social media platforms. Thus, we will analyze how these artifacts' affordances shape scientific knowledge sharing practices. Specifically, we will focus on how scientists engage with the public during the COVID-19 pandemic through mutually shaped affordances.

DOI: 10.4324/9781032678542-16

Background

In a special issue of the *Journal of Association for Information Science & Technology* (JASIST), Meyer et al. (2019) edited a volume that focuses on social informatics of knowledge. As they stated in the introduction, knowledge work research in social informatics has been primarily examined through the context of knowledge management as well as knowledge workers within organizations using the social informatics perspective. Thus, the 2019 JASIST special issue focused on knowledge work outside of organizations. For instance, Jarrahi et al. (2019) investigated how digital nomads work without the constraints of and/or support from traditional organizations. However, there were other studies that examined knowledge work occurring outside of the organizations aside from this special issue. To illustrate, Hara et al. (2010) studied Wikipedia editors who contributed to shaping the knowledge presented within Wikipedia articles in multiple languages. Their study concluded that these editors collaborate differently depending on whether they are in Eastern or Western culturally oriented countries. Hara and Sanfilippo (2016) studied how parents shared knowledge and learned from each other about the MMR vaccine in three different online communities. Another recent study focused on how scientists shared their knowledge in the Ask Me Anything (AMA) sessions of Reddit's subgroup called "subreddit science (i.e., r/science)" (Hara et al., 2019). These studies of users who work together to share and produce knowledge are called knowledge collaboration (Faraj et al., 2011).

Previous studies of knowledge collaboration have not only examined single platforms, but also compared multiple platforms and conducted cross-platform analysis using the social informatics perspective. For example, Fichman (2011) analyzed four different questions and answers (Q&A) sites and concluded that even though similar collaboration processes of identifying answers occurred, the quality of the answers significantly differed among all four sites. She also found that the sites' popularities do not necessarily correspond with answer quality. In the study of child vaccination, Hara and Sanfilippo (2016) compared three different platforms on which parents formed online communities and found that each community's norms, as well as each platform's attributes, made differences in terms of how the users share knowledge.

In social media studies, Matassi and Boczowki (2021) advocated the benefits of cross-platform analysis on social media in addition to cross-national and cross-media studies. Previous works on cross-platform analysis of social media include Fichman and Rathi (2023), who compared trolling behaviors on three social media platforms—Facebook, Instagram, and X (formerly Twitter)—and two additional media outlets—CNN and Fox News—during the 2020 Presidential election in the U.S. They found that trolling behaviors differ significantly on the two media outlets as well as the three social media platforms. The study argues that anonymity is not the only factor that enhances hostile online behaviors. Rather, they suggested that other socio-cultural context, composition of users, and socio-technical affordances make a difference concerning trolling behaviors. In the following section, we will unpack the concept of affordances.

Affordances

The literature of materiality (e.g., Leonardi, 2012; Scott & Orikowski, 2012) suggests that properties of a technological artifact influence human behaviors and vice versa. Leonardi (2012) suggested that the focus on materiality in research allows us to understand how the properties of materials affect social activities. One of the properties that artifacts provide is affordances (Faraj & Azad, 2012). In this section, we will provide an overview of affordances, although it is not a comprehensive review of affordances. The term *affordance* was coined by Gibson (1977) to describe what environments provide (i.e., afford) to animals in the context of ecological psychology. Following Gibson (1977), Valenti and Gold (1991) expanded the concept of affordances and focused on social knowing and social interaction in the context of ecological psychology. Sutcliffe et al. (2011) mentioned that the concept of "social affordances" were later defined in the context of Computer-Mediated Communication in organizations by Bradner et al. (1999) to describe social interaction enabled by some properties of technologies. Sutcliffe et al. (2011) applied social affordances to technologies that support social interactions, such as online games, Wikipedia, and Facebook.

In the late 1980s, Donald Norman (1988) introduced the concept of affordances to the Human-Computer interaction (HCI) field, which he called "perceived affordances" (Norman, 1990, p. 9). Norman's emphasis was on design. As such, he conceptualized affordances to be perceived within designs of artifacts including HCI. In line with Norman, Gaver's (1991) seminal work entitled "Technology Affordances" discussed how the concept of affordances is relevant to and useful for user-centered design of technologies. In that piece, he correctly acknowledged the dynamic interaction between tools' affordances and the users of the tools, and he noted that specific aspects of affordance may be discovered depending on the users' backgrounds.

Later in the 2000s, in the context of Science & Technology Studies (STS), Hutchby (2001), a sociologist, described how the technologies' affordances affect social behaviors, citing Kling's early work on the properties of technological artifacts (Kling, 1992). Kling (1992) challenged STS scholars who are in the camp of social constructivism and asserted that technologies' inherent properties also influence social interactions by using guns and roses as an example. Kling argued that a gun's prominent property to kill people has strong effects on young generations, including gang cultures. On the contrary, flowers, such as roses, will not have the same effects. Schrock (2015), who further developed Hutchby's (2001) use of affordances, defined "communicative affordances" as "an interaction between subjective perceptions of utility and objective qualities of the technology that alter communicative practices or habits" (p. 1232). Along the same line,

TABLE 11.1 Conceptualizing affordances

Type of affordances	Description of affordances	Scholar
Perceived affordances	How people/users understand the affordances in design work	Norman (1988)
Technology affordances	How the material properties of technologies enable actions and interaction	Gaver (1991)
Social affordances	How the affordances allow changes for social behaviors	Valenti and Gold (1991)
Communicative affordances	How the technologies alter communication practices	Hutchby (2001)
Socio-technical affordances	How the socio-technical systems provide environments to assist or hinder people	Malhotra et al. (2021)

Source: Adapted from Bucher and Helmond (2018).

Malhotra et al. (2021) began using the term *socio-technical affordances* by making reference to the socio-technical framework, which emphasizes the intertwined connection between social activities and technologies. However, Malhotra et al. did not specifically define this term and used it in the context of large-scale collaboration in organizations.

In short, these previous scholars highlighted different functions and domains of affordances. Table 11.1 shows a summary of the conceptualization of affordances in the literature. We are in agreement with Ronzhyn et al. (2023), who formulated a definition of social media affordances, which states that affordances can be either enablers or constraints. Thus, the definition of affordances in the table used neutral languages to describe each type of affordance.

Regarding affordances in social media, Bucher and Helmond (2018) have a detailed review of social media platforms' affordances. We summarized their review of affordance types in social media research in Table 11.2. Again, socio-technical affordances were not mentioned in their review, but we modified it by adding "socio-technical affordances" (Malhotra et al., 2021) to the table. Fichman and Rathi (2023) notably used the term *socio-technical affordances* to tease out how different social media platforms provide opportunities and hinderances for trolling activities.

Following Bucher and Helmond (2018), Ronzhyn et al. (2023) created an updated comprehensive review of affordances with the goal of defining affordances in the context of social media research. Their definition of social media affordances pays attention to the emerging nature of affordances that appear through the interaction between social media and their users. Thus, in this definition, affordances are inherently socio-technical. More specifically, they argue that affordances are related to "properties of technology (i.e., materiality), properties of human actors (i.e., values and attitudes), and context (i.e., how and when the relationship

TABLE 11.2 Types of affordances in social media research

Type of affordances	Description of affordances
High-level affordances	At the social media site level (e.g., persistence, replicability, scalability, and searchability (boyd, 2011, p. 46))
Low-level affordances	Specific technological features of social media platforms (e.g., Facebook's like button)
Imagined affordances	Incorporate the users' perspectives (e.g., "perceptions, attitudes, and expectations" (Nagy & Neff, 2015, p. 5) of how affordances can/may affect their activities
Vernacular affordances	Affordances rooted in specific individual users for their own purposes (McVeigh-Schultz & Baym, 2015)
Social affordances	Technology functions that support social interactions (e.g., social cues, structures, and functions (Sutcliffe et al., 2011))
Socio-technical affordances	Integrated technical and social affordances (Fichman & Rathi, 2023)

Source: Adapted from Bucher and Helmond (2018).

unfolds)" (p. 3179). Thus, we used affordances synonymously with socio-technical affordances in this chapter. In the following sections, we will describe the study's context to discuss the affordances of three social media platforms in particular—X, YouTube, and Reddit—and highlight some aspects of the affordances that were prominent. Furthermore, we will address how these affordances support or impede the interaction between scientists and the public during COVID-19.

Study context

The current observations were conducted as part of the project entitled "Identifying effective science communication outcomes with social media during the COVID-19 pandemic," which was funded by the U.S. National Science Foundation. The overarching project includes multiple studies, both quantitative and qualitative, and the quantitative studies have been published and are under review as independent studies (Chae, Hara, & Kim, 2024a; Chae, Hara, Shiroiya, Chen, & Ogihara, 2024b; Chae, Liu, Shiroiya, & Hara, 2023). Here, we share our findings mainly from our qualitative observations with some additional examples from the quantitative studies, which explored communication between scientists and the public on the three platforms: X, YouTube, and Reddit.

We chose these three platforms because of the following reasons. X has been one of the most popular platforms among scientists who communicate online (e.g., Collins et al., 2016). This popularity was also confirmed by our interviews. YouTube was selected because of its unique affordances—i.e., a combination of video-based social media and commenting capabilities (Chae & Hara, 2024). Finally, Reddit AMAs were chosen because of their established interactive format, which allows scientists and the public to directly interact with each other (Owens, 2018).

As a second part of the study, our qualitative research also focused on science communication on the three platforms. In this qualitative part, we interviewed 11 scientists who have diverse types of expertise in COVID-19; they ranged from an epidemiologist to a misinformation researcher. The interviews were conducted via Zoom and lasted between 60 and 90 minutes. We tried not only to triangulate our findings from the quantitative studies through these interviews, but also to investigate some other aspects of COVID-19 communication that we could not discover within our quantitative research designs.

These interviews with a diverse group of scientists provided insights into the conceptualization of social media platforms' affordances in practice (Felton et al., 2023). By using the interviews, we were able to understand affordances through users' perspectives. In the next section, we identified prominent themes related to affordances in this project's context from a social informatics perspective and made references to relevant literature.

Social media affordances in the context of public engagement with science

Unique affordances on different platforms

In this project that involved three different platforms, we focused on scientists' interactions with the public on social media because these platforms allow such direct exchange between scientists and the public. As the previous literature indicated, different types of affordances emerged. For example, Bucher and Helmond (2018) analyzed Twitter's decision to change the "favorite" button to the "like" button. They discussed how some Twitter users at that time expressed personal attachment to the favorite button. In that study, they advocate a "platform-sensitive approach" (p. 244). Moreover, Fichman and Rathi's (2023) systematic cross-platform analysis also revealed the similarities and differences among the three platforms that they studied (i.e., Facebook, Instagram, and X).

In the context of our study—public engagement with science—we observed that one of X's important affordances mentioned by scientists was familiarity and reachability, among other obvious affordances that others identified (e.g., persistence, replicability, scalability, and searchability (boyd, 2011, p. 46)). The interviews were conducted in mid-2023 to early 2024, during which Twitter underwent various changes such as its renaming to X and removing content moderation. Under those circumstances, we were curious to ask if they still used X. Interestingly, most of them responded "yes," albeit with some hesitation. One of the reasons that they primarily used X at the time of the pandemic was that they were already familiar with the platform and also had developed a sizable follower base through which to reach the public with their posts.

When it comes to YouTube, only one of the scientists that we interviewed used the platform. Even so, this particular scientist had access to professional production assistance. While YouTube provides richer media affordances with the video being the primary content, this again creates both positive and negative consequences. A positive consequence is that scientists (or any other YouTubers) can demonstrate visually to the public. To illustrate, in the early pandemic, there were multiple medical experts on YouTube who tried to prove the safety and necessity of COVID-19 vaccines by displaying their own vaccination moments through their videos. An example is from the channel of Doctor Mike, a medical expert (D.O.) with the greatest number of subscribers—about 11.7 million as of February 2024— on YouTube. He shared the moments of his COVID-19 vaccinations through his channel to encourage viewers to get vaccinated (Chae et al., 2024b).

Conversely, a negative consequence is that YouTube is video-based, and the audience has the expectation that these videos are high-quality. Therefore, some scientists that we interviewed mentioned their time constraints concerning producing (high-quality) videos. As one of the interviewees commented when we asked why they do not use YouTube to communicate with the public: "I have thought about it. I just haven't had the time." (Interviewee 5, Researcher in a biotechnology company). At the same time, as younger generations become more media-savvy and informal videos on TikTok that share knowledge become more common (Ghosh & Figueroa, 2023), future scientists may find this affordance less constrictive than current scientists.

Reddit is another platform that demonstrates its unique affordances. The platform's most notable affordance was shaped by its sub-communities, named subreddits (Fiesler et al., 2018). When it comes to science communication, Chae et al. (2024a) investigated how the extent of users' support for a science communication post on Reddit varies by subreddit. They investigated 92 Reddit AMA (Ask Me Anything) discussions regarding COVID-19, in which scientists answered any relevant questions from the subreddit members. As a result, the authors found that users in the COVID-related subreddits were significantly more likely to click upvote on a COVID-related AMA post than those in either science-related or other subreddits. Put differently, the study reveals that the type of subreddit where scientists upload their AMA posts is a critical factor for their engagement with users.

Enacted interactive affordances

We chose to study social media because these platforms allow direct interaction between scientists and the public. This capability is a distinctive affordance that is different from other media (such as public talks and op-eds) that scientists had used in the past to communicate with the public. Scientific blogs were popular in the early 2000s (e.g., Butler, 2005), which provided commenting features to allow readers to comment and potentially interact with the authors, including scientists. While scientific blogs are still available, in recent years, more and more people are using social media to obtain scientific information (Saks & Tyson, 2022). One of the prominent affordances of using social media for science communication is the interactive nature of platforms. This aspect allows for two-way communication, not one-way. Brossard (2013), for example, is an early advocate of noting the possibility of two-way communication between scientists and the public.

Nevertheless, the availability of interactive functions does not necessarily lead to two-way communication. Prior to the COVID-19 pandemic, many scientists used social media to primarily communicate with their peers (Collins et al., 2016). However, some of our interviewee scientists mentioned that as the global emergency hit the world, they recognized their responsibilities to communicate with the public:

> I'm on Twitter. That's the only social media that I'm on. Usually, it's just a rant about my sports teams winning or losing ... But then, with COVID, trying to dispel some rumors or things that are factually inaccurate.
>
> *- Interviewee 7, Assistant professor of anatomy,*
> *cell biology, and physiology*

> Because of the ban on the sale of tobacco products during the COVID-19 lockdown in South Africa ... I saw the need to use my Twitter handle to do a lot of communication during that period.
>
> *- Interviewee 11, Special scientist in a medical institute*

> I only got really, really active on it [Twitter] a few years ago, maybe just before COVID, because I didn't quite see any utility in it. And then, when COVID hit, it was just this place where, you know, a lot of conversations were happening, from the vaccine deniers to the people who were absolutely fascinated by what science could do. So, there were lots of conversations, and that sort of really opened another, sort of, aspect of Twitter for me.
>
> *- Interviewee 5, Researcher in a biotechnology company*

In a sense, the interactive affordances provided by social media needed to be *enacted* in order to become a reality. Once enacted, the interactive affordances have both positive and negative consequences similar to other technologies discussed in the social informatics literature (e.g., Kling et al., 2005; Fichman & Rosenbaum, 2014). A positive consequence is that the public benefited greatly from scientists who were willing to share their knowledge on accessible social media platforms. As indicated by the commenter below on one of the YouTube channels that we studied:

> Thank you very much doctor michael. I think you're awesome for sharing this information with us people. I'm just glad the world is full of people like you. I subscribe to your Channel
>
> *- Comment from Doctor Mike Hansen's video "How COVID Kills*
> *Some People But Not Others – Doctor Explaining COVID"*

A negative consequence of using social media to engage with the public is that some scientists faced harassment as a result of sharing their research that may not be supported by the biased or ill-informed public.

> I went into the crazy conspiracy theory Twitter Spaces, you know. Like, anyways, I mean, you're of course met with a lot of hate. You know, like, you say you're a researcher, and people are like 'ah, you're being paid by Pfizer,' and like, oh, that escalated, but, you know, like, people think literally that I'm driving a Porsche or Ferrari because Pfizer is paying me billions to just be on Twitter.
>
> *- Interviewee 6, Research fellow in a university*

> You get a lot of people who are just like: 'You need to be hanged.' 'We need Nuremberg 2.0 and everyone who's been involved in the vaccines are going to be put to death.' People threatening to do all sorts of things. The only thing is, the kind of—really, I find harder to ignore that do sometimes get to me is, people will say things about my family.
>
> *- Interviewee 9, Senior lecturer in reproductive immunology*

This consequence shows that interactive affordances are also enacted as a double-edged sword (Lamb & Kling, 2003), similar to other technological interventions.

Interpretive affordances

Unlike guns and roses described in Kling's (1992) article to demonstrate the fundamental properties of these artifacts, social media functionalities that are provided on these platforms allow users to interpret the platforms' affordances. In the example of Twitter's favorite button being changed to a like button (Bucher & Helmond, 2018), these buttons basically provide the same functionality—to show users' positive responses. However, users created additional interpretations of the "favorite" button. Bucher and Helmond (2018) identified several users' comments regarding users' perspectives on the "favorite" button: " 'Fav never meant favourite anyway. It means 'I agree.', 'That's funny, but not enough to RT.', or 'Let's end the conversation here.'" (p. 234).

Another interpretive affordance of X is that scientists may interpret that they are reaching a large number of public audiences based on their follower count. For instance, one of the interviewees said:

> I started off sharing content [on Twitter] with my professional circle, which was at the beginning of the pandemic about 1,000 people, and everyone who followed me, I followed back. But, because of the big public interest in this [COVID-19], I would say my followers now are about 23,000 followers now. And, I would say that probably 21,000 of those are just ordinary people. So, I

am aware that most of the people I'm speaking to now on social media aren't scientists, and it's necessitated a bit of a change in the way that I communicate, and in also the things that I share, because I know that ordinary people are interested in different things to what scientists are interested in.

- Interviewee 9, Senior lecturer in reproductive immunology

It is indeed the case that these scientists are reaching widely to the public. However, this interpretation needs to be unpacked carefully. First, previous research found that X tends to have the echo-chamber effect (e.g., Cossard et al., 2020). This result means that users on X are susceptible to follow only those with whom they agree. In a sense, the scientists are somewhat preaching to the choir. Second, another type of follower tends to take the extremely opposite position. For example, one of the interviewees commented on a case of mask wearing:

I think the best example that I had was with masking, and I know that masking was very polarizing then … people saying that if we wear masks all day every day, we're all going to die of carbon dioxide poisoning.

- Interviewee 7, Assistant professor of anatomy,
cell biology, and physiology

Thus, it is still questionable if they are reaching the right audience who are undecided—those who are between the public who support mask wearing as a preventive measure for COVID-19 and the public who, some due to politics, decided to go against wearing masks. Of course, the larger the audience they have, the likelier it is that these scientists are reaching those who are on the fence about these issues.

Similar to other social media platforms, one of the social media engagement metrics that the YouTube platform provides is the display of view numbers. This measurement sends a clear message to viewers, including social media researchers and marketing personnel. We presume that users tend to interpret the number of views as popularity. In fact, some social media researchers and marketing personnel often use this metric as a measure of engagement. However, we found that view count may not necessarily accurately represent engagement (Chae et al., 2024b). We realized that view counts are based on the view time when a video is played for at least 30 seconds. This manner of tracking views means that some views in the count may include incomplete views. We believe that this complication is a discrepancy between intended affordances (to simply capture clicks) and interpreted affordances (to measure popularity).

One of the findings that Chae et al. (2024a) identified in their study about COVID-19 communication on Reddit AMAs is that some users asked highly technical questions to the scientists who were answering the audience questions. This reality is understandable given that those AMAs were hosted by a subreddit particularly related to COVID-19 named "r/Coronavirus." In this type of subreddit where the users tend to be more knowledgeable about the specific health/scientific topic, higher-level science questions and answers emerged. This finding means that the users interpret this kind of subreddit as an affordance to be able to ask highly technical questions because the subreddit tends to attract highly educated audiences on the topic of COVID-19. Having a Reddit AMA hosted by this particular subreddit with a scientist created unique affordances that are not found in other online platforms. In fact, this finding from the qualitative observation is aligned with the authors' quantitative results showing the importance of subreddit type in science communication on Reddit (Chae et al., 2024a).

Conclusions

In this chapter, we investigated social informatics of knowledge in the context of knowledge sharing on social media. More specifically, we used the case study of how scientists interact with the public during the COVID-19 pandemic on three particular social media platforms (X, YouTube, and Reddit). In this case study, we paid attention to how the features of individual platforms (i.e., materiality), users, and surrounding environments interact with each other to create various affordances.

In light of the insights from a social informatics perspective, we identified that nuanced socio-technical milieus allow or hinder specific user actions, interactions, and interpretations as also identified by Fichman's and Rathi's (2023) cross-platform study on trolls. We then expanded social media affordances with our observations on the three social media platforms. In particular, we support Ronzhyn et al.'s (2023) notion that affordances on social media are byproducts of technology's materiality, individual users, and context. Drawing from a larger project that includes qualitative observations of the three platforms and 12 COVID-19 related scientists, we proposed the following new understanding of social media affordances: enacted interactive affordances and interpretive affordances.

Ronzhyn et al. (2023), in their thorough review of social media affordances, discussed *imagined affordances*, which "emerge between users' perceptions, attitudes, and expectations; between the materiality and functionality of technologies; and between the intentions and perceptions of designers" (Nagy & Neff, 2015, p. 5). They considered imagined affordances as similar to perceived affordances mentioned by Norman (1988). We go a step further to expand these affordances by stating that we found *emergent affordances through mutual engagement* between the technology and people drawn from another social informatics principle: "mutual shaping of technology and people" (Fichman & Rosenbaum, 2014).

As mentioned earlier, X was primarily used for scholarly communication (i.e., scientists talked to each other to share their publications) before the pandemic (Collins et al., 2016), aside from journalists. However, this unprecedented event changed the practice of some scientists, who subsequently used Twitter to share their knowledge with the public. The circumstance (i.e., global pandemic), mature technology (i.e., X), and the people who are eager to obtain up-to-date scientific knowledge about COVID-19 created the emergent affordances through mutual engagement to support direct two-way communication between scientists and the public.

These observations were driven by a social informatics perspective, mainly: mutual shaping of technologies, technologies as a double-sided sword, and questioning the standard model. By understanding that affordances are inherently socio-technical, we were able to identify enacted interactive affordances that occur among the different social media platforms, users, and surrounding communities. It is not one particular factor, such as a social media platform, that helps to manifest a specific practice as shown, for example, in the observation of the Reddit communities. Even though the users employ the same platform, the practices of how users ask questions in various subreddits differ. This finding is consistent with another study of COVID-19 discussions on Reddit (Felton et al., 2023).

Through the lens of technologies as double-sided swords, we were able to articulate the nuanced effects of the social media that we studied. On the positive side, social media allowed the public to interact directly with scientists who were engaging in innovative research at that time. Moreover, scientists were able to reach out to a larger audience than they had previously experienced to share their insights and research findings. On the negative side, social media allowed the spread of misinformation as well as the ill-intended individuals to harm scientists' reputations. Some of these individuals attempted to harass scientists who were on social media to communicate science with the public.

Finally, by questioning the standard model, we found the existing typologies of affordances to be unsatisfactory. We critically examined if they are sufficient to describe our data. As a result, we were able to advance the existing types of affordances by proposing two additional types of affordances—enacted interactive affordances and interpretive affordances.

We believe that other social informatics researchers may benefit from applying this new understanding of affordances to examine various social media platforms in different settings in the future. In addition, scientists who are willing to have dialogues with the public may wish to pay attention to emerging affordances through mutual engagement with the public.

Acknowledgments

We thank the interview participants and the reviewers of an early version of this chapter including Sarah Davies. This material is based upon work supported by the National Science Foundation under Grant No. 21-52423.

References

boyd, D. (2011). Social network sites as networked publics: Affordances, dynamics, and implications. In Z. Papacharissi (Ed.), *A networked self: Identity, community, and culture on social network sites* (pp. 39–58). Routledge.

Bradner, E., Kellogg, W. A., & Erickson, T. (1999). The adoption and use of 'BABBLE': A field study of chat in the workplace. In S. Bødker, M. Kyng, & K. Schmidt (Eds.), *Proceedings of the Sixth European Conference on Computer-Supported Cooperative Work*, 12–16 September 1999, Copenhagen, Denmark (pp. 139–158). ACM.

Brossard, D. (2013). New media landscapes and the science information consumer. *Proceedings of the National Academy of Science U S A, 110*(3), 14096–14101.

Bucher, T., & Helmond, A. (2018). The affordances of social media platforms. In J. Burgess, A. Marwick, & T. Poell (Eds.), *The SAGE handbook of social media* (pp. 233–253). SAGE Publications Ltd. https://doi.org/10.4135/9781473984066.n14

Butler, D. (2005). Science in the web age: Joint efforts. *Nature, 438*, 7068. http://dx.doi.org/10.1038/438548a

Chae, S. W., & Hara, N. (2024). Exploring how a YouTube channel's political stance is associated with early COVID-19 communication on YouTube. *Information, Communication & Society, 27*(3), 618–644. https://doi.org/10.1080/13691 18X.2023.2227674

Chae, S. W., Hara, N., & Kim, E. (2024a). Exploring science communication on community-oriented social media. *The 2024 Social Media & Society International Conference*. International Conference on Social Media & Society. London, UK.

Chae, S. W., Hara, N., Shiroiya, H., Chen, J., & Ogihara, E. (2024b). Being vulnerable with viewers: Exploring how medical YouTubers communicated about COVID-19 with the public. *PLoS ONE, 19*(12), e0313857. https://doi.org/10.1371/journal.pone.0313857

Chae, S. W., Liu, J., Shiroiya, H. R., & Hara, N. (2023). Scientists' communication with the public on Twitter during the COVID-19 pandemic: Text mining analysis of scientists' tweets. *JMIR Preprints*. http://doi.org/10.2196/preprints.45774

Chen, H., Hara, N., & McKay, C. (2021). Investigating mediated public engagement with science on the "Science" subreddit: From the participants' perspective. *PLoS One*. [Note: the author order is alphabetical.] https://journals.plos.org/plosone/article?id= 10.1371/journal.pone.0249181

Collins, K., Shiffman, D., & Rock, J. (2016). How are scientists using social media in the workplace? *PLoS One, 11*(10), e0162680. https://doi.org/10.1371/journal.pone.0162680

Cossard, A., Morales, G. D. F., Kalimeri, K., Mejova, Y., Paolotti, D., & Starnini, M. (2020). Falling into the echo chamber: The Italian vaccination debate on Twitter. *Proceedings of the International AAAI Conference on Web and Social Media (ICWSM), 14*, 130–140.

Faraj, S., & Azad, B. (2012). The materiality of technology: An affordance perspective. In P. M. Leonardi, B. A. Nardi, & J. Kallinikos (Eds.), *Materiality and organizing* (1st ed., pp. 237–258). Oxford University Press. https://doi.org/10.1093/acprof:oso/9780199664 054.003.0012

Faraj, S., Jarvenpaa, S. L., & Majchrzak, A. (2011). Knowledge collaboration in online communities. *Organization Science, 22*(5), 1224–1239. https://doi.org/10.1287/ orsc.1100.0614

Felton, M., Middaugh, E., & Fan, H. (2023). Facts do not speak for themselves: Community norms, dialog, and evidentiary practices in discussions of COVID-19 on Reddit. *Public Understanding of Science, 33*(1), 20–36. https://doi.org/10.1177/09636625231178428

Fichman, P. (2011). A comparative assessment of answer quality on four question answering sites. *Journal of Information Science, 37*(5), 476–486. https://doi-org.proxyiub.uits. iu.edu/10.1177/0165551511415584

Fichman, P., & Rathi, M. (2023). Trolling CNN and Fox News on Facebook, Instagram, and Twitter. *Journal of the Association for Information Science and Technology, 74*(5), 493–505. https://doi.org/10.1002/asi.24753

Fichman, P., & Rosenbaum, H. (2014). *Social informatics: Past, present and future.* Cambridge Scholars Publishing.

Fiesler, C., Jiang, J., McCann, J., Frye, K., & Brubaker, J. (2018). Reddit rules! Characterizing an ecosystem of governance. *Proceedings of the International AAAI Conference on Web and Social Media, 12*(1). https://doi.org/10.1609/icwsm.v12i1.15033

Gaver, W. W. (1991). Technology affordances. *Proceedings of the SIGCHI Conference on Human Factors in Computing Systems Reaching through Technology – CHI '91* (pp. 79–84). ACM. https://doi.org/10.1145/108844.108856

Ghosh, S., & Figueroa, A. (2023). Establishing TikTok as a platform for informal learning: Evidence from mixed-methods analysis of creators and viewers. *Proceedings of the 56th Hawaii International Conference on System Sciences.* University of Hawai'i at Mānoa. https://hdl.handle.net/10125/102931

Gibson, J. J. (1977). *The ecological approach to visual perception.* Lawrence Erlbaum Association.

Hara, N., Abbazio, J. M., & Perkins, K. (2019). Emerging form of science communication: Ask Me Anything (AMA) session on Reddit. *PLoS One.* https://journals.plos.org/plosone/arti cle?id=10.1371/journal.pone.0216789

Hara, N., & Sanfilippo, M. R. (2016). Co-constructing controversy: Content analysis of collaborative knowledge negotiation in online communities. *Information Communication and Society*, 1–18. https://doi.org/10.1080/1369118X.2016.1142595

Hara, N., Shachaf, P., & Hew, K. F. (2010). Cross-cultural analysis of the Wikipedia community. *Journal of the American Society for Information Science and Technology, 61*(10), 2097–2108. https://doi.org/10.1002/asi.21373

Hutchby, I. (2001). Technologies, texts and affordances. *Sociology, 35*(2), 441–456.

Jarrahi, M. H., Philips, G., Sutherland, W., Sawyer, S., & Erickson, I. (2019). Personalization of knowledge, personal knowledge ecology, and digital nomadism. *Journal of the Association for Information Science and Technology, 70*(4), 313–324.

Kling, R. (1992). Audiences, narratives, and human values in social studies of technology. *Science, Technology, & Human Values, 17*(3), 349–365. https://doi.org/10.1177/0162243 99201700305

Kling, R., Rosenbaum, H., & Sawyer, S. (2005). *Understanding and communicating social informatics: A framework for studying and teaching the human contexts of information and communication technologies.* Information Today.

Lamb, R., & Kling, R. (2003). Reconceptualizing users as social actors in information systems research. *MIS Quarterly, 27*(2), 197–235. https://doi.org/10.2307/30036529

Latour, B. (2007). *Reassembling the social: An introduction to Actor-Network Theory.* Oxford University Press.

Leonardi, P. M. (2012). Materiality, sociomateriality, and socio-technical systems: What do these terms mean? How are they different? Do we need them? In P. M. Leonardi, B. A. Nardi, & J. Kallinikos (Eds.), *Materiality and organizing* (1st ed., pp. 24–48). Oxford University Press. https://doi.org/10.1093/acprof:oso/9780199664054.003.0002

Malhotra, A., Majchrzak, A., & Lyytinen, K. (2021). Socio-technical affordances for large-scale collaborations: Introduction to a virtual special issue. *Organization Science, 32*(5), 1371–1390. https://doi.org/10.1287/orsc.2021.1457

Matassi, M., & Boczkowski, P. (2021). An agenda for comparative social media studies: The value of understanding practices from cross-national, cross-media, and cross-platform perspectives. *International Journal of Communication, 15*(0), 22.F

McVeigh-Schultz, J., & Baym, N. K. (2015). Thinking of you: Vernacular affordance in the context of the microsocial relationship app, Couple. *Social Media + Society, 1*(2), 2056305115604649. https://doi.org/10.1177/2056305115604649

Meyer, E. T. (2014). Examining the hyphen: The value of social informatics for research and teaching. In P. Fichman & H. Rosenbaum (Eds.), *Social informatics: Past, present and future* (pp. 56–72). Cambridge Scholars Publishing.

Meyer, E. T., Shankar, K., Willis, M., Sharma, S., & Sawyer, S. (2019). The social informatics of knowledge. *Journal of the Association for Information Science and Technology, 70*(4), 307–312. https://doi.org/10.1002/asi.24205

Nagy, P., & Neff, G. (2015). Imagined affordance: Reconstructing a keyword for communication theory. *Social Media + Society, 1*(2). https://doi-org.proxyiub.uits.iu.edu/10.1177/2056305115603385

Norman, D. (1988). *The psychology of everyday things*. Basic Books.

Norman, D. (1990). *The design of everyday things*. Doubleday.

Owens, S. (2018). The world's largest 2-way dialogue between scientists and the public. *Scientific American, 7*, October 2014. Retrieved on February 22 from: www.scientifica merican.com/article/the-world-s-largest-2-way-dialogue-between-scientists-and-the-public/

Ronzhyn, A., Cardenal, A. S., & Batlle Rubio, A. (2023). Defining affordances in social media research: A literature review. *New Media & Society, 25*(11), 3165–3188. https://doi.org/10.1177/14614448221135187

Saks, E., & Tyson, A. (2022). Americans report more engagement with science news than in 2017. *Pew Research Center*. www.pewresearch.org/short-reads/2022/11/10/americans-report-more-engagement-with-science-news-than-in-2017/

Schrock, A. R. (2015). Communicative affordances of mobile media: Portability, availability, locatability, and multimediality. *International Journal of Communication, 9*(2015), 1229–1246.

Scott, S. V., & Orlikowski, W. J. (2012). Great expectations: The materiality of commensurability in social media. In P. M. Leonardi, B. A. Nardi, & J. Kallinikos (Eds.), *Materiality and organizing: Social interaction in a technological world* (pp. 113–133). Oxford University Press.

Sutcliffe, A. G., Gonzalez, V., Binder, J., & Nevarez, G. (2011). Social mediating technologies: Social affordances and functionalities. *International Journal of Human–Computer Interaction, 27*(11), 1037–1065. https://doi.org/10.1080/10447 318.2011.555318

Valenti, S. S., & Gold, J. M. M. (1991). Social affordances and interaction I: Introduction. *Ecological Psychology, 3*(2), 77–98.

INDEX

Note: Page locators in **bold** and *italics* represents figures and tables, respectively. Endnotes are indicated by the page number followed by "n" and the note number e.g., 111n5 refers to note 5 on page 111.

For Product Safety Concerns and Information please contact our EU
representative GPSR@taylorandfrancis.com
Taylor & Francis Verlag GmbH, Kaufingerstraße 24, 80331 München, Germany